CISA Exam- Study Guide

2nd Edition

Aligned as per CRM - 2019

Hemang Doshi

After launch of Hemang Doshi's CISA Video series, there was huge demand for simplified text version for CISA Studies. This book has been designed on the basis of official resources of ISACA with more simplified and lucid language and explanation. Book has been designed considering following objectives:

- CISA aspirants with non-technical background can easily grasp the subject.

- Use of SmartArts to review topics at the shortest possible time.

- Topics have been profusely illustrated with diagrams and examples to make the concept more practical and simple.

- To get good score in CISA, 2 things are very important. One is to understand the concept and second is how to deal with same in exam. This book takes care of both the aspects.

- Topics are aligned as per official CISA Review Manual. This book can be used to supplement CRM.

- Questions, Answers & Explanations (QAE) are available for each topic for better understanding. QAEs are designed as per actual exam pattern.

- Book contains last minute revision for each topic.

- Book is designed as per exam perspective. We have purposefully avoided certain topics which have nil or negligible weightage in cisa exam. To cover entire syllabus, it is highly recommended to study CRM.

- We will feel immensely rewarded if CISA aspirants find this book helpful in achieving grand success in academic as well as professional world.

- We will highly appreciate the feedback and suggestions for further improvement of the book. Author can be reached at career@infosec-career.com.

About Author

Hemang has more 10 years of rich experience in field of audit, controls and risk management. Being a qualified Chartered Accountant as well as CISA, he is actively involved in mentoring cisa aspirants across globe to get qualify for this challenging certification. He is founding partner of leading cisa tutorial website www.cisaexamstudy.com.

Acknowledgement:

I would like to express my gratitude to:

- My parents Late Hasmukh Doshi and Jyoti Doshi & in-laws Chandrant Shah & Bharti Shah for their blessings & guidance in every phase of my life.

- My wife Namrata for her constant support, suggestion and encouragement in every aspect of my life.

- My darling daughter Jia (four years at the time of writing this book) for allowing me to complete this book.

- My sister Pooja and brother-in-law Hiren Shah for their invaluable advice and motivation and nephew Phenil (eight years) for always enhancing my knowledge-base. He is going to be a great author some day.

- Brother in law Ravish Shah for constant encouragement and motivation.

CONTENTS

CHAPTER 1-RISK ASSESSMENT (DOMAIN-1)

Risk Assessment is the basis on which most of the CISA questions are prepared and tested in the exam. ISACA expects CISA aspirants to have thorough understanding of various terms and elements related to risk assessment.

Important Risk Assessment concepts:

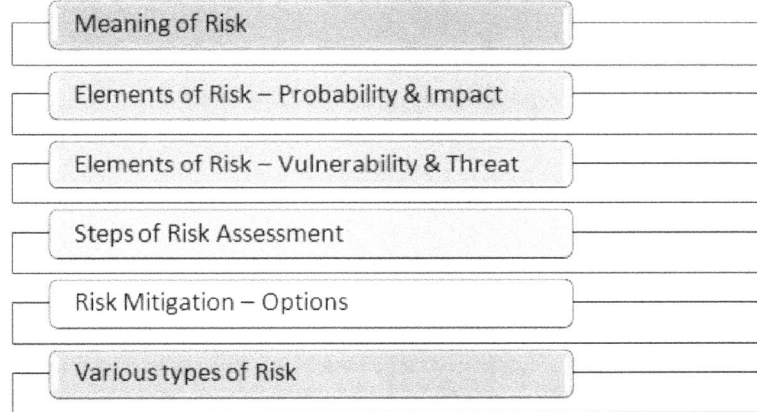

- Meaning of Risk
- Elements of Risk – Probability & Impact
- Elements of Risk – Vulnerability & Threat
- Steps of Risk Assessment
- Risk Mitigation – Options
- Various types of Risk

What is Risk?

Let us look into some of the widely accepted definition of Risk.

Source	Risk defined as	Key Words
ERM-COSO	potential events that may impact the entity.	probability/impact
Oxford Dictionary	the probability of something happening multiplied by resulting cost or benefit if it does.	probability /cost/benefit
Business Dictionary	A probability or threat of damage, injury, liability, loss, or any other negative occurrence that is caused by external or internal vulnerabilities and that may be avoided through preventive action.	probability/damage
ISO 31000	effect of uncertainty on objectives.	uncertainty/effect
Dictionary	a situation involving exposure to danger.	exposure
ISO/IEC 73	combination of an event and its consequences.	event/consequences

Risk Elements – Probability & Impact:
If you observe, almost every definition speaks directly or indirectly about two terms: **Probability** & **Impact**.
In simplest form, Risk is the product of Probability & Impact

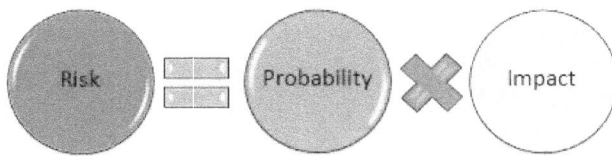

i.e. Risk= P * I

Both the terms are equally important while determining risk. Let us understand with an example. Probability of damage of a product is very high, let say 1, however that product hardly costs anything and hence Impact is Nil i.e. zero even if the product is damaged.

So risk of rain on articles will be:

Risk = P * I

i.e. Risk = 1 * 0 = 0

Risk Elements – Vulnerability & Threat:
Another approach to understand the RISK is to understand the concept of Vulnerability and Threat. In simple term, vulnerability means weak or defenseless and threat means something that can exploit the weakness. Again, there should be presence of both the elements (i.e. V*T) to constitute a risk.

There is no threat for a useless system (even though highly vulnerable). Hence risk is nil inspite of high vulnerability.

You might know end number of definitions/formulas for Risk. However, for CISA certification, please remember only below mentioned 2 formulas:

In simple term, risk is product of probability and impact.

Risk=Probability*Impact

Risk=P*I

OR

Risk is product of asset value, vulnerability and threat.

Risk=A*V*T

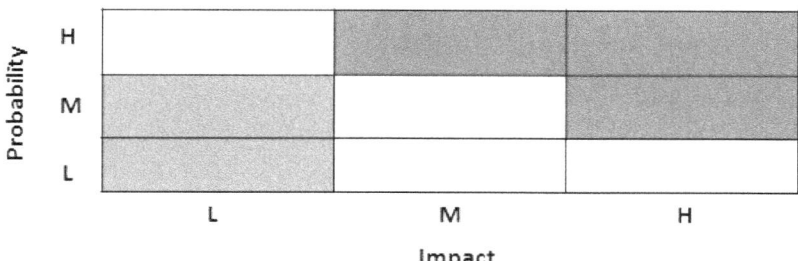

Risk Matrix

Above matrix indicates how severity of risk is aligned with severity of probability and impact. Low probability and impact leads to low risk whereas high probability and impact leads to higher risk.

Steps of Risk Assessment:

Please note down below steps for risk assessment. Invariably there will be 2 or more questions on this concept.

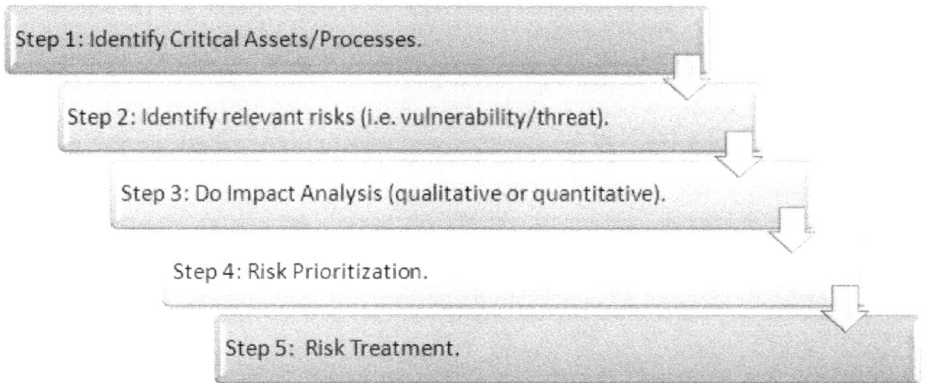

Step 1: Identify Critical Assets/Processes.

Step 2: Identify relevant risks (i.e. vulnerability/threat).

Step 3: Do Impact Analysis (qualitative or quantitative).

Step 4: Risk Prioritization.

Step 5: Risk Treatment.

Question:

IS Auditor identified certain threats and vulnerabilities in a business process. Next, an IS auditor should:

A. identify stakeholder for that business process.
B. identify information assets and the underlying systems.
C. disclose the threats and impacts to management.
D. identify and evaluate the existing controls.

(for answer & explanation refer QAE no. 4)

Clarification on Vulnerability & Threat:

One of the favorite and most preferred game of ISACA is to get us confused between the terms 'vulnerability' and 'threat' during CISA exams. Let us understand basic difference between the two so they cannot trick us anymore.

What is a threat?
A threat is what we're trying to protect against. Our enemy could be Earthquake, Fire, Hackers, Malware, System Failure, Criminals and many other unknown forces. Threats are not in our control.

What is vulnerability?
Vulnerability is a weakness or gap in our protection efforts. Vulnerability can be in form of weak coding, missing anti-virus, weak access control and other related factors. Vulnerabilities can be controlled by us.

Question:
Absence of proper security measures represents a (n):

A. threat.
B. asset.
C. impact.
D. vulnerability.

(for answer & explanation refer QAE no. 20)

Types of Risk:

- Inherent Risk: The risk that an activity would pose if no controls or other mitigating factors were in place (the gross risk or risk before controls).
- Residual Risk: The risk that remains after controls are taken into account (the net risk or risk after controls).
- Detection Risk: Risk that the auditors fail to detect a material misstatement in the financial statements.
- Control Risk: Risk that a misstatement could occur but may not be detected and corrected or prevented by entity's internal control mechanism
- Audit Risk: Inherent Risk x   Control Risk x Detection Risk

Question:

The risk of an IS auditor certifying existence of proper system and procedures without using an inadequate test procedure is an example of:

A. inherent risk.
B. control risk.
C. detection risk.
D. audit risk.

(for answer & explanation refer QAE no. 8)

Risk Treatment:
Once risks have been identified and assessed, all techniques to manage the risk fall into one or more of these four major categories:

- Risk Mitigation/Risk Reduction
- Risk Avoidance
- Risk Acceptance

- Risk Transfer

Let us take an example to understand above approaches.

Meteorological department has indicated heavy rain and we need to attend CISA classes. Risk of rain can be treated in any of the following way:

-Majority of the students will be well prepared and will arrange for umbrella or raincoat to protect them from Rain. (risk mitigation).

-Some courageous students will not bother to carry umbrella/raincoat. (risk acceptance).

-I am pretty much sure there will be some students like me who will avoid going to classes (risk avoidance)

In an organization level, it is not always possible to mitigate all the risk. Risk free business is an illusion.

Question:

Risk can be mitigated by:

A. Implementing controls
B. Insurance
C. Audit and certification
D. Contracts and service level agreements (SLAs)

(for answer & explanation refer QAE no. 23)

Question, Answer & Explanation:

(1) Most important step in a risk analysis is to identify:

A. competitors.
B. controls.
C. vulnerabilities.
D. liabilities.

Answer: C. vulnerabilities.

Explanation: If vulnerabilities are not properly identified, controls and audit planning may not be relevant. Vulnerabilities are a key element in the conduct of a risk analysis.

(2) In a risk-based audit planning, an IS auditor's first step is to identify:

A. responsibilities of stakeholders.
B. high-risk areas within the organization.
C. cost centre.
D. profit centre.

Answer: B. high-risk areas within the organization.

Explanation: The first and most critical step in the process is to identify high-risk areas within the organization. Once high-risk areas have been identified, audit planning to be done accordingly.

(3) When developing a risk-based audit strategy, an IS auditor should conduct a risk assessment to ensure that:

A. segregation of duties to mitigate risks is in place.
B. all the relevant vulnerabilities and threats are identified.
C. regularity compliance is adhered to.
D. business is profitable.

Answer: B. all the relevant vulnerabilities and threats are identified.

Explanation: In developing a risk-based audit strategy, it is critical that the risks and vulnerabilities be understood. This will determine the areas to be audited and the extent of coverage.

(4) IS Auditor identified certain threats and vulnerabilities in a business process. Next, an IS auditor should:

A. identify stakeholder for that business process.
B. identifies information assets and the underlying systems.
C. discloses the threats and impacts to management.
D. identifies and evaluates the existing controls.

Answer: D. identifies and evaluates the existing controls.

Explanation: Before reaching to any conclusion, IS Auditor should evaluate existing controls and its effectiveness. Upon completion of an audit an IS auditor should describe and discuss with management the threats and potential impacts on the assets.

(5) Major advantage of risk-based approach for audit planning is:

A. Audit planning can be communicated to client in advance.
B. Audit activity can be completed within allotted budget.
C. Use of latest technology for audit activities.
D. Appropriate utilization of resources for high risk areas.

Answer: D. Appropriate utilization of resources for high risk areas.

Explanation: The risk-based approach is designed to ensure audit time is spent on the areas of highest risk. The development of an audit schedule is not addressed by a risk-based approach. Audit schedules may be prepared months in advance using various scheduling methods. A risk approach does not have a direct correlation to the audit staff meeting time budgets on a particular audit, nor does it necessarily mean a wider variety of audits will be performed in a given year.

(6) While determining the appropriate level of protection for an information asset an IS auditor should primarily focus on:

A. Criticality of information asset.
B. Cost of information asset.
C. Owner of information asset.
D. Result of vulnerability assessment.

Answer: A. Criticality of information asset.

Explanation: The appropriate level of protection for an asset is determined based on the criticality of the assets. Other factors are not that relevant as compared to sensitivity of information asset to business.

(7) The decisions and actions of an IS auditor are MOST likely to affect which of the following risks?

A. Inherent
B. Detection
C. Control
D. Business

Answer: B. Detection

Explanation: Detection risks are directly affected by the auditor's selection of audit procedures and techniques. Inherent risks usually are not affected by the IS auditor. Control risks are controlled by the actions of the company's management. Business risks are not affected by the IS auditor.

(8) The risk of an IS auditor certifying existence of proper system and procedures without using an inadequate test procedure is an example of:

A. inherent risk.
B. control risk.
C. detection risk.
D. audit risk.

Answer: C. detection risk.

Explanation: This is an example of detection risk. Detection risk is the risk that the auditors fail to detect a material misstatement in the financial statements.

(9) Overall business risk for a particular threat can be expressed as:

A. a product of the probability and impact.
B. probability of occurrence.
C. magnitude of impact.
D. assumption of the risk assessment team.

Answer: A. a product of the probability and impact.

Explanation: Choice A takes into consideration the likelihood and magnitude of the impact and provides the best measure of the risk to an asset. Choice B provides only the likelihood of occurrence. Similarly, choice C considers only the magnitude of the damage and not the possibility of a threat exploiting vulnerability. Choice D defines the risk on an arbitrary basis and is not suitable for a scientific risk management process.

(10) An IS auditor is evaluating management's risk assessment of information systems. The IS auditor should FIRST review:

A. the controls already in place.
B. the effectiveness of the controls in place.
C. the mechanism for monitoring the risks related to the assets.
D. the threats/vulnerabilities affecting the assets.

Answer: D. the threats/vulnerabilities affecting the assets.

Explanation: One of the key factors to be considered while assessing the risks related to the use of various information systems is the threats and vulnerabilities affecting the assets. Similarly, the effectiveness of the controls should be considered during the risk mitigation stage and not during the risk assessment phase. A mechanism to continuously monitor the risks related to assets should be put in place during the risk monitoring function that follows the risk assessment phase.

(11) An IS Auditor is reviewing data centre security review. Which of the following steps would an IS auditor normally perform FIRST:

A. Evaluate physical access control.
B. Determine the vulnerabilities/threats to the data centre site.
C. Review screening process for hiring security staff
D.Evaluate logical access control.

Answer: B. Determine the risks/threats to the data centre site.

Explanation: During planning, the IS auditor should get an overview of the functions being audited and evaluate the audit and business risks. Choices A and D are part of the audit fieldwork process that occurs subsequent to this planning and preparation. Choice C is not part of a security review.

(12) Risk assessment approach is more suitable when determining the appropriate level of protection for an information asset because it ensures:

A. all information assets are protected.
B. a basic level of protection is applied regardless of asset value.
C. appropriate levels of protection are applied to information assets.
D. only most sensitive information assets are protected.

Answer: C. appropriate levels of protection are applied to information assets.

Explanation:
On the basis of risk assessment, assets are classified according to its criticality. Then appropriate level of security is provided to data as per classification.

(13) In a risk-based audit approach, an IS auditor should FIRST complete a (n):

A. inherent risk assessment.
B. control risk assessment.
C. test of control assessment.
D. substantive test assessment.

Answer: A. inherent risk assessment.

Explanation: The first step in a risk-based audit approach is to gather information about the business and industry to evaluate the inherent risks. After completing the assessment of the inherent risks, the next step is to complete an assessment of the internal control structure. The controls are then tested and, on the basis of the test results, substantive tests are carried out and assessed.

(14) In planning an audit, the MOST critical step is the identification of the:

A. areas of high risk.
B. skill sets of the audit staff.
C. test steps in the audit.
D. time allotted for the audit.

Answer: A. areas of high risk.

Explanation: When designing an audit plan, it is important to identify the areas of highest risk to determine the areas to be audited. The skill sets of the audit staff should have been considered before deciding and selecting the audit. Test steps for the audit are not as critical as identifying the areas of risk, and the time allotted for an audit is determined by the areas to be audited, which are primarily selected based on the identification of risks.

(15) Risk assessment process is:

A. subjective.
B. objective.
C. mathematical.
D. statistical.

Answer: A. subjective.

Explanation: Risk assessment is based on perception of risk officer. There is no defined mathematical or statistical formula for risk assessment. All risk assessment methodologies rely on subjective judgments at some point in the process (e.g., for assigning weightings to the various parameters).

(16) The result of risk management process is used for:

A. forecasting profit
B. post implementation review.
C. designing controls
D. user acceptance testing.

Answer: C. designing controls

Explanation:
The ultimate objective of risk management process is to ensure identified risks are managed by designing various controls. The risk management process is about making specific, security-related decisions, such as the level of acceptable risk. Choices A, B and D are not ultimate goals of the risk management process.

(17) Managing the risk up to acceptable level is the responsibility of:

A. risk management team.
B. senior business management.
C. the chief information officer.
D. the chief security officer.

Answer: B. senior business management.

Explanation:
Senior management cannot delegate their accountability for management of risk. They have the ultimate or final responsibility for the effective and efficient operation of the organization. Choices A, C and D should act as advisors to senior management in determining an acceptable risk level.

(18) Evaluation of IT risks can be done by:

A. finding threats/vulnerabilities associated with current IT assets.
B. Trend analysis on the basis of past year losses.
C. industry benchmark.
D. reviewing IT control weaknesses identified in audit reports.

Answer: A. finding threats/vulnerabilities associated with current IT assets.

Explanation: To assess IT risks, threats and vulnerabilities need to be evaluated using qualitative or quantitative risk assessment approaches. Choices B, C and D are potentially useful inputs to the risk assessment process, but by themselves not sufficient.

(19) An IS auditor is reviewing payroll application. He identified some vulnerability in the system. What would be the next task?

A. Report the vulnerabilities to the management immediately.
B. Examine application development process.
C. Identify threats and likelihood of occurrence.
D. Recommend for new application.

Answer: C. Identify threats and likelihood of occurrence.

Explanation: The IS auditor must identify the assets, look for vulnerabilities, and then identify the threats and the likelihood of occurrence.

(20) Absence of proper security measures represents a (n):

A. threat.
B. asset.
C. impact.
D. vulnerability.

Answer: D. vulnerability.

Explanation:
Vulnerability is a weakness or gap in our protection efforts. Vulnerability can be in form of weak coding, missing anti-virus, weak access control and other related factors. Vulnerabilities can be controlled by us.

A threat is what we're trying to protect against. Our enemy could be Earthquake, Fire, Hackers, Malware, System Failure, Criminals and many other unknown forces. Threats are not in our control.

Lack of adequate security functionality in this context is vulnerability.

(21) IS Auditor is developing a risk management program, the FIRST activity to be performed is a(n):

A. vulnerability assessment.
B. evaluation of control.
C. identification of assets.
D. gap analysis.

Answer: C. identification of assets.

Explanation: Identification of the assets to be protected is the first step in the development of a risk management program. CISA aspirants should know following steps of risk assessment.

- First step is to identify the assets.
- Second step is to identify relevant risk (vulnerability/threat)
- Third step is to do impact analysis

- Fourth step is to prioritize the risk on the basis of impact
- Fifth step is to evaluate controls.
- Sixth step is to apply appropriate controls.

(22) Benefit of development of organizational policies by bottom-up approach is that they:

A. covers whole organization.
B. is derived as a result of a risk assessment.
C. will be in line with overall corporate policy.
D. ensures consistency across the organization.

Answer: B. is derived as a result of a risk assessment.

Explanation:
A bottom-up approach begins by defining operational-level requirements and policies, which are derived and implemented as the result of risk assessments. Enterprise-level policies are subsequently developed based on a synthesis of existing operational policies. Choices A, C and D are advantages of a top-down approach for developing organizational policies. This approach ensures that the policies will not be in conflict with overall corporate policy and ensure consistency across the organization.

(23)Risk can be mitigated by:

A. Implementing controls
B. Insurance
C. Audit and certification
D. Contracts and service level agreements (SLAs)

Answer: A. Security and control practices

Explanation:
Risks are mitigated by implementing appropriate security and control practices. Insurance is a mechanism for transferring risk. Audit and certification are mechanisms of risk assurance, and contracts and SLAs are mechanisms of risk allocation.

(24) Most important factor while evaluating controls is to ensure that the controls:

A. addresses the risk
B. does not reduce productivity.
C. is less costly than risk.
D. is automotive.

Answer: A. addresses the risk

Explanation:
Though all of the above factors are important, it is essential that control should be able to address the risk. When designing controls, it is necessary to consider all the above aspects. In an ideal situation, controls that address all these aspects would be the best controls.

(25) The susceptibility of a business or process to make an error that is material in nature, assuming there were no internal controls.

A. Inherent risk

B. Control risk
C. Detection risk
D. Correction risk

Answer: A. Inherent risk

Explanation:
Inherent risk means the risk that an activity would pose if no controls or other mitigating factors were in place (the gross risk or risk before controls).

(26) The risk that the controls put in place will not prevent, correct, or detect errors on a timely basis.

A. Inherent risk
B. Control risk
C. Detection risk
D. Correction risk

Answer: B. Control risk

Explanation:
Control risk means the risk that a misstatement could occur but may not be detected and corrected or prevented by entity's internal control mechanism.

(27) Which of the following factors an IS auditor should primarily consider when determining the acceptable level of risk:

A. Risk acceptance is the responsibility of senior management.
B. All risks do not need to be eliminated for a business to be profitable.
C. Risks must be identified and documented in order to perform proper analysis on them.
D. Line management should be involved in the risk analysis because management sees risks daily that others would not recognize.

Answer: C. Risks must be identified and documented in order to perform proper analysis on them.

Explanation:
Though all factors are relevant, primarily consideration should be documentation of identified risk. In order to manage and control a risk, it first must be recognized as a risk. Only after documentation, other factors to be considered.

Following are some of the important aspects with respect to Audit Charter:

- Audit Charter outlines the overall authority, scope and responsibilities of the Audit Function.

- In any given scenario, audit charter should be approved by Top Management. Preferably, highest level of management and audit committee should approve this charter.

- In any given scenario, primarily auditor's action is influenced by audit charter (which defines roles and responsibilities of Audit Functions).

- Audit Charter should not be dynamic in nature and should be changed only if change can be thoroughly justified.

- Audit Charter should not include detailed yearly audit calendar, audit planning, yearly resource allocation and other routine audit activities.

- Aspects like the Professional fees payable, travel expenses budget for auditors, etc. are not included in Audit Charter.

Question, Answer & Explanation on 'Audit Charter' Concept:

(1) An audit charter should state management's objectives for and delegation of authority to IS audit and MUST be:

A. approved by the top management.
B. approved by Chief Audit Officer.
C. approved by IS department.
D. approved by IT steering committee.

Answer: A. approved by the top management.

Explanation: The audit charter should be approved by the highest level of management. Role of Chief Audit Officer is to carry out audit process as per approved audit charter. Audit charter should be independent from IS department and IT steering committee.

(2) The audit charter should be approved by the highest level of management and should:

A. is updated often to upgrade with the changing nature of technology and the audit profession.
B. include audit calendar along with resource allocation.
C. include plan of action in case of disruption of business services.
D. outlines the overall authority, scope and responsibilities of the audit function.

Answer: D. outline the overall authority, scope and responsibilities of the audit function.

Explanation:
(1) An audit charter should state management's objectives for and delegation of authority to IS audit.
(2) Charter should not be significantly changed over time. An audit charter outlines the overall authority, scope and responsibilities of the audit function. An audit charter would not be at a detailed level and therefore frequent updation is not required.
(3) Audit charter would not include detailed audit calendar and resource allocation.
(4) Action plan in case of disruption of services is included in BCP policy and not in Audit Charter.

(3) Primary purpose of an audit charter is to:

A. describe audit procedure.
B. define resource requirement for audit department.
C. prescribe the code of ethics used by the auditor
D.to prescribe authority and responsibilities of audit department.

Answer: D.to prescribe authority and responsibilities of audit department.

The correct answer is D. The charter's main purpose is to define the auditor's roles and responsibilities. It should evidence a clear mandate and authority for the auditors to perform their work. Audit procedure, resource requirements and code of ethics will not be a part of audit charter.

(4) The document used by the top management of organizations to delegate authority to the IS audit function is the:

A. audit calendar.
B. audit charter.
C. risks register.
D.audit compendium.

Answer: B. audit charter.

The audit charter outlines the overall authority, scope and responsibilities of the audit function to achieve the audit objectives stated in it. Audit Calendar will include planning of audit department. Risk register will include details of identified risk and its mitigating controls. Audit compendium includes summary of critical of audit observations for higher management.

(5) An IS auditor reviews an organization chart PRIMARILY for:

A. getting information about data-flow.
B. to assess number of employees in each department.
C. understanding the responsibilities and authority of individuals.
D. to assess number of laptops/desktops in each department.

Answer: C. understanding the responsibilities and authority of individuals.

Explanation:
An organization chart provides information about the responsibilities and authority of individuals in the organization. This helps the IS auditor to know if there is a proper segregation of functions.

(6) In a risk-based audit approach, an IS auditor, in addition to risk, would be influenced PRIMARILY by:

A. the audit charter.
B. management's representation.
C. organizational structure
D. no. of outsourcing contracts.

Answer: A. the audit charter.

Explanation:
Auditor's role and responsibility is documented in Audit Charter. The audit charter outlines the overall authority of Audit function. Hence primarily his actions will be influenced by Audit Charter.

(7) The result of risk management process is used for making:

A. business strategy plans.
B. audit charters.
C. security policy decisions.
D. decisions related to outsourcing.

Answer. security policy decisions.

Explanation:
The risk management process is about making specific, security-related decisions, such as the level of acceptable risk. Choices A, B and D are not ultimate goals of the risk management process.

(8) Audit Charter should include:

A. Yearly audit resource planning.
B. audit function's reporting structure.
C. audit report drafting guidelines.
D. Yearly audit calendar.

Answer: B. audit function's reporting structure.

Explanation:
Audit Charter outlines the overall authority, scope and responsibilities of the Audit Function. Audit Charter should include audit function's reporting structure. Ideally, Head of audit function reports to audit committee.

(9) The authority, scope and responsibility of the Information System Audit function is:

A. Defined by the audit charter approved by the senior management/Board
B. Defined by the I.T. Head of the organization, as the expert in the matter
C. Defined by the various functional divisions, depending upon criticality
D. Generated by the Audit division of the organization

Answer: A. Defined by the audit charter approved by the senior management/Board

Explanation:

The authority, scope and responsibility of the Information system audit is invariably defined by the audit charter which is approved by the senior management and, most often, by the Board of Directors. It is not left to the Audit division, the IT Head or the functional heads to decide on this. Hence, answer at Option A alone is correct.

(10) The prime objective of Audit Charter is to govern:

A. IS function
B. External Auditor
C. Internal Audit Function
D. Finance Function

Answer: C. Internal Audit Function
Explanation:
Audit Charter outlines the overall authority, scope and responsibilities of the Audit Function. Functions of External Audit are governed by Engagement letter.

Difference between Compliance Testing vis-à-vis Substantive Testing:

Compliance Testing	Substantive Testing
Involves verification of process.	Involves verification of data or transactions.
Compliance testing checks for the presence of controls.	Substantive testing checks for completeness, accuracy and validity of the data.
Attribute Sampling is used for Compliance Testing.	Variable Sampling is used for Substantive Testing.

Examples of Compliance Testing & Substantive Testing:

Compliance Testing	Substantive Testing
To verify configuration of router for controls.	Physical inventory of the tapes at the offsite storage location.
To verify change management steps to ensure controls are effective.	Confirm the validity of inventory valuation calculations.
Review of system access rights.	Conduct a bank confirmation to test ending cash balances.
Review of firewall settings.	Conduct a bank confirmation to test ending cash balances.
Review compliance with password policy.	Examining trial balance and other financial statements.

Points to remember for CISA exam:

- In any given scenario, compliance testing will be performed first. Substantive testing will be the next step.
- In any given scenario, outcome/result of compliance testing will form the basis for planning of substantive testing. For example, if compliance testing indicates strong internal control, substantive testing may be waived off or reduced. In case compliance testing indicates weak internal controls then substantive testing to be more rigorous. The development of substantive tests is often dependent on the outcome of compliance tests.
- Attribute sampling method (either control is present or absent) will be useful when testing for compliance whereas variable sampling will be useful for substantive testing.

Question, Answer and Explanation:

(1) IS auditor is reviewing the internal control of an application software. The sampling method that will be MOST useful when testing for compliance is:

A. Attribute sampling
B. Variable sampling
C. Random sampling
D. Judgmental sampling

Answer: A. Attribute sampling

Explanation:
In any given scenario, attribute sampling method (either control is present or absent) will be useful when testing for compliance. Attribute sampling is the primary sampling method used for compliance testing. Attribute sampling is a sampling model that is used to estimate the rate of occurrence of a specific quality (attribute) in a population and is used in compliance testing to confirm whether the quality exists. The other choices are used in substantive testing, which involves testing of details or quantity.

(2) Test to determine whether last 50 new user requisitions were correctly processed is an example of:

A. discovery sampling.
B. substantive testing.
C. compliance testing.
D. stop-or-go sampling.

Answer: C. compliance testing.

Explanation:
In any given scenario, compliance testing checks for the presence of controls. Compliance testing determines whether controls are being applied in compliance with policy. This includes tests to determine whether new accounts were appropriately authorized. In any given scenario, outcome/result of compliance testing will form the basis for planning of substantive testing. For example, if compliance testing indicates strong internal control, substantive testing may be waived off or reduced. In case of compliance testing indicates weak internal controls then substantive testing to be more rigorous. The development of substantive tests is often dependent on the outcome of compliance tests.

(3) Which of the following is a substantive test?

A. Reviewing compliance with firewall policy.
B. Reviewing adherence to change management policy.
C. Using a statistical sample to inventory the tape library
D. Reviewing password history reports

Answer: C. Using a statistical sample to inventory the tape library

Explanation:
In any given scenario, substantive testing checks the integrity of contents. A substantive test confirms the integrity of actual processing. A substantive test would determine if the tape library records are stated correctly.

(4) Major difference between compliance testing and substantive testing is that compliance testing tests:

A. details, while substantive testing tests controls.
B. controls, while substantive testing tests details.
C. financial statements, while substantive testing tests items in trial balance.
D. internal requirements, while substantive testing tests internal controls.

Answer: B. controls, while substantive testing tests details

Explanation:
In any given scenario, compliance testing test controls, while substantive testing tests details. Compliance testing involves determining whether controls exist as designed whereas substantive testing relates to detailed testing of transactions/procedures.

(5) When an IS auditor performs a test to ensure that only active users have access to a critical system, the IS auditor is performing a:

A. compliance test.
B. substantive test.
C. statistical sample.
D. Judgment Sampling.

Answer: A. compliance test.

Explanation:
In any given scenario, compliance testing checks for the presence of controls whereas substantive testing checks the integrity of contents. Compliance tests determine if controls are being applied in accordance with management policies and procedures. In this case, verifying that only active associates are present provides reasonable assurance that a control is in place and can be relied upon.

(6) IS auditors are MOST likely to reduce substantive test procedure if after compliance test they conclude that:

A. a substantive test would be too costly.
B. the control environment is poor.
C. inherent risk is low.
D. control risks are within the acceptable limits.

Answer: D. control risks are within the acceptable limits.

Explanation:
In any given scenario, outcome/result of compliance testing will form the basis for planning of substantive testing. For example, if compliance testing indicates strong internal control, substantive testing may be waived off or reduced. In case compliance testing indicates weak internal controls then substantive testing to be more rigorous. The development of substantive tests is often dependent on the outcome of compliance tests.

In this case, if control risks are within acceptable limits and hence substantive test procedure can be reduced.

(7) Which of the following is a substantive audit test?

A. Verifying that a management check has been performed regularly
B. Observing that user IDs and passwords are required to sign on the computer
C. Reviewing reports listing short shipments of goods received
D. Reviewing an aged trial balance of accounts receivable

Answer: D. Reviewing an aged trial balance of accounts receivable

Explanation:
In compliance testing we gather evidence with the objective of testing an organization's compliance with control procedures. In substantive testing, we gather evidence to evaluate the integrity of data, a transaction or other information. Compliance testing checks for the presence of controls whereas substantive testing checks the integrity of contents. A review of accounts receivable will provide evidence of the validity and propriety of the financial statement balance. Choices A, B and C are compliance tests to determine that policies and procedures are being followed.

(8) The objective of compliance tests is to ensure:

A. controls are implemented as prescribed.
B. documentation is complete.
C. access to users is provided as specified.
D. data validation procedures are provided.

Answer: A. controls are implemented as prescribed.

Explanation:
Compliance tests are performed primarily to verify whether controls are implemented and effective.

(9) An IS auditor is using a statistical sample to inventory the tape library. What type of test would this be considered?

A. Substantive
B. Compliance
C. Integrated
D. Continuous audit

Answer: A. Substantive

Explanation:
Using a statistical sample to inventory the tape library is an example of a substantive test.

(10) Which of the following tests is an IS auditor performing when a sample of programs is selected to determine if the source and object versions are the same?

A. A substantive test of program library controls
B. A compliance test of program library controls
C. A compliance test of the program compiler controls
D. A substantive test of the program compiler controls

Answer: B. A compliance test of program library controls

Explanation:
A compliance test determines if controls are operating as designed and are being applied in a manner that complies with management policies and procedures. For example, if the IS auditor is concerned whether program library controls are working properly, the IS auditor might select a sample of programs to determine if the source and object versions are the same. In other words, the broad objective of any compliance test is to provide auditors with reasonable assurance that a particular control on which the auditor plans to rely is operating as the auditor perceived it in the preliminary evaluation.

(11) Evidence gathering to evaluate the integrity of individual transactions, data or other information is typical of which of the following?

A. Substantive testing
B. Compliance testing
C. Detection testing
D. Control testing

Answer: A. Substantive testing

Explanation:

Evidence gathering to evaluate the integrity of individual transactions, data or other information is called substantive testing whereas evidence gathering for the purpose of testing an organization's compliance with control procedures is called compliance testing.

Last Minute Revision:

- Compliance testing involves verification of process whereas substantive testing involves verification of transactions or data.

- Attribute sampling is used for compliance testing whereas variable sampling is used for substantive testing.

- In any given scenario, outcome/result of compliance testing will form the basis for planning of substantive testing. For example, if compliance testing indicates strong internal control, substantive testing may be waived off or reduced. In case compliance testing indicates weak internal controls then substantive testing to be more rigorous. The development of substantive tests is often dependent on the outcome of compliance tests.

CHAPTER 4-CONTROL SELF ASSESSMENT (CSA) (DOMAIN-1)

What is Control Self-Assessment (CSA)?

- Control self-assessment (CSA) is a technique that allows managers and work teams directly involved in business units, functions or processes to participate in assessing the organization's risk management and control processes.

- Team understands the business process, define the controls and generate an assessment of how well the controls are working.

Details of Control Self-Assessment

CISA Question	Your Answer should be
Objectives of CSA	(1) To leverage the internal audit function by shifting some of the control monitoring responsibilities to the functional areas. (2) To concentrate on areas of high risk. (3) To enhance audit responsibilities (not replacement).
Benefits of CSA	(1) Early Detection of Risk. (2) More effective and improved Internal Controls. (3) Assurance provided to stakeholders and customers.
Disadvantages of CSA	It could be mistaken as an audit function replacement.
Auditor's Role in CSA	Facilitator
Success Factor	Involvement of line management in control monitoring.

Traditional Approach vs. Control Self-Assessment:

Traditional Approach	CSA Approach
Primary responsibility on analyzing and reporting on internal control and risk is assigned with the auditors.	Staff at all level are responsible for primary controls and risk analysis.

Question, Answer & Explanation:

(1) An IS auditor is evaluating control self-assessment program in an organization. What is MAIN objective for implementing control self-assessment (CSA) program?

A. To replace audit responsibilities
B. To enhance employee's capabilities
C. To comply with regulatory requirements
D. To concentrates on high risk area

Answer: D. To concentrates on high risk area

Explanation: In any given scenario, objective of control self assessment is to concentrate on areas of high risk. CSA involves education of line management in control responsibility and monitoring and concentration by all on areas of high risk. The objectives of CSA programs include the enhancement of audit responsibilities, not replacement of audit responsibilities.

(2) An IS Auditor has been asked by the management to support its CSA program. The role of an IS auditor in a control self-assessment (CSA) should be that of:

A. program incharge
B. program manager
C.program partner
D. program facilitator

Answer: D. program facilitator

Explanation:
Role of IS auditor is to facilitate the control self-assessment program. During a CSA workshop, they should lead and guide the clients in assessing their risks and relevant controls. Choices A, B and C should not be roles of the IS auditor. These roles are to be assumed by the client staff.

(3) For successful control self-assessment (CSA) program, it is essential to:

A. design stringent control policy
B. have auditors take responsibility for control monitoring
C. have line managers take responsibility for control monitoring
D. implement stringent control policy

Answer: C. have line managers take responsibility for control monitoring

 Explanation:
One of the success factors for effective CSA program is involvement of line management in control monitoring. The success of a control self-assessment (CSA) program depends on the degree to which line managers assume responsibility for controls.

(4) An IS auditor has been asked to participate in implementation of control self-assessment program. The auditor should participate primarily as a:

A. Team leader
B. The auditor should not participate as it would create a potential conflict of interest.
C. Facilitator
D. Project Controller

Answer: C. Facilitator

The traditional role of an IS auditor in a control self-assessment (CSA) should be that of a facilitator. During a CSA workshop, auditor should guide the clients in assessing their risks and relevant controls. Choices A, B and D should not be roles of the IS auditor. These roles are to be assumed by the client staff.

(5) An IS auditor has been asked to facilitate a control self-assessment (CSA) program. Which of the following is an objective of a CSA program?

A. Replacement of audit responsibilities
B. Enhancement of audit responsibilities
C. To evaluate risk management program
D. To provide audit training

Answer: B. Enhancement of audit responsibilities

Explanation:

Following are the major objectives of CSA program:
(1) To concentrate on area of high risk
(2) To enhance audit responsibilities
Choice C & D are the means to achieve the CSA objectives.

(6) Which of the following the BEST time to perform a control self-assessment involving all concerned parties?

A. post issuance of audit report
B. during preliminary survey
C. during compliance test
D. preparation of the audit report

Answer: B. during preliminary survey

Explanation:
Control self-assessment (CSA) is a technique that allows managers and work teams directly involved in business units, functions or processes to participate in assessing the organization's risk management and control processes. Team understand the business process, define the controls and generate an assessment of how well the controls are working. This is best achieved during preliminary survey phase.

(7) Main objective of a control self-assessment (CSA) program is to:

A. substitute audit program
B. substitute risk management program
C. support regulatory requirements
D. enhance audit responsibilities

Answer: D. enhance audit responsibilities

Explanation:
An objective associated with a CSA program is the enhancement of audit responsibilities (not a replacement). Process owner define the controls and generate an assessment of how well the controls are working. This supports the audit objective.

(8)A PRIMARY advantage of control self-assessment (CSA) techniques is that:

A. it ascertains high-risk areas that might need a detailed review later
B. risk can be assessed independently by IS auditors
C. it replaces audit activities
D. it allows management to delegate responsibility for control

Answer: A. it ascertains high-risk areas that might need a detailed review later

Explanation:
CSA helps to identify high risk area that need to be reviewed and controlled. Risk need to be assessed jointly with business staff. CSA enhances audit responsibilities (and do not replaces audit activities). Accountability for controls remains with management.

(9)IS auditor is facilitating a CSA program. Which of the following is the MOST important requirement for a successful CSA?

A. Ability of auditor to act as a workshop facilitator
B. Simplicity of the CSA program.

C. Frequency of CSA program.
D. Involvement of line managers

Answer: D. Involvement of line managers

Explanation:
Key to the success of a control self-assessment program is the support and involvement of the management and staff responsible for the process being assessed. All other options are essential for CSA to be successful, however in the absence of active involvement from those responsible, the other choices will not result in a successful CSA.

(10) Which of the following is an objective of a control self-assessment (CSA) program?

A. Concentration on areas of high risk
B. Conducting training and workshop
C. To increase risk awareness
D. To replace risk management program.

Answer: A. Concentration on areas of high risk

Explanation:
In any given scenario, objective of control self assessment is to concentrate on areas of high risk and to enhance control monitoring by functional staff.
The objectives of CSA programs include education for line management in control responsibility and monitoring and concentration by all on areas of high risk.

(11)An organization has implemented CSA programme. What is the advantage of CSA over a traditional audit?

A. Early identification of risk
B.Reduction in audit workload
C.Increase in cost of control
B.Reduction in audit resources

Answer: A. Early identification of risk

Explanation:
Control self-assessment (CSA) is a technique that allows managers and work teams directly involved in business units, functions or processes to participate in assessing the organization's risk management and control processes. Team understand the business process, define the controls and generate an assessment of how well the controls are working. This helps in early identification of risks.

Last Minute Revision:

- In any given scenario, objective of control self assessment is to concentrate on areas of high risk and to enhance control monitoring by functional staff.
- In any given scenario, role of an IS auditor in a control self-assessment (CSA) should be that of facilitator.
- In any given scenario, most important success factor for CSA is involvement of line management.
- In any given scenario, purpose of CSA is to enhance the audit responsibilities (and not audit replacement).

Difference between Statistical & Non-statistical sampling:

Statistical Sampling	Non-Statistical Sampling
Objective (no subjectivity involved)	Subjective
Also known as non-judgmental sampling	Also known as judgmental sampling
Probability of error can be objectively quantified	Cannot be objectively quantified
Each item has equal chance of selection	Sampling depends upon judgment of auditor

Difference between Attribute Sampling & Variable sampling:

Attribute Sampling	Variable Sampling
Attribute sampling is the simplest kind. We sample some number of items and classify each item as either having some attribute, like being complied, or not complied	Variable sampling contains more information than attribute data . This is because it allows us to understand "how much" or "how bad" or "how good" rather than just "yes its compling" or "no its not complied"
Generally applied in Compliance Testing	Generally applied in Substantive Testing
Expressed in Percentage	Expressed in monetary values, weight or some other measures.
Attribute sampling answers the question of " how many?"	Variable sampling answers the question of " how much?"

Difference between Stop or go sampling & Discovery sampling:

Stop or Go Sampling	Discovery Sampling
Stop-or-go-sampling is used when auditor believes that very few errors will be found. It prevents excessive sampling by allowing an audit test to be stopped at the earliest possible moment.	Discovery sampling is used when objective of audit is to discover fraud or other irregularities.

What is Confidence Co-efficient?

Confidence coefficient is a probability that sample are true representation of the population. To have high confidence correlation, you need to select high sample size or in other way, if you select high sample size your confidence co-relation will be high.

Let us see below example:

Population	Sample Size	Confidence Co-relation
	95	95 %
100	50	50 %
	25	25 %

Question, Answer & Explanation:

(1)Use of statistical sampling will be more relevant as compared to judgment (non-statistical) sampling when:

A. it is required to mitigate sampling risk
B. auditor is inexperienced
C. the probability of error must be objectively quantified
D. it is required to mitigate audit risk

Answer: C. the probability of error must be objectively quantified

Explanation:
In any given scenario, statistical sampling is to be used when the probability of error must be objectively quantified (i.e. no subjectivity is involved). Statistical sampling is an objective method of sampling in which each item has equal chance of selection. Choice A is incorrect because sampling risk is the risk of a sample not being representative of the population. This risk exists for both judgment and statistical samples. Also, audit risk is applicable for both judgment and statistical sampling.

(2)Statistical sampling reduces which of the following risk:

A. audit risk
B. detection risk
C. inherent risk
D. sampling risk

Answer: B. detection risk

Explanation:
In any given scenario, statistical sampling minimizes the detection risk. Detection risk is the chance that an auditor will not find material misstatements in an entity's financial statements. Detection risk is the risk that the auditor will conclude that no material errors are present when in fact there are. However, using statistical sampling, probability of error can be objectively quantified and hence detection risk can be minimized. Other risks cannot be minimized using statistical sampling.

(3) IS auditor is reviewing the internal control of application software. The sampling method that will be MOST useful when testing for compliance is:

A. Attribute sampling
B. Variable sampling
C. Discovery sampling
D. Stop or go sampling

Answer: A. Attribute sampling

Explanation:

In any given scenario, attribute sampling method (either control is present or absent) will be useful when testing for compliance. Variable sampling is generally used for substantive testing. Discovery sampling is used when objective of audit is to discover fraud or other irregularities. Stop-or-go-sampling is used when auditor believes that very few errors will be found. It prevents excessive sampling by allowing an audit test to be stopped at the earliest possible moment.

(4)With regard to confidence correlation, it can be said that:

A. small sample size will give high confidence correlation
B. if an auditor knows internal controls are strong, the confidence coefficient may be lowered
C. small confidence correlation will result into high sample size
D. if an auditor knows internal controls are strong, the confidence coefficient may be increased

Answer: B. if an auditor knows internal controls are strong, the confidence coefficient may be lowered

Explanation:

Confidence coefficient is a probability that sample are true representation of the populat on. In any given scenario, when internal controls are strong, confidence coefficient /sample size may be lowered. Greater the confidence coefficient, higher the sample size or in other way higher the sample size, higher the confidence coefficient.

(5) Test to determine whether last 50 new user requisitions were correctly processed is an example of:

A. discovery sampling
B. substantive testing
C. compliance testing
D. stop-or-go sampling

Answer: C. compliance testing

Explanation:

In any given scenario, compliance testing checks for the presence of controls. Compliance testing determines whether controls are being applied in compliance with policy. This includes tests to determine whether new accounts were appropriately authorized. In any given scenario, outcome/result of compliance testing will form the basis for planning of substantive testing. For example, if compliance testing indicates strong internal control, substantive testing may be waived off or reduced. In case of compliance testing indicates weak internal controls then substantive testing to be more rigorous. The development of substantive tests is often dependent on the outcome of compliance tests.

(6) IS auditor reviewing a critical financial application is concerned about fraud. Which of the following sampling methods would BEST assist the auditors?

A. Attribute sampling
B. Variable sampling
C. Discovery sampling
D. Stop or go sampling

Answer: C. Discovery sampling

Explanation:

In any given scenario, Discovery sampling is used when objective of audit is to discover fraud or other irregularities. Discovery sampling is used when an auditor is trying to determine whether a type of event has occurred, and therefore it is suited to assess the risk of fraud and to identify whether a sing e occurrence has taken place. Stop-or-go-sampling is used when auditor believes that very few errors will be found. It prevents excessive sampling by allowing an audit test to be stopped at the earliest possible moment. Attribute sampling method (either control is present or absent) will be useful when testing for compliance. Variable sampling is generally used for substantive testing.

(7) Which of the following sampling methods would be the MOST effective to determine whether access rights to staffs have been authorized as per the authorization matrix?

A. stratified mean per unit
B. attribute sampling
C. discovery sampling
D. stop or go sampling

Answer: B. attribute sampling

Explanation:
Attribute sampling method (either control is present or absent) will be useful when testing for compliance. Either access given as per authorization matrix or not given as per authorization matrix. Discovery sampling is used when an auditor is trying to determine whether a type of event has occurred, and therefore it is suited to assess the risk of fraud and to identify whether a single occurrence has taken place. Stop-or-go-sampling is used when auditor believes that very few errors will be found. It prevents excessive sampling by allowing an audit test to be stopped at the earliest possible moment. Stratified mean per unit and unstratified mean per unit are used in variable sampling.

(8) An IS auditor is determining the appropriate sample size for testing the effectiveness of change management process. No deviation noted in last 2 years audit review and management has assured no deviation in the process for the period under review. Auditor can adopt a :

A. higher confidence coefficient resulting in a smaller sample size
B. lower confidence coefficient resulting in a higher sample size
C. higher confidence coefficient resulting in a higher sample size
D. lower confidence coefficient resulting in a lower sample size

Answer: D. lower confidence coefficient resulting in a lower sample size

Explanation:
In any given scenario, when internal controls are strong, confidence coefficient /sample size may be lowered. Choice A is not correct because higher confidence correlation will always have higher sample size. Choice B is not correct because lower confidence coefficient will always have lower sample size. Choice C is not correct because where internal controls are strong, high confidence correlation or high sample size is not warranted.

Last Minute Revision:

- In any given scenario, statistical sampling is to be used when the probability of error must be objectively quantified (i.e. no subjectivity is involved).
- In any given scenario, following sampling is best suitable for compliance and substantive testing:

Situation	Sampling Technique
Compliance Testing	Attribute Sampling
Substantive Testing	Variable Sampling

- In any given scenario, best sampling technique where fraud is being suspected is Discovery Sampling.
- A higher confidence coefficient will result in the use of a larger sample size. In other way, higher sample size will give higher confidence coefficient.
- In any given scenario, when internal controls are strong, confidence coefficient /sample size may be lowered.
- In any given scenario, statistical sampling minimizes the detection risk.

Usage of Data Analytics:

Data analytics can be used for following purposes:

- To determine effectiveness of existing controls.
- To identify process lapses and area of improvements.
- To identify exceptions or deviations.
- To identify areas of fraud.
- To evaluate data quality and identify areas with poor data quality.
- To assess risk and to plan audit activities.
- Data analytics can be effective for an IS auditor in both the planning and fieldwork phases of the audit.

Process of Data Analytics:

- Determine the objectives and scope of analytics.
- Requirement gathering and obtaining the data.
- Determine the sufficiency and reliability of the data.
- Execute the test by running scripts/performing analytical tests.
- Results/conclusions of the test to be documented.
- Review of results/conclusion by a qualified person.
- Retain the results such as scripts, files, macro programs and data files.

Computer-Assisted Audit Techniques:

- CAATs helps auditor to capture and analyze the data during audit.
- This kind of software is very useful in case of complex environment or processes.
- CAATs also ensures independence of auditors while capturing the relevant data.
- CAATs provides reliability for the source of information and thus reassurance on audit findings.
- Some examples of CAAT are Generalized Audit Software (GAS), utility software, debugging and scanning software, test data, application software tracing and mapping, and expert systems.
- CAATs helps in the effective and efficient detection of exceptions or irregularities.
- CAATs can be used for following purpose:
  - Tests of the details of transactions and balances
  - Analytical review
  - Compliance tests of IS general and application controls
  - Penetration testing & application security testing

Precaution while using CAATs:

- To ensure the integrity of imported data by safeguarding their authenticity, integrity and confidentiality.
- To obtain approval for installing the CAAT software on the auditee servers
- To obtain only read only access when using CAAT on production data.
- Edit/modification should be applied to copies of production files in a controlled environment to ensure integrity of production data.

Continuous Auditing and Monitoring:

Continuous Auditing:
Audit is conducted in a real time or near real time environment. Audit is conducted within a much shorter time frame than under a traditional audit approach.

Continuous Monitoring:
Continuous monitoring refers to continuous observation of any process or system or data. For example, real-time antivirus or IDSs may operate in a continuous monitoring fashion.

Continuous auditing should be independent of continuous monitoring activities.

Continuous assurance can be established if both continuous monitoring and auditing are in place.

In general, continuous auditing is the predecessor for adoption of continuous monitoring process. Techniques used in continuous auditing is handed over to process owners for the continuous monitoring.

(1) IS auditor is performing data analytics to determine areas of high risk. Which of the following will be the first step in performing data analytics for audit?

(A)Review of results/conclusion by a qualified person.
(B)Determine the sufficiency and reliability of the data.
(C)Requirement gathering and obtaining the data.
(D)Determine the objectives and scope of analytics.

Answer: (D)Determine the objectives and scope of analytics.

Explanation: First step will be determining the objectives and scope of analytics followed by option (C), option (B) and option (A).

(2) Which of the following is the Most important aspect for considering CAAT for gathering information?

(A)CAAT is very useful in case of complex environment or processes
(B)CAAT ensures independence of auditors while capturing the relevant data.
(C)CAAT provides reliability for the source of information and thus reassurance on audit find ngs.
(D)CAAT is cost effective method for audit activities.

Answer: (C)CAAT provides reliability for the source of information and thus reassurance on audit findings.

Explanation: Most important aspect will be reliability of information. Other aspects are important but not as important as option (C).

(3) Which of the following is prime consideration while using CAAT?

(A)To ensure the integrity of imported data by safeguarding their authenticity, integrity and confidentiality.
(B)To obtain approval for installing the CAAT software on the auditee servers
(C)To provide access to CAAT to only trained and experienced auditor.
(D)To use only licensed version of CAAT.

Answer: (A)To ensure the integrity of imported data by safeguarding their authenticity, integrity and confidentiality.

Explanation: Most important aspect will be to ensure authenticity, integrity and confidentiality of the data. Others are important aspects but not as important as option A.

(4) Which of the following is the BEST way to ensure that the system calculation functions correctly?

(A)To verify existence of Segregation of Duties.
(B)Use of CAATs to perform substantive testing.
(C)To Interview process owner.
(D)To obtain post-change approval from management.

Answer:(B) Use of CAATs to perform substantive testing.

Explanation: Substantive test using CAAT will be the best way to ensure whether calculations are performed correctly by the system.

Introduction:

- EDI is the electronic transmission of transactions (information) between two organizations.
- EDI promotes a more efficient paperless environment.
- Traditional paper document exchange between organizations have been replaced with EDI platform.
- EDI system software includes transmission, translation and storage of transactions initiated by or destined for application processing.
- EDI set up can be either traditional EDI (batch transmission within each trading partner computers) or web based EDI (access through Internet Service Provider).

Following components are used in Traditional EDI process:

Communications Handler: Involves process for transmitting and receiving electronic documents between trading partners via dedicated channels.

EDI interface: Involves interface between the application system and the communications handler.

There are two components to Interface:

EDI translation: It translate the data between the standard format and a trading partner's format.

Application interface: It moves electronic transactions to or from the application systems.

EDI interface performs following functions:
- Functional acknowledgments (can be used as audit trail for EDI transactions)
- Validate the identity of partners
- Validity of transactions

Application system: It processes the data sent to, or received from the trading partner.

Risk involved in EDI Transactions:

- One of the biggest risk applicable to EDI is transaction authorization.
- Due to electronic interactions, no inherent authentication occurs.
- In absence of a trading partner agreement, there could be uncertainty related to specific, legal liability.
- Any performance related issues to EDI applications could have a negative impact on both the parties.
- Other EDI related risk include unauthorized access, data integrity and confidentiality, loss or duplication of EDI transactions.

Controls for EDI Transactions:

- Appropriate control to ensure integrity of message format and content and to avoid transmission errors.
- Appropriate control at receiving organization to validate reasonableness of messages received.
- Appropriate controls should be established to ensure data integrity in active transactions, files and archives. Logs to be maintained and monitored for any modification/changes.
- Process to be placed to determine messages are only from authorized parties and transmissions are properly authorized.

- Availability of direct transmission channels among the parties to reduce risk of wiretapping.
- Use of appropriate encryption technique for data protection.
- Use of electronic signatures to identify the source and destination.
- Use of message authentication codes to ensure that what is sent is received.
- Use of methods such as batch total, run to run total and functional acknowledgement for positive assurance that transmissions have been completed.
- Trading partner agreement should define written business terms and conditions associated with the transactions.

EDI – IS Auditor's Role

Following controls to be reviewed by an IS auditor:

Control	Objective
Internet Encryption	To ensure authenticity, integrity, confidentiality and nonrepudiation of transactions.
Edit Checks	To identify invalid transactions prior to updating the application.
Computerized Checking	To assess transaction reasonableness and validity.
Control Totals	To verify and reconcile totals between applications and with trading partners.

Also, IS auditor to ensure use of following controls to validate the sender:

- Use of control fields within an EDI message.
- Use of VAN sequential control numbers or reports.
- Use of acknowledgment transaction to sender.

Control Consideration for Inbound Transactions:

- Log of each inbound transaction on receipt
- Build segment count totals into transaction set trailer by the sender.
- Use of check digit to detect transposition and transcription error.

Control Consideration for Outbound Transactions:

- Transaction to be compared with trading partner's profile.
- Proper segregation of duties for high risk transactions.
- Log to be maintained for outbound transactions.

EDI audits also involves use of audit monitors (to capture EDI transactions) and expert systems (to evaluate transactions).

Question, Answer & Explanation:

(1) An IS auditor is reviewing the EDI process of an organization. Which of the following is the most concern area?

(A)EDI transactions are not logged and monitored.
(B)EDI process has not been approved by senior management.

(C)Trading partner agreement is not entered.
(D)Dedicated channel communication channel is used for EDI.

Answer: (C)Trading partner agreement is not entered.

Explanation: In absence of a trading partner agreement, there could be uncertainty relatec to specific, legal liability. This is the area of most concern. Having a dedicated communication channel is a better control on EDI transactions. Options (A) & options (B) though areas of concern but most important concern is option (C).

(2) An IS auditor reviewed EDI process and noted use of appropriate encryption technique? Encryption helps in achieving which of the following objective?

(A)To ensure integrity and confidentiality of transactions.
(B)To identify invalid transactions prior to updating the application.
(C)To verify and reconcile totals between applications and with trading partners.
(D)To ensure functional acknowledgement to sender.

Answer: (A)To ensure integrity and confidentiality of transactions.

Explanation: Internet encryption processes is placed to ensure authenticity, integrity, confidentiality and nonrepudiation of transactions.

(3) Which of the following procedures ensure completeness of inbound transaction in an EDI environment?

(A)Log of each inbound transaction on receipt.
(B)Build segment count totals into transaction set trailer by the sender.
(C)Maintenance of audit trail.
(D)Matching acknowledgment transactions received to the log of EDI messages sent.

Answer: (B)Build segment count totals into transaction set trailer by the sender. Other procedures provide supporting evidence but their findings are not complete to ascertain the above objective.

As per CRM 'A CISA candidate should be familiar with the integrated audit process and steps.'

Integrated Audit:

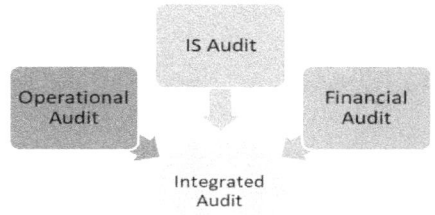

- Integrated auditing aims to assess key internal controls of operation or process or entity and focuses on risk.
- The role of an IS auditor is to understand and identify risk applicable to information management, IT infrastructure, IT governance and IT operations.
- Other audit and assurance specialists will understand and identify business risk and business controls.
- Using this approach permits a single audit of an entity with one comprehensive report.

Process of Integrated Audits:
- To identify risk faced by the organization.
- To identify relevant key controls.
- To understand design of key controls.
- To test whether Key controls are supported by the IT system.
- To test controls are operating effectively.
- To issue a combined report on risk, control and weakness.

Advantages of Integrated Audits:
- Easy to link controls and audit procedures and thus process owners better understand the objectives of an audit.
- Integrated audit helps to identify and implement better allocation and utilization of IT resources.
- Ability to establish linkage between good corporate governance and reliable financial statements.

(1) Which of the following is the primary advantage of integrated audits?

(A)Availability of single comprehensive report
(B)Reduction in audit fatigue.
(C)Ability to establish linkage between good corporate governance and reliable financial statements.
(D)Utilization of expertize audit staff.

Answer: (C)Ability to establish linkage between good corporate governance and reliable financial statements.

Explanation: Integrated audits helps to establish linkage between good corporate governance and reliable financial statements.

CISA Aspirant should be aware about following important terms with respect to outsourcing:

In-sourced	• Activity performed by Organization's staff.
Outsourced	• Activity performed by Vendor's staff
Hybrid	• Activity performed jointly by organization's staff & vendor's staff
Onsite	• Staff works onsite in IT department
Offsite	• Staff works from remote location in same geographical area. Also known as near-shore.
Offshore	• Staff works from remote location from different geographical area.

Evaluation Criteria for Outsourcing:

Function(s) should not be outsourced in following situation:
- In case of core functions of the organization.
- If function requires specific knowledge, processes and critical staffs that cannot be replicated externally or in another location.
- In case of contractual or regulatory restrictions preventing outsourcing.

Function(s) can be outsourced if:
- It can be performed with same quality (or higher quality) with same price (or lower price) by another party without increasing the risk.
- Organization has sufficient experience of managing third parties performing on behalf of organization.

Steps for Outsourcing:

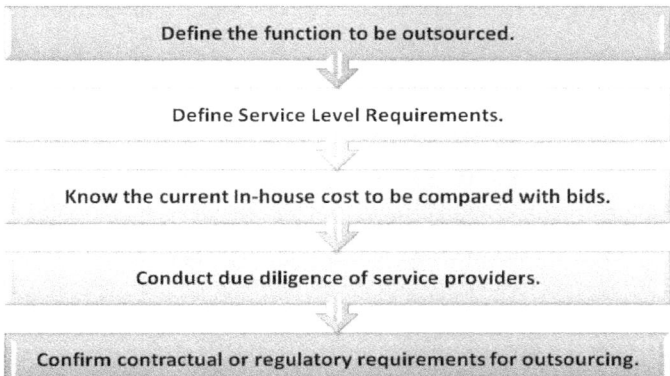

Define the function to be outsourced.

Define Service Level Requirements.

Know the current In-house cost to be compared with bids.

Conduct due diligence of service providers.

Confirm contractual or regulatory requirements for outsourcing.

Above steps will help to determine whether outsourcing will allow the organization to meet desired objective considering the cost and risk involved.

Outsourcing – Risk Reduction Options:
- Service level Agreement to contain measurable performance requirements.
- Escrow arrangement for propriety software.
- Use of multiple suppliers to reduce risk of dependency.
- Periodic performance review.
- Establishing cross-functional contract management team.
- Establishing necessary controls for foreseen contingencies.

Provisions in Outsourcing Contracts:
Service level Agreement should serve as instrument for control. It should contain atleast below mentioned clauses:
- Service level Agreement to contain measurable performance requirements.
- Confidentiality agreements protecting both the parties.
- 'Right to Audit' clause.
- Business Continuity & Disaster Recovery Provisions.
- Protecting Intellectual Property Rights.
- Requirements for confidentiality, Integrity & Availability (CIA) of resources/systems/data.

Role of IS Auditor-Monitoring of Outsourced Activities:
- Regular review of contracts and service levels.
- Review of outsourcer's documented procedures and outcome of their quality programs.
- Regular audits to certify that the process and procedures meet the quality standards.

Globalization of IT functions:
- Globalization requires setting up IT function at remote or offshore location.
- Globalization may or may not involve outsourcing.
- Many organizations globalize their IT function for the same reasons cited for outsourcing.
- Following issues need to be addressed for smooth functioning of IT function from offsite location:
  -Legal & Regulatory issues.

-Continuity of Operations.
-Telecommunication issues.
-Cross-border and cross-cultural issues.

Question, Answer & Explanation:

(1) Which of the following clauses in outsourcing contract help MOST to improve service level and minimize the costs?

A. use of latest O/S and hardware
B. Gain-sharing performance bonuses
C. Penalties for noncompliance
D. training to outsourced staff

Answer: Gain-sharing performance bonuses

Explanation:
Other clauses are important and must be in an outsourcing agreement but element of borus will provide a financial incentive to go beyond stated terms of the agreement.

(2) An organization has outsourced some of its IS processes. What is the MOST important function to be performed by IS management in such scenario?

A. Ensuring that outsourcing charges are paid as per SLA.
B. Training to staffs of outsourced vendors.
C. Levy of penalty for non-compliances
D. Monitoring the outsourcing provider's performance

Answer: D. Monitoring the outsourcing provider's performance

Explanation:
Though other parameters are important, the most important function of IS management is to monitor the performance of vendors. It is critical the outsourcing provider's performance be monitored tc ensure that services are delivered to the company as required.

(3) IS auditor observed that outsourcing vendors have been appointed without formal written agreements? The IS auditor should recommend that management:

A. obtains independent assurance of the third-party service providers.
B. sets up a process for monitoring the service delivery of the third party.
C. ensures that formal contracts are in place.
D. appointment of outsourcing vendors to be revoked.

Answer. ensures that formal contracts are in place.

Explanation:
It is difficult to enforce the terms of contract in absence of formal written agreement. Written agreements would assist management in ensuring compliance with contractual requirements.

(4) An organization has outsourced IT support service. A probable advantage of outsourcing is that:

A. reliance can be placed on expertise of outsourcing vendors.

B. more control can be exercised over IT processing.
C. organization can transfer their accountability in terms of privacy laws.
D. employee satisfaction may increase.

The correct answer is: A. reliance can be placed on expertise of outsourcing vendors.

Explanation:
Through outsourcing arrangement, service of an expert can be obtained in absence of in-house expertise. No organization can transfer their accountability through outsourcing.

(5) An organization has outsourced designing of IT security policy. Which of the following function cannot be outsourced?

A. Accountability for the IT security policy
B. Benchmarking security policy with other organization in industry
C. Implementing the IT security policy
D. User awareness for IT security policy.

Answer: A. Accountability for the IT security policy

Explanation:
In no circumstance, accountability can be transferred to external parties. Other functions can be outsourced as long as accountability remains within the organization.

(6) An organization has outsourced IT support service to a provider in another country. Which of the following conclusions should be the main concern of the IS auditor?

A. Legal jurisdiction can be questioned.
B. Increase in overall cost.
C. Delay in providing service due to time difference.
D. Difficult to monitor performance of outsourced vendor due to geographical distance.

Answer: A. Legal jurisdiction can be questioned.

Explanation:
Here main concern is legal jurisdiction. In absence of proper clarification there can be compliance as well as legal issues. The other choices are not as relevant as legal jurisdiction. Also, even if service provider is in different country, that not necessarily indicate delay in service or difficulty in monitoring. Generally, outsourcing to other countries is done to save cost.

(7) An IS auditor reviewing an outsourcing contract of IT facilities. He should be MOST concerned if which of the following clause is not included in contract:

A. types of hardware
B. software configuration
C. ownership of intellectual property
D. employee training policy

Answer: C. ownership of intellectual property

Explanation:
Clause with respect to ownership of intellectual property is a must in an outsourcing contract. The contract specifies who owns the intellectual property. Ownership of intellectual property will have a significant cost and

is a key aspect to be defined in an outsourcing contract. Other choices though important may not have that much significance as compared to intellectual property clause.

(8) An organization has outsourced data operations service to a provider in another country. Which of the following conclusions should be the main concern of the IS auditor?

A. Communication issues due to geographical differences.
B. Scope creep due to cross-border differences in project implementation.
C. Privacy laws could prevent cross-border flow of information.
D. Dissatisfaction of in-house IT team.

Answer: C. Privacy laws could prevent cross-border flow of information.

Explanation:
Main concern will be regulatory issue that can prohibit flow of information.

(9) An IS auditor is reviewing request for proposal (RFP) floated by IT department to procure services from independent service provider. Inclusion of which of the below clause is MOST important while floating such RFP?

A. Details about Maintenance plan
B. Details about Proof of Concept (POC)
C. References from other customers
D. Details about BCP

The correct answer is: C. References from other customers

Explanation:
Reference from other customers will help IT department to get idea about performance level of service provider. Checking references is a means of obtaining an independent verification that the vendor can perform the services it says it can. Other options are important and needs to be understood before awarding contracts. However, most important clause will be references from other customers.

(10) An organization has outsourced IT support service to an independent service provider. Which of the following clause would be the best to define in the SLA to control performance of service provider?

A. Total number of users to be supported
B. Minimum percentage of incidents solved in the first call
C. Minimum percentage of incidents reported to the help desk
D. Minimum percentage of agents answering the phones

Answer: B. Minimum percentage of incidents solved in the first call

Explanation:
Since it is about service level (performance) indicators, the percentage of incidents solved on the first call is the most relevant control. It helps to control performance of the service provider. Other options are not relevant.

(11) An organization is in process of entering into agreement with outsourced vendor. Which of the following should occur FIRST?

A. Deciding periodicity of contract
B. Approval from compliance team.

C. Decide the level of penalties.
D. Finalize the service level requirements.

Answer: D. Draft the service level requirements.

Explanation:
Out of options given, very first step should be finalizing the service level requirements. This SLR will form part of SLA. Other options are performed once the service level requirements are finalized.

(12) Which of the following document will serve the purpose for vendor performance review by an IS Auditor?

A. Market Feedback of the vendor.
B. Service level agreement (SLA)
C. Penalty levied reports
D. Performance report submitted by vendor.

Answer: B. Service level agreement (SLA)

Explanation:
A Service Level Agreement (SLA) is considered as most independent document for performance review of the vendor.

(13) An IS auditor has been asked to recommend effective control for providing temporary access rights to outsourced vendors. Which of the following is the MOST effective control?

A. Penalty clause in service level agreement (SLA).
B. User accounts are created as per defined role (least privilege) with expiration dates.
C. Full access is provided for a limited period.
D. Vendor Management to be given right to delete Ids when work is completed.

Answer: B. User accounts are created as per defined role (least privilege) with expiration dates

Explanation:
(1) Creation of need-based user ID and automated revocation of IDs as per expiration date will serve as most effective control under the given scenario and options.
(2) Penalty clause in SLA may act as a deterrent control but automated revocations of Ids are more effective method of control.
(3) Providing full access is a risky affair.
(4) Control in terms of providing rights to vendor management for deletion of IDs may not be reliable.

(14) Which of the following is the GREATEST concern in reviewing system development approach?

A. User manages acceptance testing.
B. A quality plan is not part of the contracted deliverables.
C. Application will be rolled out in 3 phases.
D. Compliance with business requirements are done through prototyping.

Answer: B. A quality plan is not part of the contracted deliverables.

Explanation:
A quality plan is critical element to be included in contracted deliverables. It is critical that the contracted supplier be required to produce such a plan. Other areas are not point of concerns.

(15) An IS Auditor is reviewing process of acquisition of application software. Which of the following is MOST important consideration?

A. documented operating procedure to be available.
B. a backup server be loaded with all the relevant software and data.
C. training to staff.
D. escrow arrangement for source code.

Answer: D. escrow arrangement for source code.

Explanation:
Source code escrow is the deposit of the source code of software with a third-party escrow agent. The software source code is released to the licensee if the licensor files for bankruptcy or otherwise fails to maintain and update the software as promised in the software license agreement. Escrow arrangement is very important in such cases. This will ensure that the purchasing company will have the opportunity to modify the software should the vendor cease to be in business.

Last Minute Revision:

(1) Following clauses are must in any outsourcing contracts from IS auditor point of view:
- clause with respect to 'Right to Audit'.
- clause with respect to ownership of intellectual property rights.
- clause with respect to data confidentiality and privacy.
- clause with respect to BCP & DRP.
(2) In any given scenario, two main advantage of outsourcing in their preferential order are:
- Expert service can be obtained from outside (so organization can concentrate on its core business)
- Cost Saving.
(3) In any given scenario, no organization can have outsourced or transfer its accountability. Even if any process has been outsourced, final accountability lies with the organization.
(4) In any given scenario, if service provider is in other country, then main concern of IS Auditor will be legal jurisdiction. In absence of proper clarification on legal jurisdiction, it can have compliance and legal issues.

Relationship between IT Strategy Committee & IT Steering Committee:

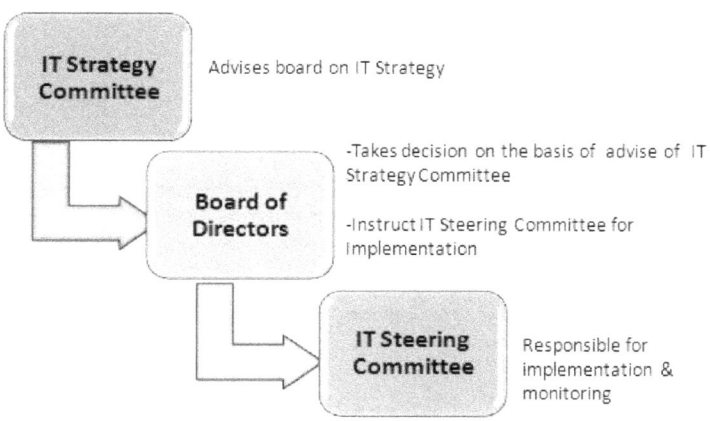

Difference between IT Strategy Committee & IT Steering Committee:

Strategy Committee	Steering Committee
Member includes Board Members & Specialized Officer.	Members includes Executives, CIO and other functionaries as required.
Advises Board on IT Strategies.	Focus on implementation & monitoring of IT projects.
Responsibilities -Alignment of IT with business objectives	Responsibilities: -Approves project plans and budget
-Exposure to IT risks	-setting priorities and milestones
-Direction to management related to IT strategy	-Acquires and assigns appropriate resources
-Contribution of IT to the business	-Ensures project meets the business requirement and continuous monitoring
	-Ensure efficient use of IT resources
In short, strategy committee shows direction for IT.	In short, steering committee drives the IT implementation

Question, Answer & Explanation:

(1) Which of the following is the role of IT Steering Committee?

A. Advise board on IT Strategy.
B. Approve & monitor funds for IT Strategy.
C. Scheduling meetings.
D. Monitoring of outsourcing agreements.

Answer: B. Approve & monitor funds for IT Strategy.

Explanation:
A. IT Strategy Committee advises board on IT Strategy.
B. IT Steering committee responsibilities include approving project plan and budget, setting priorities and milestone, appropriate use of resources and ensuring that project meets the business requirement.
C. Scheduling meetings is the routing activity to be taken care by IT executives.
D. Monitoring of outsourcing agreements to be done on continuous basis by IT executives.

(2) Which of the following authority is responsible for monitoring the overall project, achievement of milestones and alignment of project with business requirements?

A. User Management
B. IT steering committee
C. IT strategy committee
D. System Development Management

Answer: B. IT steering committee

Explanation:
A. User management provides functional requirements and approves the UAT.
B. IT steering committee is responsible for monitoring the overall project, achievement of milestones and alignment of project with business requirements.
C. IT strategy committee advises board on IT strategy. They are not involved in implementation.
D. System Development Management provides technical support for hardware and software.

(3) Which of the following is the role of IT Steering Committee?

A. Issuance of Purchase Order (PO) to empanelled vendor.
B. Providing hardware support.
C. Prioritization of IT projects as per business requirement.
D. Advises board on IT strategy.

Answer: C. Prioritization of IT projects as per business requirement.

Explanation:
A. Issuance of Purchase Order (PO) to empanelled vendor is a routine activity to be performed by IT dept.
B. Providing hardware support is also a routine activity to be performed by IT dept.
C. Responsibilities of IT steering committee include prioritization of IT projects as per business requirement.
D. IT strategy committee advises board on IT strategy.

(4) The chairperson for steering committee who can have significant impact on a business area would be the:

A. Board Member.
B. Executive level Officer
C. Chief Information Officer (CIO)
D. Business Analyst

Answer: B. Executive level Officer

Explanation:
A. Board Members generally are not expected to be involved in implementation.
B. The chair of the steering committee should be a senior person (executive level manager) with the authority to make decisions.
C. The chief information officer (CIO) would not normally be the chair, although the CIO or his representative would be a member to provide input on organization wide strategies.
D. Business Analyst do not have an appropriate level of authority within the organization.

(5) An IS steering committee should constitute of:

A. Board Members
B. User Management
C. Key executives and representative from user management
D. Members from IT dept.

Answer: C. Key executives and representative from user management

Explanation:
A. Board Members generally are not expected to be involved in implementation.
B. Only User Management will not serve the objective of the committee.
C. Steering committee should consist of Key executives and representative from user management.
D. Only IT dept. will not serve the objective of the committee.

(6) Which of the following is a PRIME role of an IT steering committee?

A. IT support to user management.
B. Monitoring IT priorities and milestones.
C. Monitoring IT vendors.
D. Advise board members about new projects.

Answer: B. Monitoring IT priorities and milestones.

Explanation:
A. IT support to user management is routine activity to be managed by IT team.
B. Monitoring IT priorities and milestones is the responsibility of IT steering committee.
C. Monitoring IT vendors is routine activity to be managed by IT team.
D. Advise board members about new projects is the responsibility of IT strategy committee.

(7) An IT steering committee should review the IT process to determine:

A. Alignment of IT processes with business requirement.
B. Capacity management.
C. Functionality of existing software.
D. Stability of installed technology.

Answer: A. Alignment of IT processes with business requirement.

Explanation:
A. The role of an IT steering committee is to determine whether IT processes are aligned with business requirement.
B. Capacity management is not Prime objective of IT steering committee.
C. Functionality of existing software is not Prime objective of IT steering committee.
D. Stability of installed technology is not Prime objective of IT steering committee.

(8) Which of the following is a function of an IS steering committee?

A. Monitoring change management & control testing.
B. Monitoring role conflict assessment.
C. Approving and monitoring major projects, the status of IS plans and budgets
D. Monitoring service level agreements with third party vendors.

Answer: C. Approving and monitoring major projects, the status of IS plans and budgets

Explanation:
A. Monitoring change management & control testing is a routine activity to be managed by IT dept.
Routine activity to be managed by IT dept.
Approving and monitoring major projects, the status of IS plans and budgets is the responsibility of IT Steering Committee.
Routine activity to be managed by IT dept.

(9) IS department is in process of floating the request for proposal (RFP) for the acquisition of an application system. Who would MOST likely to approve content of RFP:

A. project steering committee.
B. project sponsor.
C. project manager.
D. IS Strategy committee.

Answer: A. project steering committee.

Explanation:
The project steering committee provides overall direction and is also responsible for monitoring project costs and project schedules .A project steering committee usually consists of a senior representative from each function that will be affected by the new system and would be the most appropriate group to approve the RFP. The project sponsor provides funding for the project. IS strategy committee advices board of directors on IT initiatives.

(10) Which of the following is a major control weakness that can adversely affect a system development project?

A. Out of 10 recommendation from IT strategy committee, board has approved only 8 recommendations.
B. Project deadlines have not been specified in project approval plan.
C. Project Manager has not been specified in project approval plan.
D. The organization has decided that a project steering committee is not required.

Answer:D. The organization has decided that a project steering committee is not required.

Explanation:

A. Board can adopt recommendation as per its requirement. This is not a control weakness.

B. This is control weakness but not as critical as not having project steering committee.

C. This is control weakness but not as critical as not having project steering committee.

D. The project steering committee provides overall direction and is also responsible for monitoring.

project costs and project schedules. Absence of such committee can be considered as major weakness.

(11)An organization has established a steering committee to oversee its application development program. Following is the function of the steering committee:

A. documentation of requirements.

B. escalation of project issues.

C. design of interface controls.

D. specification of reports.

Answer: B. escalation of project issues.

Explanation:

The function of the steering committee is to ensure the success of the project. If there are factors or issues that potentially could affect planned results, the steering committee should escalate them.

Last Minute Revision for CISA Exam:

- IT Strategy committee advises board on various IT strategy and initiatives whereas IT Steering committee focuses on implementation part.
- Responsibilities of Strategy Committee include determining exposure of IT and strategic direction to board.
- Responsibilities of Steering Committee include setting priorities and milestone, monitoring and approving funds and efficient use of IT resources.

A CISA aspirant is expected to understand following aspects for alignment of IT with business objectives:

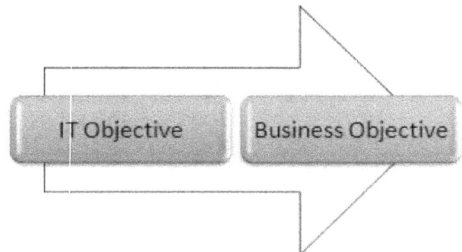

IT should support business and to align as per business objective

(1)In any given scenario, IT processes should be aligned as per business requirement. Close alignment is evident when there is a clear mapping, linking or cascading of IT strategy to business strategy hence ensuring that IT supports business objectives.

(2)In any given scenario, business processes and objectives should always be driver for IT requirement. When formulating the IT strategy, the prime consideration should be business objectives.

(3)In any given scenario, the very first step in reviewing an organization's IT strategic plan is to review/understand the business plan.

(4)Information security to be effective should be in line with enterprise requirements. Hence enterprise requirements should form the basis of security requirements.

(5)To govern IT effectively, IT and business should be moving in the same direction, requiring that the IT plans should be aligned with an organization's business plans.

(6)In any given scenario, IT alignment with business objective can be best assured by involvement of top management. Top management who are very well aware of business objectives can derive maximum benefit from information system by way of structure alignment.

(7)When formulating the IT strategy, the enterprise must consider:
- business objectives
- risks and benefits they can bring to the business;
- cost of current IT and whether this provides sufficient value to the business

Question, Answer & Explanation:

(1)The prime objective of review of information systems by IT steering committee should be to assess:

A. alignment of IT processes as per business requirement.
B. alignment of business process as per IT requirement.

C. the capacity of existing software.
D. the capacity of installed technology.

Answer: A. alignment of IT processes as per business requirement.

Explanation:
(A)IT steering committee must determine that IT processes are designed as per business requirement and that whether IS processes support the business requirement. The role of an IT steering committee is to ensure that the IS objectives are in line with business objectives.
(B)In no case business process should be defined as per IT requirement.
(C)Capacity of existing software and installed technology are important consideration. However prime objective should be to assess alignment of IT processes as per business requirement.

(2) An IS auditor is reviewing an organization's IT strategic plan. He should FIRST review:

A. alignment of IT processes as per business requirement.
B. the business plan.
C. the capacity of installed technology.
D. latest technology trends.

Answer: B. the business plan.

Explanation:
(A)The very first step in reviewing an organization's IT strategic plan is to review/understand the business plan. Without understanding the context in which business operates and its expansion plan, review of strategic plan may not be that effective. To evaluate the IT strategic plan, the IS auditor would first need to familiarize him/herself with the business plan.
(B)Alignment of IT processes as per business is an important consideration. However, first one needs to understand the business.
(C)Impact and capacity of technology depends on nature of business and business plan. Hence understanding of business plan should be first step.

(3) Information security governance requires strategic alignment in terms of:

A. enterprise requirements are the basis for security requirements.
B. security requirements are the basis for enterprise requirements.
C. current technology trend.
D. benchmarking with industry standards.

Answer: A. enterprise requirements are the basis for security requirements.

Explanation:
(1)Information security to be effective should be in line with enterprise requirements. Hence enterprise requirements should form the basis of security requirements. Other options are not relevant.
(2)Security requirements should not form the basis for enterprise requirements. It should be other way round.
(3)Current technology and benchmarking are important consideration though prime consideration should be alignment of security requirements in terms of enterprise objectives.

(4)As a part of effective IT governance, IT Plan should be consistent with the organization's:

A. business plan.
B. information security plan.
C. business continuity plan.

D. risk management plan.

Answer: A. business plan.

Explanation:
To govern IT effectively, IT and business should be moving in the same direction, requiring that the IT plans are aligned with an organization's business plans. Information security, business continuity and risk management should be considered while developing IT plan, but all this will add value only if IT plan is in line with business plan.

(5)Best way to determine that whether IS functions support the organization's business objective is to ensure that:

A. IS has latest available equipments.
B. IS plans are designed as per business objectives.
C. all resources are utilized effectively and efficiently.
D. IS has proper control over outsourcing partners.

Answer: B. IS plans are designed as per business objectives.

Explanation:
To govern IT effectively, IT and business should be moving in the same direction, requiring that the IT plans are aligned with an organization's business plans.

(6) To improve the IS alignment with business, which of the following is the best practice:

A. Outsourcing risks are managed.
B. Use of latest technology to operate business.
C. Structured way of sharing of business information.
D. Involvement of top management to mediate between business and information system.

Answer: D. Involvement of top management to mediate between business and information system.

Explanation:
(1)Strategic alignment can be best assured by involvement of top management. Top management who are very well aware of business objectives can derive maximum benefit from information system by way of structure alignment.
(2)Management of outsourcing risk is a good practice however it does not necessarily ensures IS alignment with business.
(3)Use of latest technology and structured way of information sharing may not be effective in absence of mandate from top management.

(7)An IS auditor is evaluating an organization's IS strategy. Which of the following would be the MOST important consideration?

A. Organization's IS strategy has been approved by CIO.
B. Organization's IS strategy is designed as per IS department's budget.
C. Organization's IS strategy is considered on the basis of latest technology available in the market.
D. Organization's IS strategy supports the business objectives of the organization.

Answer: D. Organization's IS strategy supports the business objectives of the organization.

Explanation:

It must be noted that IS function will not effective if same does not supports the business objectives of the organization. Other factors are important consideration but they can be meaningless in absence of IS alignment with business objectives.

(8) An IS auditor is evaluating an organization's IT security policy. The PRIMARY objective is to ensure that:

A. IT security policy is available with all the users.
B. IT security policy support business and IT objectives.
C. IT security policy is considered on the basis of latest technology available in the market.
D. IT security policy is approved by top management.

Answer: IT security policy support business and IT objectives.

Explanation:
It must be noted that IT security function will not effective if same does not supports the business objectives of the organization. Other factors are important consideration but they can be meaningless in absence of proper alignment of IT security with business and IT objectives. Even if top management approves the policy which is not in line with business objective, same should be questionable.

(9)IT governance to be effective requires that:

A. the business strategies and objectives supports the IT strategy.
B. the business strategy is derived from an IT strategy.
C. Cost effective IT governance.
D. the IT strategy supports the business strategies and objectives.

Answer: D. the IT strategy supports the business strategies and objectives.

Explanation:
Effective IT governance need to manage two dimensions of governance. First and primary, governance is a decision-making framework that reflects the organization's goals and priorities, and how the organization intends to achieve them. Second, governance processes, covers the structures and methods the organization uses to execute and institutionalize the governance framework. In essence, the framework is what the organization has decided, while the process is how the organization will institutionalize those decisions.

(10)IS auditor is reviewing software development process. Which of the following is best way to ensure that business requirements are met during software development?

A. Proper training to developer.
B. Programmers with good business knowledge.
C. Adequate documentation.
D. user engagement in development process.

Answer: D. user engagement in development process.

Explanation:
Though other factors are important to ensure all the requirements have been considered, best way is to ensure that users are frequently engaged from early stage of software development. End users anchor the value stream. Most software requirements techniques start by asking users what they want or need the system to do.

(11) An IS auditor is reviewing an organization's IS strategy. Which among below is the most important criteria for such review?

A. It includes a mission statement.
B. It includes usage of latest technology.
C. It includes best security practices.
D. It supports the business objectives.

Answer: D It supports the business objectives.

Explanation:
The correct answer is D. Other factors are important consideration but if IS strategy is not in ine with business objectives, IS strategy will not add value to the business.

Objective of IT balanced Scorecard:

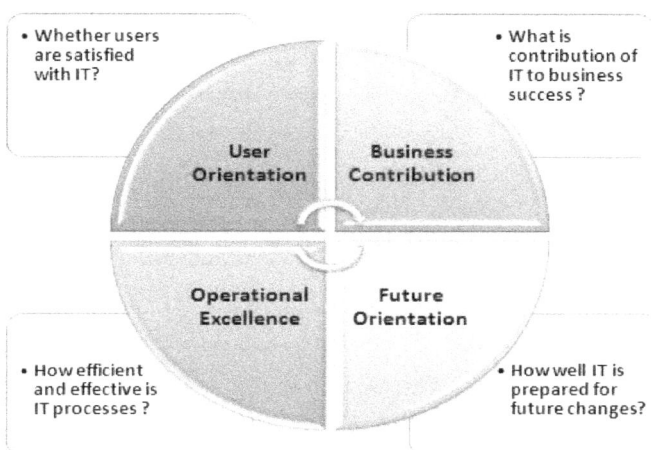

The objective of IT balanced score card is to establish, monitor and evaluate IT performance in terms of (i) business contribution (ii) future orientation, (iii) operational excellence & (iv) user orientation.

Performance Indicators of IT balanced Scorecard

-Customer Satisfaction
-Internal Processes
-Ability to innovate

CISA aspirants to understand following aspects of Balanced Score Card:

(1)In any given scenario, three indicators of IT balanced scorecard are (a) customer satisfaction (b) internal processes and (c) ability to innovate.

(2)Though financial performance is an indicator of generic balanced scorecard, it is not part of IT balanced scorecard.

(3)In any given scenario, use of IT balanced scorecard is the most effective means to aid the IT strategy committee and management in achieving the IT governance through proper IT & business alignment.

(4)In any given scenario, success of IT scorecard depends upon involvement of senior management in IT strategy planning.

(5)In any given scenario, primary objective of IT balanced scorecard is to optimize the performance.

(6)In any given scenario, key performance indicators (KPIs) need to be defined before implementing IT balanced scorecard.

Question, Answer & Explanation:

(1)The purpose of IT balanced scorecard is to evaluate and monitor performance indicators other than:

A. financial performance.
B. customer satisfaction.
C. internal processes.
D. innovation capacity.

Answer: A. financial results

.
Explanation:
The IT BSC considers factor such as customer satisfaction, innovation capacity and internal processes. Financial performance are not part of IT balanced score card.
.

(2)Following is the pre-requisite before implementing an IT balanced scorecard:

A. existence of effective and efficient IT services.
B. define key performance indicators.
C. IT projects should add value to the business.
D. IT expenses within allotted budget.

Answer: B. define key performance indicators.

Explanation:
For measuring the performance of IT services, it is required to define the key performance area along with benchmark or expected performance level. Other choices are the objective of IT balanced score card.

(3) IS Auditor observed lack of senior management's involvement in IT strategy planning. The MOST likely risk is:

A. a lack of investment in technology.
B. absence of structured methodology for IT security.
C. absence of IT alignment with business objectives.
D. an absence of control over outsourced vendors.

Answer: C. absence of IT alignment with business objectives.

Explanation:
Major risk can be absence of IT alignment with business objectives. A steering committee should exist to ensure that the IT strategies support the organization's goals.

(4) Which of the following is the PRIMARY objective of an IT performance measurement process?

A. To reduce error.

B. To obtain performance data.
C. To finalize the requirement baseline.
D. To improve performance.

Answer: D. To improve performance.

Explanation:
Prime objective for IT measurement process is to optimize the performance of IT services. An IT performance measurement process can be used to optimize performance, measure and manage products/services, assure accountability, and make budget decisions. Other options are aspects of performance measurement but not prime objective.

Roles of Important functions:

Board of directors:
IT governance is primarily the responsibility of the board of directors.

Strategy Committee:
Role of strategy committee is to advise board on IT initiative. Strategy committee generally consists of board members and specialized non-board members.

Steering Committee:
The role of an IT steering committee is to ensure that the IS department is in harmony with the organization's mission and objectives. To ensure this, the committee must determine whether IS processes support the business requirements.

The IT steering committee monitors and facilitates deployment of IT resources for specific projects in support of business plans.

Project Steering Committee:
A project steering committee usually consists of a senior representative from each function that will be affected by the new system. They provide overall direction and monitors costs and project schedules & timetables.

The project steering committee is ultimately responsible for all costs and timetables of the project. The function of the steering committee is to ensure the success of the project. If there are factors or issues that potentially could affect planned results, the steering committee should escalate them.

User Management:
User management assumes ownership of the project and the resulting system. They review and approve deliverables as they are defined and accomplished.

System Development Management:
System development management provides technical support for the hardware and software environments by developing, installing and operating the requested system.

Project Sponsor:
The project sponsor is the manager in charge of the business function, the owner of the data and the owner of the system under development. Providing functional specifications through functional users is the responsibility of the project sponsor.

Question, Answer & Explanation:

(1)Which of the following authority is ultimately responsible for the development of an IS security policy:

A. IS department.
B. security committee.
C. IS audit department.
D. board of directors.

Answer: D. board of directors.

Explanation:
Board of directors in any organization have ultimate responsibility for the development of IS security function. Security committee performs as per the direction of board. The IS department is responsible for the execution of the policy. IS audit department need to ensure proper implementation of IS security policy and in case of any deviation need to report to management.

(2)Senior Management's involvement is very vital in the development of:

A. strategic plans.
B. IS security guidelines.
C. IS security procedures.
D. IS Functions.

Answer: A. strategic plans.

Explanation:
Strategic plans are the basis for achieving organization's goal and objectives. Involvement of senior management is critical for ensuring that the plan is aligned with business objectives. Other options are all structured to support the overall strategic plan.

(3)Which of the following is a function of an IS steering committee?

A. Managing outsourced vendors for IS services.
B. Proper segregation of duties for IS processes.
C. Approving and monitoring major projects, the status of IS plans and budgets.
D. Implementing IS security procedures.

Answer: C. Approving and monitoring major projects, the status of IS plans and budgets

Explanation:
IS steering committee basically monitors the implementation of IT projects in the organizations. The IS steering committee typically serves as a general review board for major IS projects and should not become involved in routine operations; therefore, one of its functions is to approve and monitor major projects, the status of IS plans and budgets. Other functions are not the function of IS steering committee.

(4) Who is primarily responsible for IT governance:

A. IT strategy committee.
B. board of directors.
C. IT steering committee.
D. audit committee.

Answer: B. board of directors.

Explanation:
Board of directors in any organization have ultimate responsibility for the IT governance. IT strategy committee advises the board and IT steering committee monitors the board approved IT governance policy and facilitates deployment of IT resources for specific projects in support of business plans. The audit committee looks after audit issues and control part.

(5) Which of the following team should assume overall responsibility for system development projects?

A. audit committee
B. project steering committee
C. user management
D. Systems development management

Answer: B. Project steering committee

Explanation:
Project steering committee is ultimately responsible for total project management for IT related projects. They provide direction and monitors costs and project schedules. Audit committee do not involve in monitoring the projects. User management and system development management are involved in projects to the extent of their role however responsibility lies with project steering committee. User management assumes ownership of the project and resulting system. They should review and approve deliverables as they are defined and accomplished.

(6) Which of the following should take ownership of project for system development?

A. User management
B. Project strategy committee.
C. Project steering committee
D. Systems development management

Answer: A. User management

Explanation:
User management assumes ownership of the project. Project should be defined by user management. Also, they should review and approve deliverables to ensure that project is as per their requirement. Role of Strategy Committee is to advise board on IT initiatives. The project steering committee provides overall direction and is also responsible for monitoring project costs and project schedules. Systems development management is responsible for providing technical support.

(7)IS department is in process of floating the request for proposal (RFP) for the acquisition of an application system. Who would MOST likely to approve content of RFP:

A. project steering committee.
B. project sponsor.
C. project manager.
D. IS Strategy committee.

Answer: A. project steering committee.

Explanation:
The project steering committee provides overall direction and is also responsible for monitoring project costs and project schedules .A project steering committee usually consists of a senior representative from each function that will be affected by the new system and would be the most appropriate group to approve the RFP. The project sponsor provides funding for the project. IS strategy committee advices board of directors on IT initiatives.

(8) Who among the following is responsible for internal control in the organization:

A. Accounting department.
B. management.

C. the external auditor.
D. IS auditor.

Answer: B. management.

Explanation:
Management is ultimately responsible for effectiveness of internal control mechanism. Designing, implementing and maintaining a system of internal controls, including the prevention and detection of fraud is the responsibility of management.

(9)Requirement specifications is ultimately responsibility of :

A. Top Management
B. Project sponsor
C. System analyst
D. Steering committee

Answer: B. Project sponsor

Explanation:
The project sponsor is the manager in charge of the business function, the owner of the data and the owner of the system under development. Providing functional specifications through functional users is the responsibility of the project sponsor.

(10)An organization has established a steering committee to oversee its application development program. Following is the function of the steering committee:

A. documentation of requirements.
B. escalation of project issues.
C. design of interface controls.
D. specification of reports.

Answer: B. escalation of project issues.

Explanation:
The function of the steering committee is to ensure the success of the project. If there are factors or issues that potentially could affect planned results, the steering committee should escalate them.

(11) Accountability for the maintenance of appropriate security measures over information assets resides with the:

A. security administrator.
B. database administrator.
C. resource owners.
D. IT group.

Answer: C. resource owners.

Explanation:
Resource owners are accountable for protection of their resources. Management should ensure that all information assets (data and systems) have an appointed owner who makes decisions about classification and access rights. System owners typically delegate day-to-day custodianship to the systems delivery/operations

group and security responsibilities to a security administrator. Owners, however, remain accountable for the maintenance of appropriate security measures.

(12) Who of the following is ultimately responsible for providing requirement specifications to the software development project team?

A. Team leader
B. Project sponsor
C. System analyst
D. Steering committee

Answer: B. Project sponsor

Explanation:
The project sponsor is the manager in charge of the business function, the owner of the data and the owner of the system under development. Providing functional specifications through functional users is the responsibility of the project sponsor. The other choices are incorrect.

(13)Who assumes ownership of a systems-development project and the resulting system?

A. User management
B. Project steering committee
C. IT management
D. Systems developers

Answer: A

Explanation:
User management assumes ownership of a systems-development project and the resulting system.

Last Minute Revision:

Function	Role
Board of Directors	Ultimate responsibility for IT governance.
IT Strategy Committee	Advises board on IT Strategy.
IT Steering Committee	Monitors IT projects, costs and timelines. Ensures alignment between IT and business objectives.
Project Sponsor	Assumes ownership of project and resulting systems. Providing functional requirements. To review and approve deliverables.
System Development Management	Provides technical support for hardware and software.

As per CRM 'For the CISA exam, the IS auditor must be aware of these globally recognized concepts; however, knowledge of specific legislation and regulations will not be tested.'

Introduction:

- Some of the global compliance requirement includes protection of privacy and confidentiality of personal data, intellectual property rights and reliability of financial information.
- IS auditor to ensure that requirements pertaining to the use of IT resources, systems and data should be reviewed to assess whether organization is effectively managing associated risk.
- Some organizations are operating in multiple jurisdictions. They must be aware of the legal and regulatory requirements in those areas in which they operate.
- In few scenario, laws and regulations may apply to organizations even if they do not operate in the jurisdiction where the law or regulation was created. For example, GDPR applies not only to organizations within the European Union, but organizations that do business with individuals in the European Union as well.
- Governance, risk management and compliance (GRC) is an integrated approach for managing three areas. GRC includes multiple overlapping and related activities within an organization, which may include internal audit, compliance requirements, ERM, operational risk, incident management and other activities.
- Examples of laws that may require audit include:
  - Financial Services Modernization Act of 1999, better known as the Gramm-Leach-Bliley Act (GLBA)
  - Family Educational Rights and Privacy Act (FERPA)
  - Children's Online Privacy Protection Act (COPPA)
  - Children's Internet Protection Act (CIPA)
  - Health Insurance Portability and Accountability Act (HIPAA)
  - The Federal Information Security Management Act of 2002 (FISMA)
  - Canada's Personal Information Protection and Electronic Documents Act (PIPEDA)
  - South Korea's Personal Information Protection Act (PIPA)
  - South Africa's Protection of Personal Information (POPI) Act
  - The UK Ministry of Defence's (MOD) DEFCON 658
  - The European Union's GDPR

Following guidelines (issued by IIA) to be considered when auditing regulatory compliance:

- **Standards and procedure:** Availability of compliance standards and procedures which employees and other entities should follow to reduce the risk of regulatory breach.

- **Assignment of responsibility to senior personnel:** Compliance responsibility should be assigned to individual(s) within senior management of the organization.

- **Reliable background of staff:** Proper background verification to be conducted prior to establishing access or authority roles to ensure that such power is not delegated to individuals who have conducted illegal activity.

- **Communication of procedures:** Standards and procedures should be communicated effectively to all employees and other stakeholders.

- **Compliance monitoring and auditing:** Appropriate steps with respect to monitoring and reporting to be taken to achieve compliance with its standards.

- **Consistent enforcement**: Organization should ensure that compliance is enforced consistently throughout the organization with appropriate disciplinary action taken toward offenders.

- **Appropriate response to an offense and prevention of similar offenses:** Organizations report to proper authorities once an offense is detected/occurs and act to prevent future offenses in a timely manner.

(1) An IS auditor is reviewing regulatory compliance of an organization. Which of the following is the major concern?

(A)Organization do not have documented process to report offence(s) to respective regulator.
(B)Standards and procedures are not communicated to all employees and other stakeholders.
(C)Compliance responsibility is assigned to a junior staff member.
(D)Organization do not have list of applicable laws and regulations.

Answer: (D)Organization do not have list of applicable laws and regulations.

Explanation: In absence of list of all applicable laws and regulations, it is not possible to monitor the compliance level and ensue adherence to respective laws and regulation. Other options are not as critical as option (D).

(2) Which of the following is MOST essential to optimize IT activities?

(A)Performance metrics
(B)IT budget variance analysis
(C)Compliance with regulatory requirements
(D)Optimum IT resource utilization

Answer: (C)Compliance with regulatory requirements

Explanation: Utmost important and essential option will be compliance with regulatory requirements.

As per CRM 'The IS auditor needs to understand the QA and quality management concepts, structures, and roles and responsibilities within the organization.'

Quality Assurance:

- Quality assurance is a process to provide adequate confidence that an item or product conforms to established requirements.
- QA personnel verify that system changes are authorized, tested and implemented in a controlled manner.
- Quality Control (QC) is process for conducting tests or reviews to verify and ensure that product is defect free and as per requirement of the user.
- Generally, two distinct tasks are performed by quality assurance personnel:
  - **Quality assurance (QA):** Provides assurance that an item or product conforms to the set down requirements.
  - **Quality control (QC):** Observation techniques or activities to ensure that requirements of quality are fulfilled.

Quality Assurance	Quality Control
Pro-active	Reactive
Prevent Defects	Find Defects
More focused on process	More focused on product

- QC is responsible to ensure that software is free from defects and meets user expectations.
- QC must be done before the programs are moved into production.
- For effective quality assurance, it is recommended to have independent QA group independent within the organization.
- QC role should not be performed by an individual whose role would create a segregation of duties (SoD) conflict. Under no circumstances should an individual review his/her own work.
- For example, quality review by a database administrator for processes that would impact database.

Quality Management:

- Through quality management processes are controlled, measured and improved.
- Some areas for quality management may include:
  - Software development, maintenance and implementation
  - Purchase of hardware and software
  - Operational activities
  - Service management
  - Security
  - HR management

(1) An IS auditor is reviewing quality assurance process of an organization. Which of the following will area of major concern?

(A)Quality Assurance processes have not been documented.
(B)Outcome of quality checks are not presented to senior management.
(C)QA is performed by member nominated by Business Manager.
(D)QA parameters are not benchmarked with industry standards.

Answer: (C)QA is performed by member nominated by Business Manager.

Explanation: For effective quality assurance, it is recommended to have independent QA group independent within the organization. QC role should not be performed by an individual whose role would create a segregation of duties (SoD) conflict. Under no circumstances should an individual review his/her own work. Other options though have concerns; however major area of concern will be option (C).

(2) An IS auditor is reviewing quality control process of a software developing company. Which of the following will area of major concern?

(A)Quality controls parameters are not documented.
(B)Quality control activity is outsourced.
(C)QC parameters are not benchmarked with industry standards.
(D)QC is done after 3 months of program being moved to production.

Answer: (D)QC is done after 3 months of program being moved to production.

Explanation: QC is responsible to ensure that software is free from defects and meets user expectations.
QC must be done before the programs are moved into production. Option (A) and (C) have concerns; however major area of concern will be option (D). There is nothing wrong in QC being outsourced, provided appropriate outsourcing controls are in place.

CRM covers following Online Auditing Techniques:

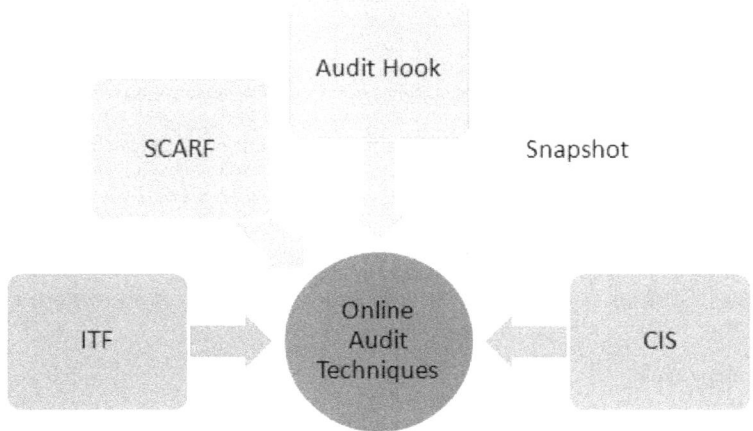

Integrated Test Facility (ITF):
- Fictitious entity is created in LIVE environment.
- This technique allows auditor to open a dummy account.
- Auditor can enter dummy or test transactions and verify the processing and results of these transactions for correctness.
- Processed results and expected results are compared to verify that systems are operating correctly.
- Example: A dummy asset of $ 100000/- is entered into system to verify whether same is being capitalized under correct head and depreciation is calculated properly as per correct rate. Subsequently this dummy transaction is removed after verification of system controls.

System Control Audit Review File (SCARF):
- SCARF stands for System Control Audit Review File.
- In this technique an embedded (inbuilt) audit module is used to continuously monitor transactions.
- This technique is used to collect data for special audit purpose.
- SCARF files records only those transactions which are of special audit significance such transactions above specified limit or transactions related to deviation/exception.
- On regular basis, auditor gets a printout of the SCARF file for examination and verification.

Snapshot Technique:
- In this technique, snaps (pictures) are taken of the transactions as transaction moves through various stages in the application system.
- Both before -processing and after -processing images of the transactions are captured.-Auditor can verify the correctness of the processing by checking before-processing and after-processing images of the transactions.
- In this technique, three important considerations are (i)location where snaps to be taken (ii)time of capturing snaps and (iii) reporting of snapshot data captured.

Audit Hook:

- These are audit software that captures suspicious transactions.
- Criteria for suspicious transactions are designed by auditors as per their requirement.
- For example, in most of the organizations, cash transactions are monitored closely. Criteria can be designed to capture cash transaction exceeding $ 50000/- All such captured transactions are subsequently verified by auditor to identify fraud, if any.
- Audit hook is useful when early detection of error or fraud is required.

Continuous and Intermittent Simulation (CIS):
- This technique is variation of SCARF technique.
- This technique can be used whenever the application system uses the database management system (DBMS).
- DBMS reads the transaction which is passed to CIS. If transaction is as per selected criteria, then CIS examines the transaction for correctness.
- CIS determines whether any discrepancies exist between the results it produces and those the application system produces.
- Such discrepancies are written to exception log file.
- Thus, CIS replicates or simulates the application system processing.
- As high complex criteria can be set in CIS, it is the best technique to identify transactions as per pre-defined criteria.

Question, Answer & Explanation:

(1)Management of an organization is evaluating automated audit tool for its critical business processes. Which of the following audit tools is MOST useful when an audit trail is required?

A. Integrated test facility (ITF)
B. Continuous and intermittent simulation (CIS)
C. Audit hooks
D. Snapshots

Answer: D. Snapshots

Explanation:
In snapshot technique, snaps (pictures) are taken of the transactions as transaction moves through various stages in the application system. Both before -processing and after -processing images of the transactions are captured. Auditor can verify the correctness of the processing by checking before-processing and after-processing images of the transactions.

(2)Integrated test facility (ITF) has advantage over other automated audit tools because of its following characteristics:

A. Creation of dummies/fictitious entity is not required as testing is done on actual master files.
B. ITF does not require setting up separate test environment/test processes.
C. ITF is continuous audit tool and validates the ongoing operation of the system.
D. ITF eliminates the need to prepare test data.

Answer: B. ITF does not require setting up separate test environment/test processes.

Explanation:
Fictitious entity is created in LIVE environment. As live environment is used, there is no need to create separate test processes. However, careful planning is necessary and test data must be isolated from production data.

(3)Characteristics that BEST describes an integrated test facility:

A. Technique to verify system processing.
B. Technique to verify system integration.
C. Technique to generate test data.
D. Technique to validate the ongoing operation of the system.

Answer: A. Technique to verify system processing.

Explanation:
In ITF, fictitious entity is created in LIVE environment. Auditor can enter dummy or test transactions and verify the processing and results of these transactions for correctness. Processed results and expected results are compared to verify that systems are operating correctly. ITF does not verify system integration neither it is used to generate test data. ITF does not validate the ongoing operation of the system.

(4) Management of an organization is evaluating automated audit tool for its critical business processes. Which of the following audit tools is MOST useful for the early detection of errors or irregularities?

A. Embedded audit module
B. Integrated test facility
C. Snapshots
D. Audit hooks

Answer: D. Audit hooks

Explanation:
The audit hook technique involves embedding code in application systems for the examination of selected transactions. This helps the IS auditor to act before an error or an irregularity gets out of hand. Audit hooks have very low complexity in designing criteria and hence most useful tool when early detection is warranted.

(5)Which of the below online auditing tool would best identify transactions as per predefined criteria?

A. Systems Control Audit Review File and Embedded Audit Modules (SCARF/EAM)
B. Continuous and Intermittent Simulation (CIS)
C. Integrated Test Facilities (ITF)
D. Audit hooks

Answer: B. Continuous and Intermittent Simulation (CIS)

Explanation:
As high complex criteria can be set in CIS, it is the best technique to identify transactions as per pre-defined criteria. Continuous and Intermittent Simulation (CIS) is a moderately complex set of programs that during a process run of a transaction, simulates the instruction execution of its application. As each transaction is entered, the simulator decides whether the transaction meets certain predetermined criteria and if so, audits the transaction. If not, the simulator waits until it encounters the next transaction that meets the criteria. Audits hooks which are of low complexity focus on specific conditions instead of detailed criteria in identifying transactions for review. ITF is incorrect because its focus is on test versus live data.

(6)Characteristics that BEST describes an integrated test facility:

A. actual transactions are validated on ongoing basis.
B. enables the IS auditors to generate test data.
C. pre-determined results are compared with processing output to ascertain correctness of

system processing.
D. enables the IS auditors to analyse large range of information.

Answer: C. pre-determined results are compared with processing output to ascertain correctness of system processing.

Explanation:
In ITF technique, auditor can enter dummy or test transactions and verify the processing and results of these transactions for correctness. Processed results and expected results are compared to verify that systems are operating correctly. Other options are not correct in view of ITF characteristics.

(7) To identify excess inventory for the previous year, which online auditing technique can be used?

A. Test data
B. Generalized audit software
C. Integrated test facility
D. Embedded audit module

Answer: B. Generalized audit software

Explanation: The IS auditor, using generalized audit software, could design appropriate tests to identify excess inventory. Test data would not be relevant here as audit will be required on actual data. ITF and EAM cannot detect errors for a previous period.

Last Minute Revision:

ITF	SCARF	Audit Hook	Snapshot	CIS
• Dummy entities are created in live production environment	• Inbuilt audit software used when regular processing cannot be interrupted	• Audit hook is useful when early detection of error or fraud is required.	• Take pictures • (snaps) • Used when audit trial is required.	• Used with DBMS. • CIS simulates the application system processing. • As high complex criteria can be set in CIS, it is the best technique to identify transactions as per pre-defined criteria.

Following diagram depicts the stages of Software Development Testing:

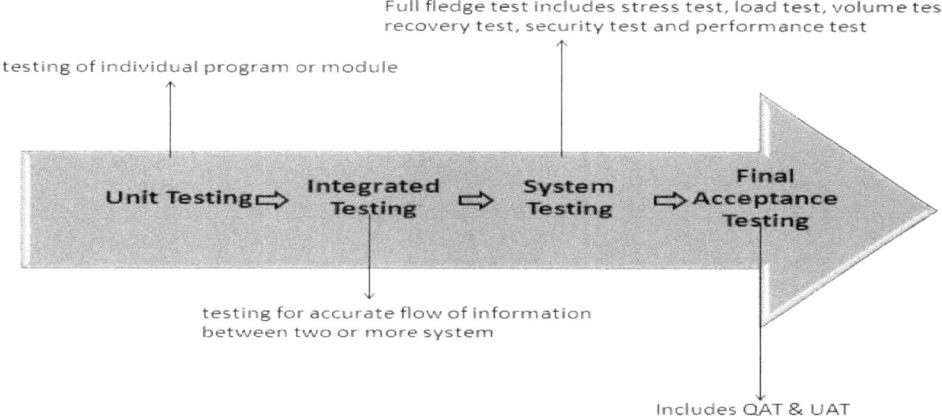

Unit Testing:

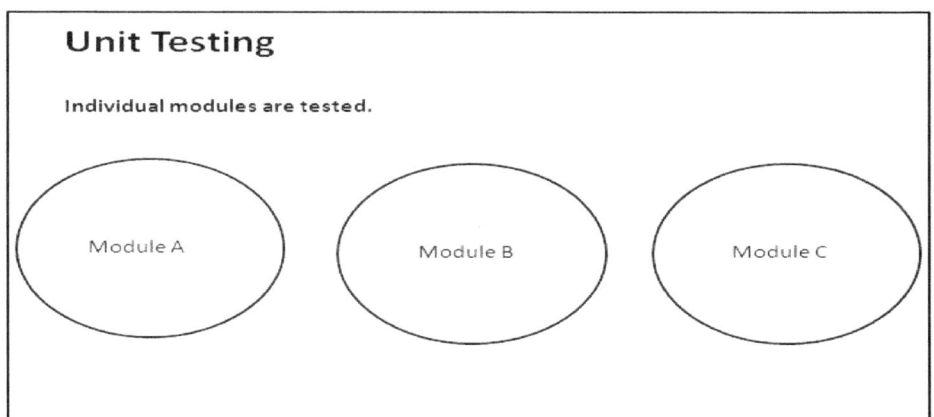

Unit testing involves testing of individual program or module.

Characteristics of unit testing:

- Testing is done by developer as and when individual program or module is ready. No need to wait till completion of full software.
- White box approach (i.e. testing of internal program logic) is applied in unit testing.

Integrated Testing/Interface Testing:

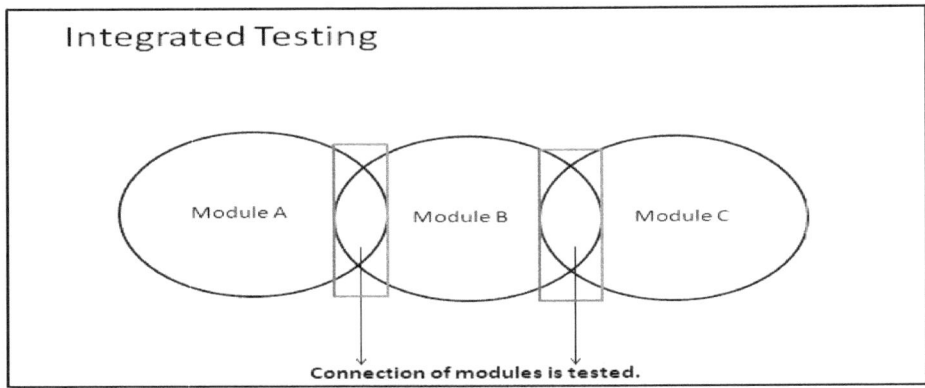

Dictionary meaning of integrate is 'to connect'. Integrated testing involves testing of connection of two or more module or components that pass information from one area to another.

System Testing:

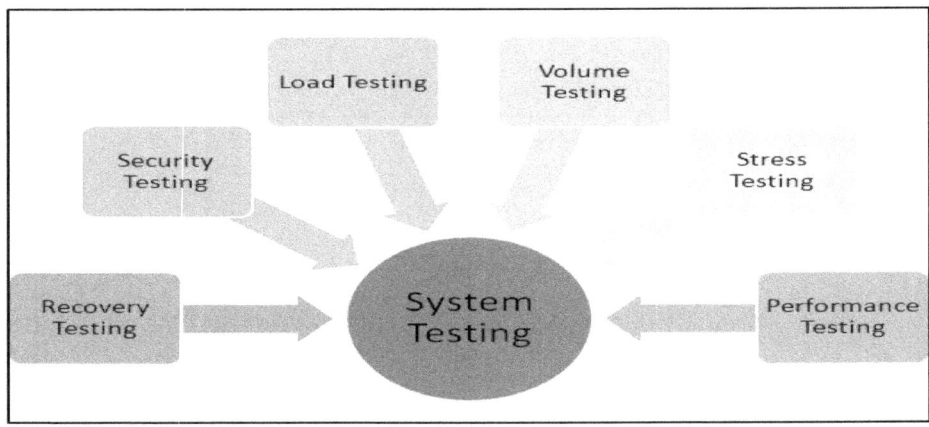

The primary reason for system testing is to evaluate the entire system functionality. System testing includes (i)Recovery testing (ii)Security testing (iii)Load testing (iv)Volume testing (v)Stress testing & (vi)Performance testing.

Final Acceptance Testing:

Final Acceptance Testing includes (i) Quality Assurance Testing (QAT) & (ii) User Acceptance Testing (UAT)

Other Types of Testing:

Regression Testing:

Dictionary meaning of regression is 'act of going back' or 'to return'. Thus in regression testing, testing done again to ensure that changes or corrections in a program have not introduced new errors.

Data used for regression testing should be same data as used in previous test. Regression testing ensures that changes or corrections in a program have not introduced new errors. Therefore, this would be achieved only if the data used for regression testing are the same as the data used in previous tests.

Sociability Testing:

Dictionary meaning of sociability is 'ability to have companionship with others'. Sociability test is a test to ensure that new or modified system can work in the specified environment without adversely impacting existing system.

Pilot Testing:

Pilot testing takes place first at one location to review the performance. The purpose is to see if the new system operates satisfactorily in one place before implementing it at other locations.

Parallel Testing:

Parallel testing is the process of comparing results of the old and new system. The purpose of parallel testing is to ensure that the implementation of a new system meets user requirements.

White Box Testing vis-a-vis Black Box Testing:

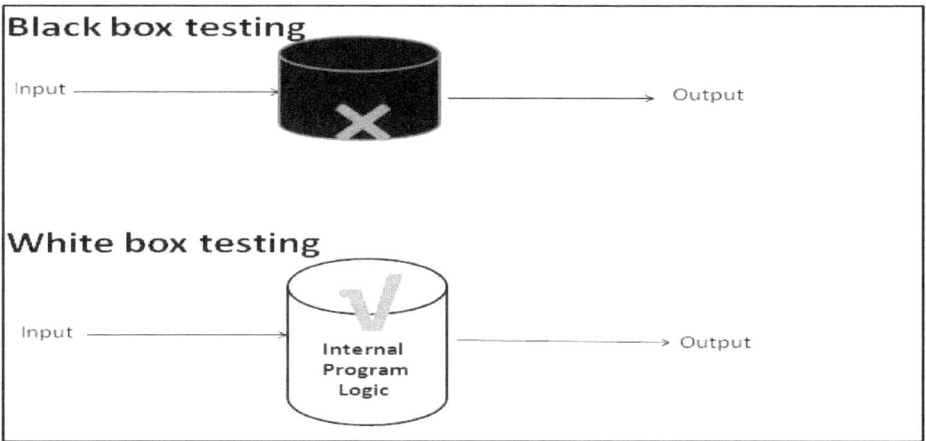

White Box Testing	Black Box Testing
Program logic is tested.	Only functionality is tested. Program logics are not tested.
Applicable for unit testing and interface testing	Applicable for user acceptance testing(UAT) and interface testing
Detailed knowledge of programming is required.	Testing can be performed without knowledge of programming.

Alpha Testing vis-a-vis Beta Testing:

Alpha Testing	Beta Testing
Testing done by internal user.	Testing done by external user.
Alpha testing is done prior to beta testing.	Beta testing is done after alpha testing.
Alpha testing may not involve testing of full functionality.	Generally, beta testing involves testing of full functionality.

Top-Down Approach vis-a-vis Bottom-Up Approach:

Bottom-Up Approach	Top-Down Approach
Begin testing of individual units such as programs or modules and work upward until a complete system is tested.	Opposite of bottom-up approach. Test starts from broader level and then gradually moves towards individual programs and modules.
Advantages: (i) Test can be started even before all programs are complete (ii) Errors in critical modules can be found early.	Advantages: (i) Interface error can be detected earlier (ii) confidence in the system is achieved earlier.
-	More appropriate for prototype development.

Regression Testing vis-a-vis Sociability Testing:

Regression Testing	Sociability Testing
Test to ensure that corrections or changes done have not introduced new errors.	Test to ensure that new or modified system can work without adversely impacting existing system.

Unit Testing vis-a-vis Interface Testing/Integrate Testing:

Unit Testing	Interface Testing/Integrate Testing
Involves testing of individual program or module.	Involves testing of connection of two or more components that pass information from one area to another. Test of integrated system.

Question, Answer & Explanation:

(1)A system is in development phase. Which of the following test is MOST likely to be conducted?

A. User acceptance test
B. Stress test
C. Regression test
D. Unit test

Answer: D. Unit test

Explanation:
Unit test involves testing of individual program or module. During the development stage, the development team should ensure that individual module or programs should be tested to ensure that code is working correctly. Stress test, regression test and acceptance test would normally occur later once system is developed and ready for implementation.

(2) Which of the following approach is applied during unit testing?

A. top-down
B. black box
C. bottom-up
D. white box

Answer: D. white box

Explanation:
In any given scenario, for unit testing appropriate strategy is white box approach (as both involve testing of internal logic).Unit testing involves testing of individual program or module. In white box testing, program logic is tested. It is applicable for unit testing and interface testing. White box testing examines the internal structure of a module. In black box, only functionality is tested. Program logics are not tested and hence not relevant for unit testing.

(3)Testing the network of two or more system for accurate flow of information between them is:

A. unit testing
B. interface testing
C. sociability testing
D. regression testing

Answer: B. interface testing

Explanation:
Interface testing is a hardware or software test that evaluates the connection of two or more components that pass information from one area to another.

(4)In several instances, system interface failures are occurred when corrections to previously detected errors are resubmitted. This would indicate absence of which of the following types of testing?

A. Pilot testing
B. Integration testing
C. Parallel testing
D. Unit testing

Answer: B. Integration testing

Explanation:
Integration testing/interface testing is done to ensure flow of information between two or more system is correct and accurate. Integration testing aims at ensuring that the major components of the system interface correctly. Pilot testing takes place first at one location to review the performance. The purpose is to see if the new system operates satisfactorily in one place before implementing it at other locations.
Parallel testing is the process of comparing results of the old and new system.
Unit test involves testing of individual program or module. During the development stage, the development team should ensure that individual module or programs should be tested to ensure that code is working correctly.

(5)Unit testing indicates that individual modules are operating correctly. The IS auditor should:

A. conclude that system as a whole can produce the desired results.
B. document the test result as a proof for system functionality.

C. review the findings of integrated test.
D. conduct the test again to confirm the findings.

Answer: C. review the findings of integrated test.

Explanation:
After unit testing, next stage is integrated test. Integrated testing involves testing of connection of two or more module or components that pass information from one area to another. Modules that have been tested individually can have interface problems, causing adverse affects on other modules. Therefore, the most appropriate action for the IS auditor is to review results of integrated test.

(6)Purpose of regression testing is to determine if:

A. new or modified system can work without adversely impacting existing system.
B. flow of information between two or more system is correct and accurate.
C. new requirements have been met.
D. changes have not introduced any new errors in the unchanged code.

Answer: D. changes have not introduced any new errors in the unchanged code.

Explanation:
Regression testing is done to ensure that changes or corrections have not introduced new errors. Sociability testing is done to ensure that new or modified system can work without adversely impacting existing system. Integration testing is done to ensure flow of information between two or more system is correct and accurate.

(7) An organization is conducting regression testing for rectified bugs in the system. What data should be used for regression testing?

A. Same data as used in previous test
B. Random data
C. Different data as used in previous test
D. Data produced by a test data generator

Answer: A. Same data as used in previous test

Explanation:
Dictionary meaning of regression is 'act of going back' or to 'return'. Regression testing ensures that changes or corrections in a program have not introduced new errors. Therefore, this would be achieved only if the data used for regression testing are the same as the data used in previous tests.

(8)A new system has been added to client-server environment. Which of the following tests would confirm that modification in window registry will not impact performance of existing environment?

A. Regression testing
B. Parallel testing
C. White box testing
D. Sociability testing

Answer: D. Sociability testing

Explanation:

Sociability testing helps to ensure that new or modified system can work without adversely impacting existing system. When implementing a new system in an client-server environment, sociability testing would confirm that the system can operate in the environment without adversely impacting other systems.

(9)An organization wants to evaluate whether a new or modified system can operate in its target environment without adversely impacting other existing systems. Which of the following testing would be relevant?

A. Regression testing
B. Sociability testing
C. Interface/integration testing
D Pilot testing

Answer: B. Sociability testing

Explanation:
Sociability testing is done to ensure that new or modified system can work without adversely impacting existing system. The purpose of sociability testing is to confirm that a new or modified system can operate in its target environment without adversely impacting existing systems. Regression testing is done to ensure that changes or corrections have not introduced new errors. Integration testing/interface testing is done to ensure flow of information between two or more system is correct and accurate.

Pilot testing takes place first at one location to review the performance. The purpose is to see if the new system operates satisfactorily in one place before implementing it at other locations.

(10)Which of the following characteristic of white box testing differentiates between white box testing and black box testing?

A. white-box testing involves IS auditor.
B. white-box testing involves testing of program's logical structure.
C. white-box testing involves bottom-up approach.
D. white-box testing does not involve testing of program's logical structure.

Answer: B. white-box testing involves testing of program's logical structure.

Explanation:
In white-box testing, program logic is tested whereas in black-box testing only functionality is tested. In black-box testing, program logic is not tested. White box testing requires knowledge of the internals of the program or the module to be implemented/tested. Black box testing requires that the functionality of the program be known. The IS auditor need not be involved in either testing method.
The bottom-up approach can be used in both tests.

(11)An organization implementing a new system adopted parallel testing. Which of the following is the PRIMARY purpose for conducting parallel testing?

A. To ensure cost is within the budget.
B. To document system functionality.
C. To highlight errors in the program logic.
D. To validate system functionality with user requirements.

Answer: D. To validate system functionality with user requirements.

Explanation:

Parallel testing is the process of comparing results of the old and new system. The purpose of parallel testing is to ensure that the implementation of a new system will meet user requirements. Unit testing is used to validate program logic of individual module or system.

(12) An organization is implementing bottom-up approach for software testing. An advantage in using a bottom-up as against a top-down approach is that:

A. errors in critical modules can be found early.
B. test can be performed only once all programs are complete.
C. errors in interface can be found early.
D. confidence in the system is achieved earlier.

Answer: A. errors in critical modules can be found early.

Explanation:
Bottom-Up Approach: Start with testing of individual units such as programs or modules and work upward until a complete system is tested. Advantages of bottom-up: (i) Test can be started even before all programs are complete (ii) Errors in critical modules can be found early. Top-Down Approach: Opposite of bottom-up approach. Test starts from broader level and then gradually moves towards individual programs and modules. Advantages of top-down: (i) Interface error can be detected earlier (ii) confidence in the system is achieved earlier.

(13) An IS auditor is reviewing process of acceptance testing. What should be the IS auditor's major concern?

A. Test objectives not documented.
B. Expected test results not documented by user.
C. Test problem log not updated.
D. unsolved major issues.

Answer: D. unsolved major issues.

Explanation:
All the options are concern for IS auditor reviewing process of acceptance testing. However major concern is option D i.e. major issues are still pending. The IS auditor should then determine the impact of the unresolved issues on system functionality and usability.

(14)For a software development, an organization has planned following test. Failure in which stage can have the GREATEST adverse impact on cost and time budget?

A. Unit testing
B. Integration testing
C. System testing
D. Acceptance testing

Answer: D. Acceptance testing

Explanation:
First stage of testing is unit testing. Second stage is integrated testing. Third stage is system testing and fourth one is final acceptance testing. Acceptance testing is the final stage before the software is installed and is available for use. The greatest impact would occur if the software fails at the acceptance testing level, as this could result in delays and cost overruns. Unit, Integration and System testing is conducted by developer at different stages of development and impact of failure is comparatively less than acceptance testing.

(15)An organization is conducting system testing for newly developed software. The primary purpose of a system test is to:

A. test efficiency of security controls built in the system.
B. determine appropriate documentation of system functionality.
C. evaluate the system functionality.
D. identify and document the benefit of new system.

Answer: C. evaluate the system functionality.

Explanation:
System testing includes (i) Recovery testing (ii) Security testing (iii) Load testing (iv) Volume testing (v) Stress testing & (vi)Performance testing. The primary reason why a system is tested is to evaluate the entire system functionality.

(16) A major vulnerability was observed in a application by IS team. To mitigate risk, a patch was applied to a significant number of modules. Which of the following tests should an IS auditor recommend?

A. Security testing
B. load testing
C. System testing
D. Interface testing

Answer: C. System testing

Explanation:
System testing includes (i) Recovery testing (ii)Security testing (iii)Load testing (iv)Volume testing (v) Stress testing & (vi) Performance testing. Given the extensiveness of the patch system testing is most appropriate. Interface testing is not enough, and security and load testing are part of system testing.

(17) An organization has implemented prototyping approach for development of system. Which of the following testing methods is MOST effective during the initial phases of prototyping?

A. bottom-up
B. parallel
C. volume
D. top-down

Answer: D.top-down

Explanation:
In top-down, test starts from broader level and then gradually moves towards individual programs and modules. Advantages of top-down approach are (i) Interface error can be detected earlier (ii) confidence in the system is achieved earlier. A prototype is an early sample, model, or release of a product built to test a concept or process or to act as a thing to be replicated or learned from. The initial emphasis when using prototyping is to create screens and reports, thus shaping most of the proposed system's features in a short period. Top-down testing method is most effective for prototype development.

(18)Best approach for conducting stress testing is:

A. using test data and in test environment.
B. using live data and in production environment.

C. using live data and in test environment.
D. using test data and in production environment.

Answer: C. using live data and in test environment.

Explanation:
Stress testing is carried out to determine maximum number of concurrent users/services the application can process. A test environment should always be used to avoid damaging the production environment. Test data may not cover the entire scenario in accordance with live workload and hence live data gives accurate result for stress testing.

(19)In final acceptance testing, QAT and UAT were combined. The MAJOR concern will be:

A. increase in cost of testing.
B. inadequate documentation.
C. insufficient functional testing.
D. delays in test results.

Answer: C. insufficient functional testing.
Explanation:
The major concern of combining quality assurance testing and user acceptance testing is that functional testing may not be sufficient for accurate result. Other options are not as important.

(20) When creating data for testing the logic in a new system, which of the following is MOST critical?

A. quantity of the data.
B. data designed as per expected live processing.
C. sample of actual data
D. completing the test as per schedule.

Answer: B. data designed as per expected live processing.

Explanation:
Data designed as per expected live processing gives accurate result. Quality is more important than quantity. Sample of actual data may not cover all the scenarios in the live environment.

Last Minute Revision:

- ISACA will try to confuse us with three terms i.e. regression testing, sociability testing and interface testing.
- Please remember difference between the three. Regression (dictionary meaning-'to return') is test to check again that changes/modifications have not introduced any new errors. Sociability (dictionary meaning- "ability to have companionship with others') is test to determine adoptability of new system to settle in existing environment. Integration (dictionary meaning-'to connect') is test to ensure flow of information between two or more system is correct and accurate.
- In any given scenario, for unit testing appropriate strategy is white box approach (as both involve testing of internal logic).
- In any given scenario, test data should be designed as per live workload for accurate test result.
- In any given scenario, test environment should always be used (i.e. test should not be conducted in live/production environment).

Following are some of the important technical controls covered in CISA Review Manual (CRM):

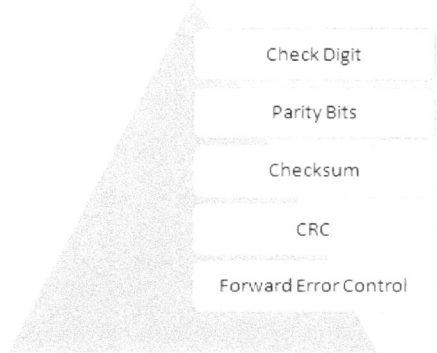

Check Digit

Parity Bits

Checksum

CRC

Forward Error Control

Check Digit:

A check digit is a mathematically calculated value that is added to data to ensure that the original data have not been altered. This helps in avoiding transposition and transcription errors.

Example:
Check digit is used by bank to ensure the correctness of bank account numbers assigned to customers, thereby helping to avoid transposition and transcription errors.

For instance, a bank account number is "630000241453". The last digit is the check digit "3", and if the other numbers are correct then the check digit calculation must produce 3.

Step 1: Add the numbers placed in odd digits: 6+0+0+2+1+5 = 14.
Step 2: Add the numbers placed in even digits: 3+0+0+4+4 = 11.
Step 3: Deduct result of step 2 from step 1 : 14 - 11 = 3.

Therefore, the check digit value is 3.

Here we have given simple calculation for understanding. In real scenarios, calculations are more complicated.

Please note above calculation is only for understanding purpose. In CISA exam, such calculation will not be tested.

Parity Bits:

The parity method of error detection is quite simple and simply requires adding an extra bit on the data. This extra bit is called a parity bit. This bit simply says whether the number of 1 bits is odd or even. Generally the parity bit is 1 if the number of 1 bits is odd and 0 if the sum of the 1 bits is even.

This parity is verified by receiving computer to ensure data completeness and data ntegrity during transmission.

Parity bits are used to check for completeness of data transmissions. A parity check is a hardware control that detects data errors when data are read from one computer to another, from memory or during transmission.

Checksum:

Checksums are exactly same as parity but able to identify complex errors also by increasing the complexity of the arithmetic.

Cyclic Redundancy Checksums (CRC)/Redundancy Checksums:

More advanced version of checksums by increasing the complexity of the arithmetic.

Forward Error Control:

Works on same principle as CRC. However FEC also corrects the error. FEC provides the receiver with the ability to correct errors.

Atomicity:

Atomicity is a feature of databases systems where a transaction must be all-or-nothing. That is, the transaction must either fully happen, or not happens at all. The principle of atomicity requires that a transaction be completed in its entirety or not at all. If an error or interruption occurs, all changes made up to that points are backed out.

Question, Answer & Explanation:

(1)An IS auditor should recommend which of following check (control) for completeness of data transmission?

A. Check digits
B. One-for-one checking
C. Parity bits
D. Atom City

Answer: C. Parity bits

Explanation:
When objective is to identify transmission error, relevant control out of above options is parity bits. A parity check is a hardware control that detects data errors when data are read from one computer to another, from memory or during transmission. Parity bits are used to check for completeness of data transmissions. Objective of check digit is to identify transcription and transposition error.

(2)An IS auditor should suggest which of the following data validation edits for banks to avoid transposition and transcription errors and thereby ensuring the correctness of bank account numbers assigned to customers?

A. Parity check
B. Checksum
C. Check digit
D. Existence check

Answer: C. Check digit

Explanation:
When objective is to identify transcription and transposition error, best validation control is check digit. A check digit is a mathematically calculated value that is added to data to ensure that the original data have not been altered. This helps in avoiding transposition and transcription errors. Bank uses check digit to check for accuracy.

(3)An IS auditor is reviewing a process where frequency of transposition and transcription errors are very high for data entry. Which of the following data validation edits will be effective in detecting such errors?

A. Parity check
B. Duplicate check
C. Validity check
D. Check Digit

Answer: D. Check Digit

Explanation:
Check digit is effective in detecting transposition and transcription errors. A check digit is a mathematically calculated value that is added to data to ensure that the original data have not been altered. This helps in avoiding transposition and transcription errors. Parity bit is used to detect data transmission error. A validity check helps to validate the data in accordance with predetermined criteria. Duplicate check helps to prevent data duplication.

(4)An IS auditor is reviewing EDI application and observed that validation edit 'checksum' has been implemented for communication of financial transactions. Purpose of 'checksum' is to ensure:

A. source validation.
B. authenticity.
C. integrity.
D. non-repudiation.

Answer: C. integrity.

Explanation:
Checksum is used for data integrity and data completeness. Extra bit is added to the data while data transmission. This bit is verified by receiving computer to ensure data completeness and data integrity during transmission. Thus a checksum calculated on an amount field and included in the EDI communication can be used to identify unauthorized modifications. Source validation and authenticity cannot be established by a checksum alone and need other controls. Non-repudiation can be ensured by using digital signatures.

(5)Principle of data integrity that a transaction is either completed in its entirety or not at all is known as:

A. atomicity.
B. consistency.
C. isolation.
D. durability.

Answer: A. atomicity.

Explanation:
Following is the concept of ACID (atomicity, completeness, isolation and durability) principle for data integrity:

Atomicity:
Atomicity is a feature of databases systems where a transaction must be all-or-nothing. That is, the transaction must either fully happen, or not happens at all. The principle of atomicity requires that a transaction be completed in its entirety or not at all. If an error or interruption occurs, all changes made upto that points are backed out.

Consistency:
Consistency ensures that all integrity conditions in the database be maintained with each transaction.

Isolation:
Isolation means that each transaction is separated from other transactions.

Durability:
Durability means that the database survives failures (hardware or software).

(6)Main reason for implementing parity bits as a control is to validate:

A. Data source
B. Data completeness
C. Data availability
D. Data accuracy

Answer: B. Data completeness

Explanation:
Parity bits are a control used to validate data completeness. The parity method of error detection is quite simple and simply requires adding an extra bit on the data. This extra bit is called a parity bit. This bit simply says whether the number of 1 bits is odd or even. Generally the parity bit is 1 if the number of 1 bits is odd and 0 if the sum of the 1 bits is even.

This parity is verified by receiving computer to ensure data completeness and data integrity during transmission.

Parity bits are used to check for completeness of data transmissions. A parity check is a hardware control that detects data errors when data are read from one computer to another, from memory or during transmission.

(7) Which of the following control BEST detects transmission error by appending extra bits onto the end of each segment?

A.Checksum
B. parity check
C. redundancy check
D. check digits

Answer: C. redundancy check.

Explanation:
Parity check, checksum and redundancy check detects transmission error by appending extra bits. However, CRC/Redundancy check is best method to detect transmission error as it applies advanced arithmetic calculation.

Please note, when objective is to ensure completeness, control should be either parity bits or checksum (higher version of parity bit) or CRC (higher version of checksum) with following preferences for BEST detection:
- First preference to CRC.
- If CRC is not there as option then preference to be given to Checksum.
- If CRC and Checksum both are not there in option then preference to be given to Parity Bits.

(8)Detection of bursts of errors in network transmissions is Best ensured by:

A. Parity check
B. Echo check
C. Checksum
D. Cyclic redundancy check

Answer: D. Cyclic redundancy check

Explanation:
Parity check, checksum and redundancy check detects transmission error by appending extra bits. However, CRC/Redundancy check is best method to detect transmission error as it applies advanced arithmetic calculation.
The cyclic redundancy check (CRC) can check for a block of transmitted data. The workstations generate the CRC and transmit it with the data. The receiving workstation computes a CRC and compares it to the transmitted CRC. If both of them are equal, then the block is assumed error free.

(9)To ensure detection and correction of errors, redundant information is transmitted with each character or frame. This control is known as:

A. Parity bits
B. block sum check
C. forward error control
D. cyclic redundancy check

Answer: C. forward error control.

Explanation:
When objective is to correct (detect & correct) transmission error, best control will be Forward Error Control (FEC).Forward error control involves transmitting additional redundant information with each character or frame to facilitate detection and correction of errors. Other controls help to detect the error, but automatic correction will not happen.

(10) An IS auditor is reviewing a ERP system. To evaluate data integrity he should review atomicity to ensure that:

A. hardware or software failure will not impact the database.
B. each transaction is isolated from other transactions.
C. database consistency is maintained.
D. a transaction is completed in its entirety.

Answer: D. a transaction is completed in its entirety.

Explanation:

Atomicity is a feature of databases systems where a transaction must be all-or-nothing. That is, the transaction must either fully happen, or not happens at all. The principle of atomicity requires that a transaction be completed in its entirety or not at all. If an error or interruption occurs, all changes made upto that points are backed out.

This concept is included in the atomicity, completeness, isolation and durability (ACID) principle. Durability means that the database survives failures (hardware or software). Isolation means that each transaction is separated from other transactions. Consistency means that integrity conditions are maintained.

(11) An IS auditor is reviewing EDI application and observed that validation edit 'Check Digit' has been implemented for financial transactions. Purpose of 'Check Digit' is to:

A. Detect only data-transcription errors
B. Detect data-transposition and transcription errors
C. Detect data-transmission error.
D. Detect only data-transposition errors

Answer: B. Detect data-transposition and transcription errors

Explanation:
A check digit is an effective edit check to detect data-transposition and transcription errors.

Last Minute Revision:

Objective	Relevant Control
To identify transcription & transpositions error (accuracy).	Check Digit
To identify data transmission error (completeness & integrity).	•First preference to CRC. •If CRC is not there as option then preference to be given to Checksum. •If CRC and Checksum both are not there in option then preference to be given to Parity Bits.
To correct data transmission error.	Forward Error Control (FEC)
To ensure that a transaction must either fully happen or not happen at all.	Atomicity

- When objective is to identify transcription and transposition error, answer should be check digit.
- When objective is to ensure accuracy, answer should be check digit.
- When objective is to identify transmission error, answer should be parity bits or checksum (higher version of parity bit) or CRC (higher version of checksum).
- When objective is to ensure completeness, answer should be parity bits or checksum (higher version of parity bit) or CRC (higher version of checksum).
- When objective is to ensure integrity, answer should be parity bits or checksum (higher version of parity bit) or CRC (higher version of checksum).
- For point no. (3), (4) and (5), first preferences to be given as follow:(i)First preference to CRC(ii)If CRC is not there as option then preference to be given to Checksum(iii)If CRC and Checksum both are not there in option then preference to be given to Parity Bits.
- When objective is to correct (detect & correct) transmission error, answer should be Forward Error Control (FEC).
- When objective is to ensure that a transaction must either fully happen, or not happens at all, answer should be atomicity.

CRM covers following project evaluations techniques:

- **Critical Path Methodology (CPM)**

- CPM is a technique for estimating project duration. All projects have atleast one critical path.
- Critical path is sequence of activities where duration is longest as compared other path.
- Thus, CPM represents the shortest possible time required for completing the project.
- Activities on Critical Path have zero slack time.
- Alternatively, it can be said that activities with zero slack time are on a critical path.
- Slack time can be defined as the amount of time an activity can be delayed without impacting the completion date of the project. Thus zero slack time makes an activity critical and concentration on such activities will help to reduce overall project completion time.

- **Program Evaluation Review Technique (PERT)**

- PERT is a CPM type technique. PERT is a technique for estimating project duration.
- Advantage of PERT over CPM is that in CPM only single duration is considered while PERT considers three different scenarios i.e. optimistic (best), pessimistic (worst) and normal (most likely) and on the basis of three scenarios, a single critical path is arrived.
- PERT is more reliable than CPM for estimating project duration.

- **Gantt chart**

- Progress of the entire project can be read from Gantt chart to determine whether the project is behind, ahead or on schedule compared to baseline project plan.
- Gantt chart can also be used to track the achievement of milestone.

- **Function Point Analysis (FPA)**

- Indirect method of software size estimation.
- Function points are a unit measure for software size much like an hour is to measuring time, miles are to measuring distance or Celsius is to measuring temperature.
- FPA is arrived on the basis of number and complexity of inputs, outputs, files, interfaces and queries.
- FPA is more reliable than SLOC.

- **Counting source lines of code (SLOC)**

- SLOC is a direct method of software size estimation.
- FPA is more reliable as compared to SLOC specially for complex projects.

- **Earned Value Analysis (EVA)**

- EVA compares following metrics at regular interval:
  -Budget to date
  -Actual spending to date

-Estimate to complete

-Estimate at completion

- It compares the planned amount of work with what has actually been completed to determine if the cost, schedule and work accomplished are progressing in accordance with the plan.
- EVA is based on the premise that if a project task is assigned 24 hours for completion, it can be reasonably completed during that time frame. For example, a development team has spent eight hours of activity on the first day against a budget of 24 hours (over three days). The projected time to complete the remainder of the activity is 20 hours, then according to EVA following is the analysis:

Particulars	Hours	Remarks
Budgeted hours	8 hours	24 hours for 3 days i.e. 8 hour per day
Value of actual work completed	4 hours	Total budgeted hours – Pending hours i.e. (24 hours – 20 hours)
Delay in schedule	By 4 hours	

Thus value of actual work completed indicates delay of 4 hours from schedule.

- **Time- box Management**

- Major advantage of this approach is that it prevents project cost overruns and delays from scheduled delivery.
- It is used for prototyping or rapid application development where project need to be completed within timeframe.
- It integrates system and user acceptance testing, but does not eliminate the need for a quality process.

Question, Answer & Explanation:

(1) An IS auditor evaluating how the project manager has monitored the progress of the project. Which of the following is MOST relevant in this context?

A. Critical Path Methodologies
B. PERT
C. Gantt Chart
D. Function Point Analysis (FPA)

Answer: C. Gantt Chart

Explanation:
Progress of the entire project can be read from Gantt Chart to determine whether the project is behind, ahead or on schedule compared to baseline project plan. Gantt Chart can also be used to track the achievement of milestone. **Gantt charts help to identify activities that have been completed early or late through comparison to a baseline.** Following table shows objective of each of the above mentioned options:

Technique	Objective
Critical Path Methodology (CPM) PERT	To estimate project duration. PERT is more reliable than CPM
Gantt Chart	To monitor progress of project
Function Point Analysis	To estimate software size

(2)Which of the following should an IS auditor review to understand project progress in terms of time, budget and deliverables and for projecting estimates at completion (EACs) ?

A. Earned Value Analysis (EVA)
B. PERT
C. Gantt Chart
D. Function Point Analysis (FPA)

Answer: A. Earned Value Analysis (EVA)

Explanation:
EVA compares following metrics at regular interval:

-Budget to date
-Actual spending to date
-Estimate to complete
-Estimate at completion

It compares the planned amount of work with what has actually been completed to determine if the cost, schedule and work accomplished are progressing in accordance with the plan. Following table shows objective of each of the above mentioned options:

Technique	Objective
Earned Value Analysis Gantt Chart	Both EVA & Gantt Chart is used to monitor progress of the project. However EVA emphasis on earned value upto date and estimate at completion. Choose EVA when question hints about budget to date or actual spending to date or estimate at completion.
Function Point Analysis	To estimate software size
PERT	To estimate project duration. PERT is more reliable than CPM

(3)The purpose of Function Point Analysis (FPA) is:

A.to define functionalities of a software
B.to identify risk in software development program
C.to estimate efforts required to develop software
D.to monitor the progress the software development

Answer: C.To estimate efforts required to develop software

Explanation:
FPA is an indirect method of software size estimation. Function points are a unit measure for software size much like an hour is to measuring time, miles are to measuring distance or Celsius is to measuring

temperature. FPA is arrived on the basis of number and complexity of inputs, outputs, files, interfaces and queries.

(4)Which of the following is a advantage of the program evaluation review technique (PERT) over other techniques? PERT:

A. considers single scenario for planning and control projects
B. considers different scenarios for planning and control projects
C.defines functionalities of the software under development
D.allows the user to define program and system parameters

Answer: B. considers different scenarios for planning and control projects.

Explanation:
Advantage of PERT over CPM is that in CPM only single duration is considered while PERT considers three different scenarios i.e. optimistic (best), pessimistic (worst) and normal (most likely) and on the basis of three scenarios, a single critical path is arrived.
PERT considers different scenarios for planning and controlling projects. Three time estimates—optimistic, pessimistic and most likely—are used to create a level of uncertainty in the estimation of the time for individual activities.

(5)A system under development has multiple linked modules which will handle several million queries and transactions a year. Which of these techniques could the IS auditor use to estimate the size of the development effort?

A. Critical Path Methodology (CPM)
B. Counting source lines of code (SLOC)
C. Function point analysis
D. Program evaluation review technique (PERT)

Answer: C. Function point analysis

Explanation:
FPA is an indirect method of software size estimation. FPA is arrived on the basis of number and complexity of inputs, outputs, files, interfaces and queries. It is useful for evaluating complex applications. SLOC gives a direct measure of program size, but does not allow for the complexity that may be caused by having multiple, linked modules and a variety of inputs and outputs.

(6) Which of the following techniques would provide the GREATEST assistance in developing an estimate of project duration?

A. Function point analysis
B. PERT
C. Critical Path Methodology (CPM)
D. Object-oriented system development

Answer: B. PERT

Explanation:
A PERT chart will help determine project duration once all the activities and the work involved in the activities are known. PERT is more reliable than CPM for estimating project duration. Advantage of PERT over CPM is that in CPM only single duration is considered while PERT considers three different scenarios i.e. optimistic

(best), pessimistic (worst) and normal (most likely) and on the basis of three scenarios, a single critical path is arrived.

(7)When identifying an earlier project completion time, the activities that should be selected for early completion and more concentration are those:

A. activities with shortest completion time
B. activities with zero slack time
C. activities with longest completion time including slack time
D. activities with highest slack time

Answer: B. activities with zero slack time

Explanation:
Activities on Critical Path have zero slack time. Alternatively, it can be said that activities with zero slack time are on a critical path. Slack time can be defined as the amount of time an activity can be delayed without impacting the completion date of the project. Thus zero slack time makes an activity critical and concentration on such activities will help to reduce overall project completion time. This path is important because if everything goes as scheduled, its length gives the shortest possible completion time for the overall project. Activities on the critical path become candidates for crashing, i.e., for reduction in their time by payment of a premium for early completion.

(8) A project has budget of 16 hours (over 2 days). While reviewing, the IS auditor notes that the development team has spent eight hours of activity at the end of first day. The projected time to complete the remainder of the activity is 12 hours. The IS auditor should report that the project:

A. is ahead schedule
B. is behind of schedule
C. is on schedule
D. to be evaluated only after activity is completed.

Answer: B. is behind schedule

Explanation:

Particulars	Hours	Remarks
Budgeted hours	8 hours	16 hours for 2 days i.e. 8 hour per day
Value of actual work completed	4 hours	Total budgeted hours – Pending hours i.e. (16 hours – 12 hours)
Delay in schedule	By 4 hours	

In the given scenario, work should have completed at the end of day 1 is 8 hours (i.e. total 16 hours for 2 days and 8 hours per day). However actual work completed is only 4 hours i.e. 16 (total hours required) - 12 (work hours still pending). Hence it can be said against 8 hours of work required to be completed only 4 hours of work has been completed. So project is behind schedule.
Earned value analysis (EVA) is based on the premise that if a project task is assigned 24 hours for completion, it can be reasonably completed during that time frame. According to EVA, the project is behind schedule because the value of the eight hours spent on the task should be only four hours, considering that 12 hours of effort remain to be completed.

(9)An IS auditor is reviewing a project controlled through timebox management. Which of the following is a characteristic of timebox management?

A. Not suitable for prototyping or rapid application development where project need to be completed within timeframe
B. It prevents project cost overruns and delays from scheduled delivery
C. It requires separate system testing & user accepting testing
D. Performance can be evaluated only after activity is completed

Answer: B. It prevents project cost overruns and delays from scheduled delivery

Explanation:
The major advantage of timebox management approach is that it prevents project cost overruns and delays from scheduled delivery. It is used for prototyping or rapid application development where project need to be completed within timeframe. It integrates system and user acceptance testing, but does not eliminate the need for a quality process
.
(10)An organization is planning to add personnel to activities imposing time constraints on the duration of a project, which of the following should be revalidated FIRST?

A. budget of the project
B. critical path of the project
C. duration for remaining task
D. resources availability for the project

Answer: B. critical path of the project

Explanation:
Critical path must be re-evaluated to ensure that additional resources will in fact shorten the project duration. Given that there may be slack time available on some of the other tasks not on the critical path, factors such as the project budget, the length of other tasks and the personnel assigned to them may or may not be affected.

(11) Which of the following would BEST help to determine the timeline for a project and prioritize project activities ?

A.CPM
B. PERT
C. Gantt Chart
D. FPA (Function Point Analysis)

Answer: B. PERT

Explanation:
Both CPM & PERT is a technique for estimating project duration and timeline. However, PERT is more reliable than CPM for estimating project duration. Advantage of PERT over CPM is that in CPM only single duration is considered while PERT considers three different scenarios i.e. optimistic (best), pessimistic (worst) and normal (most likely) and on the basis of three scenarios, a single critical path is arrived.

Last Minute Revision:

CISA Question Objective	Your Answer
To estimate project duration or timelines	PERT/CPM. First preference to PERT
To monitor progress of the project	Gantt Chart
Earned value by calculating following:	Earned Value Analysis (EVA)
-Budget to date -Actual spending to date -Estimate to complete -Estimate at completion	
To estimate size of software development efforts	Function Point Analysis
To prevent cost overruns & delivery delays	Timebox Management

Following table shows objective of each of the above mentioned options:

Technique	Objective
Critical Path Methodology (CPM) PERT	To estimate project duration/timelines. PERT is more reliable than CPM
Gantt Chart	To monitor progress of project
FPA (Function Point Analysis)	To estimate software size

- In any given scenario, when objective is to estimate project duration or timeless, answer should be PERT or CPM. However, first preference to be given to PERT.
- In any given scenario, when objective is to monitor the project or track any milestone, answer should be Gantt chart.
- In any given scenario, when objective is to consider earned value by calculating any of the following, answer should be Earned Value Analysis (EVA).

- Budget to date
- Actual spending to date
- Estimate to complete
- Estimate at completion

- In any given scenario, when objective is to estimate software size, answer should be FPA or SLOC. However, first preference to be given to FPA.
- In any given scenario, when objective is to prevent project cost overruns and delays from scheduled delivery, answer should be Timebox Management.

What is Decision Support System (DSS)?
- DSS is an interactive system which support semi-structured decision making. It collects data from varied sources and provides useful information to managers.

- Examples of information that a DSS provides:

    -Comparative sales figures between one week and the next.
    -Projected revenue figures based on various assumptions.
    -Evaluation of various alternatives on the basis of past experience

- Characteristics of DSS:

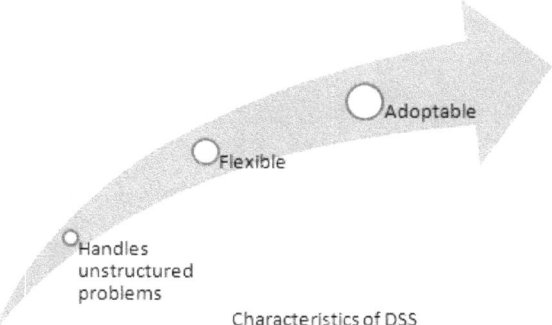

Characteristics of DSS

    -DSS supports semi-structured or less structured decisions.
    -DSS uses techniques with traditional data access and retrieval function.
    -DSS is flexible and adoptable in changing environment and decision making approach of the users.

Efficiency vs. Effectiveness:
A principle of DSS design is to concentrate less on efficiency (i.e. performing tasks quickly and reducing the costs) and more on effectiveness (i.e. performing the right task).

Design & Development:
Prototyping is the most popular approach to DSS design and development.

Risk Factors:
Developers should be prepared for following eight implementation risk factors:

(1)Non-existent or unwilling users
(2)Multiple users or implementers
(3)Disappearing users, implementers and maintainers
(3)Inability to specify purpose or usage patterns in advance
(4)Inability to predict and cushion impact on all parties
(5)Lack or loss of support
(6)Lack of experience with similar systems

(7)Technical problems and cost effectiveness issues.

Last Minute Revision:

- In any given scenario, DSS supports the semi-structured problem (and not only structured problem).
- In any given scenario, DSS should be flexible and adoptable to changing requirements and scenarios.
- In any given scenario, Decision tree is used as a questionnaire to lead a user through a series of choices until a conclusion is reached.

Question, Answer & Explanation:

(1)Which of the following is a characteristic of decision support system (DSS)?

A. DSS allows flexibility in the decision-making approach of users.
B. DSS supports only structured decision-making tasks.
C. DSS is aimed at solving highly structured problems.
D. DSS uses techniques with non-traditional data access and retrieval function.

Answer: A. DSS allows flexibility in the decision-making approach of users.

Explanation:
Following are the characteristics of DSS:
-DSS supports semi-structured or less structured decisions.
-DSS uses techniques with traditional data access and retrieval function.
-DSS is flexible and adoptable in changing environment and decision making approach of the users.

(2)Expert system's knowledge base that uses questionnaires to lead the user through a series of choices before a conclusion is reached is known as:

A. diagram trees
B. decision trees.
C. semantic nets.
D. networks trees.

Answer: B. decision trees.

Explanation:
Decision trees use questionnaires to lead a user through a series of choices until a conclusion is reached.

(3)Major risk of implementation of decision support system is:

A. Not able to specify purpose and usage requirements.
B. decision making is of Semi-structured dimensions
C. Inability to specify purpose and usage patterns
D. Frequent changes in decision processes

Answer: C. Inability to specify purpose and usage patterns

Explanation:
The inability to specify purpose and usage patterns is a risk that developers need to anticipate while implementing a decision support system (DSS). Choices A, B and D are not risks, but characteristics of a DSS.

(4)Questionnaires to lead the user through a series of choices to reach a conclusion are used by:

A. Network trees
B. Decision trees
C. Logic trees
D. Logic algorithms

Answer: B. Decision trees
Explanation:
Decision trees use questionnaires to lead the user through a series of choices to reach a conclusion.

(5)A decision support system (DSS):

A. concentrates on highly structured problems.
B. supports the requirements of only top management.
C. emphasizes flexibility in the decision making approach of users.
D. fails to survive in changing environment.

Answer: C. emphasizes flexibility in the decision making approach of users.
Explanation:
DSS emphasizes flexibility in the decision-making approach of users. Following are the characteristics of DSS:
-DSS supports semi-structured or less structured decisions.
-DSS uses techniques with traditional data access and retrieval function.
-DSS is flexible and adoptable in changing environment and decision making approach of the users.

(6)The Business Information System which provides answers to semi-structured problems & for validation of business decisions is:

A. Decision Support System
B. Structured Information System
C. Transaction Processing System
D. Executive Support System

Answer: A. Decision Support System
Explanation:
The Business Information System used for handling semi-structured problems & for validation of business decisions is the Decision Support System or DSS. TPS address lower level needs while ESS deals with higher level systems which aim more at problem solving & also address strategic concerns. Hence, the correct answer is as in Option A.

(7)An IS auditor reviewing the decision support system should be MOST concerned with the:

A. quality of input data.
B. level of experience and skills contained in the knowledge base.
C. logical access control of the system.
D. processing controls implemented in the system.

Answer: B.level of experience and skills contained in the knowledge base.
Explanation:
The level of experience or intelligence in the knowledge base is a key concern for the IS auditor, as decision errors based on a lack of knowledge could have a severe impact on the organization. Choices A, C and D are not as important as B.

Following are the some of the important system development methodologies:

- **Agile Development:**
- Dictionary meaning of agile is 'able to move quickly and easily'.
- Agile allows the programmer to just start writing a program without spending much time on preplanning documentation.
- Less importance is placed on formal paper-based deliverables, with the preference being to produce releasable software in short iterations, typically ranging from 4 to 8 weeks.
- At the end of each iteration, the team considers and documents what worked well and what could have worked better and identifies improvements to be implemented in subsequent iterations.
- Programmers generally prefer agile because they do not want to be involved in tedious planning exercises.

- **Prototyping:**
- Prototyping is the process of creating systems through controlled trial and error.
- A prototype is an early sample or model to test a concept or process. A prototype is a small scale working system used to test the assumptions. Assumptions may be about user requirements, program design or internal logic.
- This method of system development can provide the organization with significant time and cost savings.
- By focusing mainly on what the user wants and sees, developers may miss some of the controls that come from the traditional systems development approach; therefore, a potential risk is that the finished system will have poor controls.

- **Rapid Application Development:**
- RAD includes use of:
  -Small and well trained development teams.
  -Prototypes
  -Tools to support modelling, prototyping and component reusability.
  -Central repository.
  -Rigid limits on development time frames.

- RAD enables the organization to develop systems quickly while reducing development cost and maintaining quality. This is achieved by use of above techniques.
- RAD relies on the usage of a prototype that can be updated continually to meet changing user or business requirements.

- **Object Oriented System Development:**
- OOSD is a programming technique and not a software development methodology.
- Object here refers to small piece of program that can be used individually or in combination with other objects.
- In Object oriented language, application is made up of smaller components (objects).
- One of the major benefits of object-oriented design and development is the ability to reuse objects.
- OO uses a technique known as 'encapsulation' in which one object interacts with another object. This is a common practice whereby any particular object may call other object to perform its work.

- **Component based Development:**
- Component-based development can be regarded as an outgrowth of object-oriented development.

- **Software Reengineering:**
- Reengineering is the process of updating an existing system by extracting and reusing design and program components.
- This process is used to support major changes in the way an organization operates.

- **Reverse Engineering:**
- Reverse engineering is the process of studying and analyzing an application and the information is used to develop a similar system.

Question, Answer & Explanation:

(1)An organization is developing one of its applications using agile approach. Which of the following would be a risk in agile development process?

A. Insufficient documentation.
B. Insufficient testing.
C. Poor requirements definition.
D. Insufficient user involvement.

Answer: A. Insufficient documentation.

Explanation:
Agile allows the programmer to just start writing a program without spending much time on preplanning documentation. Less importance is placed on formal paper-based deliverables, with the preference being to produce releasable software in short iterations, typically ranging from 4 to 8 weeks.
Lack of testing might be an issue but without formal documentation it is difficult for an auditor to gather objective evidence.

(2)Which of the following is the characteristic of agile software development approach?

A. Systematic Documentation.
B. More importance is placed on formal paper-based deliverables.
C. Extensive use of software development tools to maximize team productivity.
D. Reviews at the end of each iteration to identify lessons learned for future use in the project.

Answer: D. Reviews at the end of each iteration to identify lessons learned for future use in the project.

Explanation:
Dictionary meaning of agile is 'able to move quickly and easily'. Agile allows the programmer to just start writing a program without spending much time on preplanning documentation. Less importance is placed on formal paper-based deliverables, with the preference being to produce releasable software in short iterations, typically ranging from 4 to 8 weeks. At the end of each iteration, the team considers and documents what worked well and what could have worked better, and identifies improvements to be implemented in subsequent iterations. Agile projects do make use of suitable development tools; however, tools are not seen as the primary means of achieving productivity.

(3)Which of the following is considered as limitation of the Agile Software development methodology?

A. Quality of system may be impacted due to speed of development and limited budget.
B. Absence of well-defined requirements may end up with more requirements than needed.
C. Absence of review mechanism to identify lesions learned for future use in the project.
D. Incomplete documentation due to time management.

Answer: D. Incomplete documentation due to time management.

Explanation:
In the above scenario, major risk associated with agile development is lack of documentation.

(4)An organization is developing one of its applications using prototyping approach. Which of the following would be an advantage of using prototyping for systems development?

A. Sufficient controls will be built in the system.
B. Sufficient audit trial will be built in the system.
C. Reduction in deployment time.
D. Sufficient change control will be built in the system.

Answer: C. Reduction in deployment time.

Explanation:
A prototype is a small scale working system used to test the assumptions. Assumptions may be about user requirements, program design or internal logic. This method of system development can provide the organization with significant time and cost savings. Prototyping is the process of creating systems through controlled trial and error. By focusing mainly on what the user wants and sees, developers may miss some of the controls that come from the traditional systems development approach; therefore, a potential risk is that the finished system will have poor controls. In prototyping, changes in the designs and requirements occur quickly and are seldom documented or approved; hence, change control becomes more complicated with prototyped systems.

(5)An organization is developing one of its applications using prototyping approach. Which of the following testing methods is MOST effective during the initial phases of prototyping?

A. Bottom-up
B. Parallel
C. Volume
D. Top-down

Answer: D. Top-down

Explanation:

In any given scenario, Top-down testing methods is MOST effective during the initial phases of Prototyping. Top-down testing starts with the system's major functions and works downward. The initial emphasis when using prototyping is to create screens and reports, thus shaping most of the proposed system's features in a short period.

(6)Which of the following techniques uses a prototype that can be updated regularly to meet ever changing user or business requirements?

A. Reverse Engineering
B. Object-oriented system development (OOD)
C. Software reengineering (BPR)
D. Rapid application development (RAD)

Answer: D. Rapid application development (RAD)

Explanation:
RAD enables the organization to develop systems quickly while reducing development cost and maintaining quality. Rapid Application Development (RAD) uses a prototype approach that can be updated continually to meet changing user or business requirements.RAD uses prototyping as its core development tool no matter which underlying technology is used.

(7)Which of the following is an advantage of prototyping?

A. Prototyping ensures strong internal controls.
B. Prototyping ensures significant time and cost savings.
C. Prototyping ensures strong change controls.
D. Prototyping ensures that extra functions are not added to the intended system.

Answer: B. Prototyping ensures significant time and cost savings.

Explanation:
Prototyping is the process of creating systems through controlled trial and error. Prototype systems can provide significant time and cost savings; however, other options are not the characteristics of prototyping. They often have poor internal controls, change control becomes much more complicated,
and it often leads to functions or extras being added to the system that were not originally intended.

(8)An organization is developing one of its applications using prototyping approach. Change control can be impacted by the:

A. involvement of user in prototyping.
B. rapid pace of modifications in requirements and design.
C. trial and error approach in prototyping.
D. absence of integrated tools.

Answer: B. rapid pace of modifications in requirements and design.

Explanation:
In prototyping, changes in the designs and requirements occur quickly and are seldom documented or approved; hence, change control becomes more complicated with prototyped systems. Chcices A, C and D are characteristics of prototyping, but they do not have an adverse effect on change control.

(9)An organization considering development of system should use which of the below methodology to develop systems faster, reduce development costs, and still maintain high quality?

A. CPM
B. Rapid application development (RAD)
C. PERT
D. Function Point Analysis

Answer: B. Rapid application development (RAD)

Explanation: -RAD enables the organization to develop systems quickly while reducing development cost and maintaining quality. This is achieved by use of below techniques:
-RAD includes use of:
- Small and well trained development teams.
- Prototypes
- Tools to support modelling, prototyping and component reusability.
- Central repository
- Rigid limits on development time frames

(10)Which of the following uses a prototype that can be updated continually to meet changing user or business requirements?

A. Critical Path Methodology (CPM)
B. Rapid application development (RAD)
C. Function point analysis (FPA)
D. Earned Value Analysis (EVM)

Answer: B. Rapid application development (RAD)

Explanation:
Explanation: Rapid application development (RAD) uses a prototype that can be updated continually to meet changing user or business requirements.

(11)Which of the following is the main advantage of rapid application development (RAD) over the traditional system development life cycle (SDLC)?

A. engages user in system development.
B. prioritizes testing of technical features.
C. simplifies conversion to the new system.
D. shortens the development time frame.

Answer: D. shortens the development time frame.

Explanation:
The greatest advantage of RAD is the shorter time frame for the development of a system. Choices A and B are true, but they are also true for the traditional systems development life cycle. Choice C is not necessarily always true.

(12)Which of the following technology or approach will facilitate the speedy delivery of information systems to the business user community?

A. Business process reengineering (BPR)
B. Computer-aided software engineering (CASE)
C. Rapid application prototyping (RAP)
D. Waterfall Approach

Answer: C. Rapid application prototyping (RAP)

Explanation:
RAD enables the organization to develop systems quickly while reducing development cost and maintaining quality. This is achieved by use of below techniques:
- Small and well trained development teams.
- Prototypes
- Tools to support modelling, prototyping and component reusability.
- Central repository
- Rigid limits on development time frames

(13)Which of the following is a advantage of using of object-oriented development technique?

A. ability to reuse modules.
B. improvement in system performance.
C. increase control effectiveness.
D. rapid system development process.

Answer: A. ability to reuse modules.

Explanation:
One of the major benefits of object-oriented design and development is the ability to reuse modules. The other options are not normally benefit of the object-oriented technique.

(14)Which of the following is an object-oriented technology characteristic that permits an enhanced degree of security over data?

A. Inheritance
B. Dynamic warehousing
C. Encapsulation
D. Polymorphism

Answer: C. Encapsulation

Explanation:
OO uses a technique known as 'encapsulation' in which one object interacts with another object. This is a common practice whereby any particular object may call other object to perform its work.
Encapsulation prevents accessing either properties or methods that have not been previously defined as public. This means that any implementation of the behaviour of an object is not accessible.

(15)In which of the below mentioned scenario, waterfall life cycle approach for system development is most likely to be used:

A. requirements are well defined and no changes are expected.
B. requirements are well defined and the project is subject to time pressures.
C. requirements are not finalized and subject to frequent changes.
D. the project will involve the use of new technology.

Answer: A. requirements are well defined and no changes are expected.

Explanation:

In any given scenario, waterfall approach is most suitable when requirements are well defined and understood and no major changes are expected. When requirements changes frequently, the waterfall model has not been successful. In these circumstances the various forms of iterative development life cycle gives the advantage of breaking down the scope of the overall system to be delivered, making the requirements gathering and design activities more manageable.

(16)Which of the following technique is used to study a application or software to see how it functions and to use that information to develop a similar system?

A. Object oriented.
B. Reverse Engineering.
C. Software Reengineering.
D. Agile development.

Answer: B. Reverse Engineering.

Explanation:
Reverse engineering is the process of studying and analyzing an application and the information is used to develop a similar system.

(17)Which of the following technique is used to enhance the system by extracting and reusing design and program components?

A. Object oriented.
B. Reverse Engineering.
C. Software Reengineering.
D. Agile development.

Answer: C. Software Reengineering.

Explanation:
Reengineering is the process of updating an existing system by extracting and reusing design and program components. This process is used to support major changes in the way an organization operates.

(18)An IS auditor reviewing the system development approach should be concerned about:

A. UAT is managed by user group.
B. A quality plan is not part of the contracted deliverables.
C. Module is released in phases instead of full implementation.
D. Prototyping is used to ensure that system is aligned with business objectives.

Answer: B. A quality plan is not part of the contracted deliverables.

Explanation:
For better deliverable, a quality plan is an essential element of all projects. Detailed quality plan for the proposed development contract should be documented and should encompass all phases of the development. UAT is normally managed by the user area to ensure systems are as per user requirements. If the system is large, a phased-in approach to implementing the application is a reasonable approach. Prototyping is a valid method to ensure that system is aligned with business objectives.

(19)Which of the following is the MAJOR advantage of a component-based development?

A. ability to manage multiple data types.

B. ability to model complex relationships.
C. ability to meet the demands of a changing environment.
D. ability to support multiple development environments.

Answer :D. ability to support multiple development environments.

Explanation:
In any given scenario, the major advantage of a component-based development approach is the support of multiple development environments. Components written in one language can interact with components written in other languages or running on other machines, which can increase the speed of development. Software developers can then focus on business logic. The other choices are not the most significant advantages of a component-based development approach.

(20) Which of the following would be the IS auditor's main concern while reviewing the business process reengineering process?

A. Appropriate Key controls are in place to protect assets and information resources.
B. Requirements of the new system are appropriately documented.
C. Time and resource budget is adhered to.
D. Roles and responsibilities assigned for new process.

Answer: A. Appropriate Key controls are in place to protect assets and information resources.

Explanation:
The audit team should be concerned about the key controls and verify that the controls are in place before implementing the new process. Choices B, C and D are objectives that the BPR process should achieve, but they are not the auditor's primary concern.

(21) An organization is implementing business process reengineering (BPR) project for its critical system. Which of the following is the impact of BPR?

A. business processes will remain stable.
B. information technologies will not change.
C. the process will improve performance of product & services.
D. input from clients and customers will no longer be necessary.

Answer: C. the process will improve performance of product & services.

Explanation:
As a reengineering process takes hold, certain key results will begin to emerge, including a concentration on process as a means of improving product, service and profitability. In addition, new business priorities and approaches to the use of information as well as powerful and more accessible information technologies will emerge. Often, the roles of client and customers will be redefined providing them with more direct and active participation in the enterprise's business process.

(22)An organization is implementing business process reengineering (BPR) project for its critical system. Which of the following is the FIRST step?

A. Defining the scope and areas to be reviewed.
B. Designing a project plan.
C. Analyzing the process under review.
D. Reengineering the process under review.

Answer: A. Defining the scope and areas to be reviewed.

Explanation:
First step will be to understand the scope and area for which BPR is required. On the basis of the definition of the areas to be reviewed, the project plan is developed. Thereafter, the process can be reengineered, implemented and monitored for continuous improvement.

(23) Which of the following represents a typical prototype of an interactive application?

A. Program logic and screens
B. Interactive Edits and Screens
C. Interactive edits program logic and sample reports
D. Screens, interactive edits, program logics and sample reports

Answer B. Interactive Edits and Screens

Explanation:
Program logics are not produced by a prototyping tool. This often leads to confusion for the end user who expects quick implementation of program logics.

Last Minute Revision:

- In any given scenario, major risk associated with agile development is lack of documentation.
- In any given scenario, in agile approach reviews are done to identify lessons learned for future use in the project.
- In any given scenario, waterfall approach is most suitable when requirements are well defined and understood. Waterfall approach is not successful when requirements are changing frequently.
- In any given scenario, reengineering refers to process of major changes in system and reverse engineering refers to studying and analyzing software to see how it functions and to use that information to develop a similar system.
- In any given scenario, important advantage of prototyping is that it provides significant cost and time savings.
- In any given scenario, Top-down testing methods is MOST effective during the initial phases of Prototyping.
- In any given scenario, Rapid Application Development (RAD) uses a prototype approach that can be updated continually to meet changing user or business requirements.
- In any given scenario, a major benefit of object-oriented development is the ability to reuse objects.
- In any given scenario, the major advantage of a component-based development approach is the support of multiple development environments.

CISA aspirants should be aware of two very important terms i.e. RTO & RPO and should be able to differentiate between them:

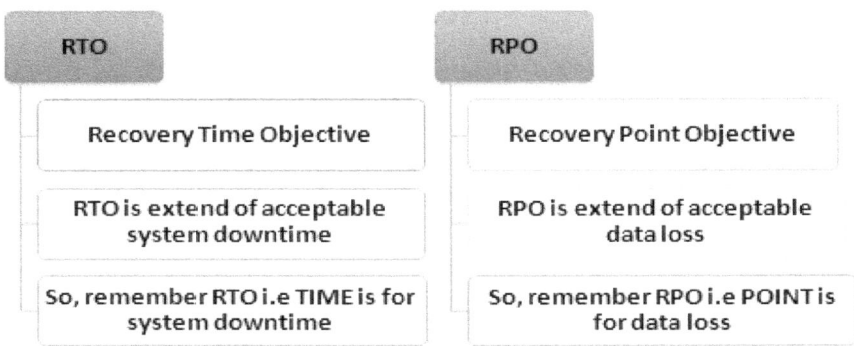

Exercise to understand RTO & RPO:

Find RTO & RPO from below statements:

(1)An organization cannot afford to have any downtime and can afford data loss upto 2 hours.

Solution:
RTO- 0 hours
RPO-2 hours

(2) In a day, back-up is taken twice i.e. at 12 AM & at 12 PM. What is RPO?

Solution:
RPO-12 hours
Here data back-up is done every 12 hours and hence maximum data loss can be for 12 hours.

(3) Daily back-up schedule is follow: First back-up at 8.00, second back-up at 16.00 and third back-up is at 24.00. What is RPO?

Solution:
RPO-8 hours
Here data back-up is done every 8 hours and hence maximum data loss can be for 8 hours.

(4) Systems at the main site went down at 13:00 and systems resumed from alternate site at 16.00 as per defined RTO. What is RTO?

Solution:
RTO-3 hours

(5)A disaster recovery plan (DRP) for an organization's financial system specifies that there should not be any data loss and service should be resumed within 72 hours.

Solution:
RTO- 72 hours
RPO-0 hours

(6) If RTO and RPO are low (i.e. zero or near zero) then systems and data are critical/non-critical.

Solution:
Critical
For critical systems RTO will be low. Similarly, for critical data RPO will be low.

(7) If RTO and RPO are low (i.e. zero or near zero) then cost of maintaining the environment is high/low.

Solution:
High
Lower the RTO/RPO, higher the cost of maintenance of environment.

Question, Answer & Explanation:

(1)What is Recovery Time Objective (RTO)?

A. The extent of acceptable system downtime.
B. The time period the crisis is expected to last
C. The extent of acceptable data loss.
D. The time required for the crisis management team to respond

Answer: A. The extent of acceptable system downtime.

Explanation:
The RTO is a measure of the user's tolerance to downtime. This is the amount of downtime of the business process that the business can tolerate and still remain viable .RTO is basically extent of system downtime that is acceptable by the organization. In case of critical systems, generally RTO is zero or near to zero. RPO is extent of acceptable data loss.

(2)What level of Recovery Time Objective (RTO) will a critical monitoring system have?

A. Very high RTO
B. Very low RTO, close to zero
C. Close to a year
D. Medium level of RTO, close to 50 %

Answer: B. Very low RTO, close to zero

Explanation:
The RTO is a measure of the user's tolerance to downtime. In case of critical systems, generally RTO is zero or near to zero. Low RTO indicates that system should be resumed at the earliest. For example, if RTO is 2 hours, system should be resumed within 2 hours and if RTO is 72 hours, system should be resumed within 72 hours. Thus, in case of critical system generally RTO is kept low to ensure immediate resumption of services.

(3) What is Recovery Point Objective (RPO)?

A. The extent of acceptable system downtime.
B. The time period the crisis is expected to last
C. The extent of acceptable data loss.
D. The date by which lost data can be recovered by Recovery team

Answer: C. The extent of acceptable data loss.

Explanation:
RPO is extent of acceptable data loss. For example, if RPO is 2 hours, then organization can afford to loss at the most data captured during last 2 hours. They need to design back-up strategy in such a way that back-up should be taken every 2 hours. Back-up is taken at 2.00 PM, 4.00 PM, 6.00 PM and so on. In this case, if data is corrupted at 5.59 then back-up data up-to 4.00 will be available with the organization. Hence data loss will not be more than 2 hours.

(4)A Recovery Point Objective (RPO) will be deemed critical if it is?

A. Small
B. Large
C. Medium
D. Large than industry standards

Answer: A. Small

Explanation:
RPO is the extent of acceptable data loss to a business. The lower the extent of acceptable data loss, the more critical the situation. For example, an organization having RPO of 0 hours need to ensure that there should not be any data loss at all. They should work on stringent back-up strategy. Hence small RPO indicates that systems are critical for the organization.

(5)If the Recovery Point Objective (RPO) is close to zero, how will the overall cost of maintaining the environment for recovery be?

A. High
B. Low
C. Medium
D. There is no relation between RPO and cost.

Answer: A. High

Explanation:
RPO is the extent of acceptable data loss to a business. The lower the extent of acceptable data loss, the more critical the situation. For example, an organization having RPO of 0 hours need to ensure that there should not be any data loss at all. They should work on stringent back-up strategy. Hence cost of maintaining the environment will high in case RPO is zero or close to zero.

(6)A hot site should be implemented as a recovery strategy when the:

A. recovery time objective (RTO) is low.
B. recovery point objective (RPO) is high.
C. recovery time objective (RTO) is high.
D. disaster tolerance is high.

Answer: A. recovery time objective (RTO) is low.

Explanation:
A low RTO means disaster tolerance is also low. If this time gap is low, recovery strategies that can be implemented within a short period of time, such as a hot site, should be used. Cold site can be used (which takes more time for resumption of services) when RTO is high.

(7) In which of the following situations is it MOST appropriate to implement data mirroring as the recovery strategy?

A. Disaster tolerance is high.
B. Recovery time objective is high.
C. Recovery point objective is low.
D. Recovery point objective is high.

Answer: C. Recovery point objective is low

Explanation:
Data mirroring is the technique in which data are backed-up concurrently without any time gap. Such techniques are costly to implement and generally used for critical data where RPO is low.
RPO is the extent of acceptable data loss to a business. For example, an organization having RPO of 0 hours need to ensure that there should not be any data loss at all. They should work on stringent back-up strategy.

(8)Following is the RTO and RPO of a financial system:
  RTO-96 hours
  RPO-0 hours (No data loss)

Which of the following is the MOST cost-effective solution?

A. A hot site that can be operational in two hours with data backup every 2 hours.
B. Reciprocal agreement for alternate site with data backup every 2 hours.
C. Synchronous backup of the data and standby active systems in a hot site
D. Synchronous backup of the data in a warm site that can be operational in 48 hours

Answer: D. Synchronous backup of the data in a warm site that can be operational in 48 hours

Explanation:
Synchronous backup of the data in a warm site that can be operational in 48 hours meets both RPO and RTO. Also, option C meets the RPO and RTO but is more costly than option D. Option A and B does not meet RPO.

(9) A hot site should be implemented as a recovery strategy when the:

A. disaster tolerance is low.
B. recovery point objective (RPO) is high.
C. recovery time objective (RTO) is high.
D. disaster tolerance is high.

Answer: A. disaster tolerance is low.

Explanation:
Disaster tolerance is the time gap during which the business can accept non availability of IT facilities. If this time gap is low, recovery strategies that can be implemented within a short period of time, such as a hot site,

should be used. A high RPO/RTO means that the process can wait for a longer time. In such cases, other recovery alternatives, such as warm or cold sites, should be considered.

Last Minute Revision:

- RTO of 2 hours indicates that organization needs to ensure that their system downtime should not exceed 2 hours.
- RPO of 2 hours indicates that organization needs to ensure that their data loss should not exceed 2 hours of data captured.
- In any given scenario, for critical systems, RTO is zero or near zero. Similarly, for critical data, RPO is zero or near zero.
- In any given scenario, lower the RTO/RPO, higher the cost of maintenance of environment.
- In any given scenario, low RTO/RPO indicates that disaster tolerance is low. Other way round, if disaster tolerance is low, RTO/RPO should be low.
- In any given scenario, when RTO is low, mirrored site or hot site is recommended.
- In any given scenario, when RPO is low, mirror imaging or real time replication for data back-up is recommended.
- In any given scenario, where RPO is zero, synchronous data backup strategy to be used.
- Both RTO & RPO are based on time parameters. The lower the time requirements, the higher the cost of recovery strategies.

Types of Alternate Recovery Site:

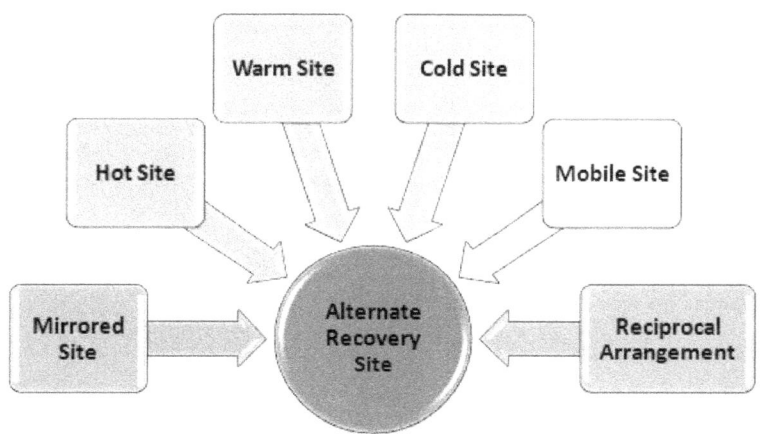

Mirrored Site

Already available at site:
- Space and basic infrastructure
- All applications
- Updated data back-up

Further requirement for resumption of service:
- Hardly anything

Hot Site

Already available at site:
- Space and basic infrastructure
- All applications

Further requirement for resumption of service:
- Updated data back-up

Warm Site

Already available at site:
- Space and basic infrastructure
- Few IT Applications

Further requirement for resumption of service:
- Required IT Applications

- Updated data back-up

Cold Site
Already available at site:
- Space and basic infrastructure

Further requirement for resumption of service:
- Required IT Applications
- Updated data back-up

Mobile Site
Mobile sites are processing facilities mounted on a transportable vehicle and kept ready to be delivered. A mobile site is a vehicle ready with all necessary computer equipment, and it can be moved to any cold or warm site depending upon the need. The need for a mobile site depends upon the scale of operations.

Reciprocal Agreement
Reciprocal agreements are the agreements wherein two organizations (mostly having similar processing) agree to help each other in case of emergency. Reciprocal agreements are the least expensive because they usually rely on agreement between two firms. However, they are the least reliable.

Expenses for maintaining alternate recovery site:
Most Expensive- Mirror Site
Least Expensive-Reciprocal Agreement

Last Minute Revision:

Parameters/Type of Alternate Sites	Mirrored Site	Hot Site	Warm Site	Cold Site
Space & basic infrastructure	Available	Available	Available	Available
IT Equipment for processing	Available	Available	Only few equipments available	Not Available
Database	Available	Not Available	Not Available	Not Available
Maintenance Cost	Costliest	-	-	Cheapest
Recovery Time	Fastest	-	-	Slowest

- In any given scenario, mirrored site is fastest mode of recovery and then hot site.
- In any given scenario, cold site is slowest mode of recovery.
- In any given scenario, for critical system, mirrored/hot sites are appropriate option.
- In any given scenario, for non-critical system, cold site is appropriate option.
- In any given scenario, reciprocal agreement will have lowest expenditure in terms of recovery arrangement.

Question, Answer & Explanation:

(1)An organization has done provision for hot sit as an alternate arrangement. An advantage of the use of hot sites as a backup alternative is that:

A. cost of maintaining the environment is low.
B. hot sites can be arranged in or near primary site.
C. hot sites can be made ready for operation within a short period of time.
D. system compatibility is not an requirement in case of hot site.

Answer: C. hot sites can be made ready for operation within a short period of time.
Explanation:
Hot sites can be made ready for operation normally within hours. But cost of maintaining the alternate site is high in case of hot site as compared to warm or cold sites. No alternate site should be in or near primary site. Also, systems at hot site should be compatible with the primary site.

(2)For recovering a non-critical system, which of the following is appropriate option?

A. Cold Site
B. Mirrored Site
C. Hot site
D. Warm site

Answer: A. Cold site
Explanation:
Cold site is most appropriate option for non-critical system. In cold site only space and basic infrastructures are available. Mirrored site and hot site are expensive option and mostly used for critical systems/functions. A warm site is generally available at a medium cost, requires less time to become operational and is suitable for sensitive operations.

(3)Which of the following situation is MOST suitable for implementation of hot site as a recovery strategy?

A. disaster tolerance is high
B. recovery point objective (RPO) is high.
C. recovery time objective (RTO) is high.
D. disaster tolerance is low

Answer: D. disaster tolerance is low
Explanation:
Low disaster tolerance indicates that systems are critical and has to be resumed at the earliest. RTO is low for such systems. Hot sites are used for critical systems where disaster tolerance is low. In case if disaster tolerance is high (i.e. RTO/RPO are high), hot site may not be required and arrangement can be made through cold/warm site.

(4)An alternate recovery site with space and basic infrastructure like electrical wiring, air-conditioning and flooring, but no computer or communications equipment is a:

A. cold site.
B. warm site.
C. hot site
D. mirrored site

Answer: A. cold site.
Explanation:

A cold site is basically availability of space and basic infrastructure. No communication equipments and computers are installed. On the other hand, other mirrored and hot site are fully prepared alternate recovery site. A warm site is an offsite backup facility that is partially configured with required equipments.

(5)What is GREATEST concern when implementing warm site as a recovery site?

A. Timely availability of hardware
B. Availability of heat, humidity and air conditioning equipment
C. Adequacy of electrical power connections
D. Space arrangement.

Answer: A. Timely availability of hardware
Explanation:
A warm site has the basic infrastructure facilities, such as power, air conditioning and networking and some of computers. However, all computing device are not installed. Hence before resumption of services from warm site, timely availability of hardware is major concern.

(6)Which among the following will have lowest expenditure in terms of recovery arrangement?

A. Warm site facility
B. Cold Site
C. Hot site
D. Reciprocal agreement
Answer: D
Reciprocal agreements are the agreements wherein two organizations (mostly having similar processing) agree to help each other in case of emergency. Reciprocal agreements are the least expensive because they usually rely on agreement between two firms. However, they are the least reliable.

(7)In which of the following recovery processing site, only arrangement for electricity and HVAC is available?

A. Cold site
B. Mirrored site
C. Hot site
D. Warm site

Answer: A
Explanation:
Cold site is characterized by at least providing for electricity and HVAC (heat, ventilation and air-conditioning).No other computing facilities are available at cold site.

(8) Which of the following is the GREATEST concern when an organization's backup facility is at a hot site?

A. Timely availability of hardware
B. Availability of heat, humidity and air conditioning equipment
C. Adequacy of electrical power connections
D. Requirement of updated database.

Answer: D. Requirement of updated database.
Explanation:
Hot site is basically ready to use alternate recovery site with all the arrangements like space, infrastructure and required computers and communication devices. However, before resumption of service from hot site, data back-up should be installed at the hot site. Therefore, the availability of data becomes a primary concern.

CRM covers following types of network physical media specifications:
- Twisted Pairs (shielded twisted pairs and unshielded twisted pairs)
- Fiber-optics
- Co-axial

Twisted Pair:

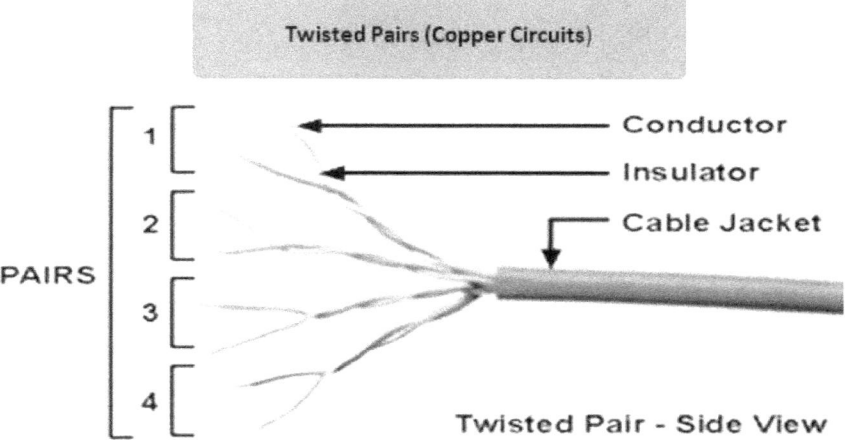

Two insulated wires are twisted around each other, with current flowing through them in opposite directions.

- Twisted pairs are also known as copper circuits.
- Twisted pair can be either shielded twisted pair or unshielded twisted pair.

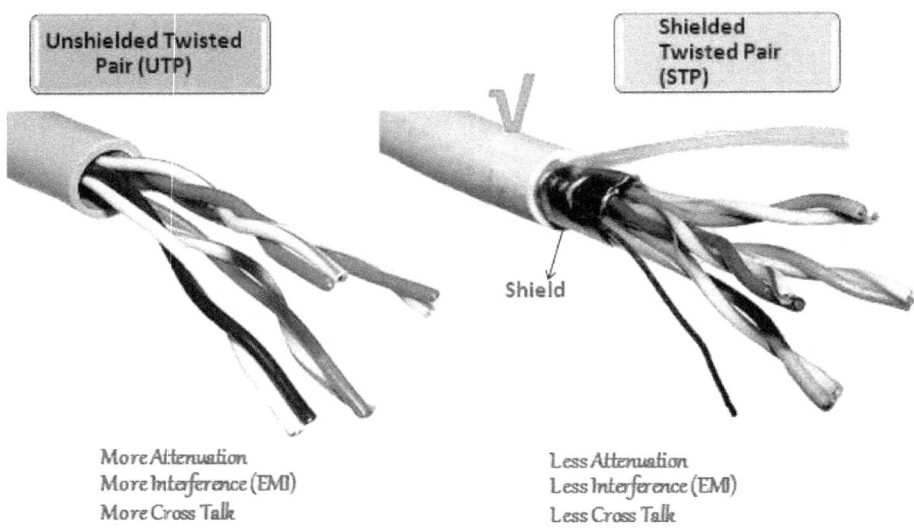

Unshielded Twisted Pair (UTP)	Shielded Twisted Pair (STP)

Shield

More Attenuation
More Interference (EMI)
More Cross Talk

Less Attenuation
Less Interference (EMI)
Less Cross Talk

Shielded Twisted Pair (STP):

- Two insulated wires are twisted around each other, with current flowing through them in opposite direction.
- This reduces the opportunity for cross talk and allows for lower sensitivity for electromagnetic disturbances.

Unshielded Twisted Pair (UTP):

- For unshielded twisted pair a disadvantage is that it is not immune to effect of electromagnetic interface (EMI).
- Unshielded twisted pair should be away from potential interference such as fluorescent lights.
- Parallel runs of cable over long distances should be avoided since the signals on one cable can interfere with signals on adjacent cables (i.e. cross talk).

Fiber-Optic:

Fiber-optic: Most secured mode of data transmission

- Glass fibers are used to carry binary signals as flashes of light.
- Fiber-optic systems have very low transmission loss.
- Fiber-optics are not affected by electromagnetic interference (EMI).
- Fiber-optic cables have proven to be more secure than the other media.
- Fiber is preferred choice for high volume and long distance calls.

Coaxial Cables:

Co-Axial Cables

Advantages

Easy Installation &
Ready Available

Disadvantages

Expensive
Distance Sensitive
Difficult to modify
Does not support many LANs

CISA aspirants should also understand following Important Terms:

Attenuation:

- Attenuation is the weakening of signals during transmission.
- Attenuation exists in both wired and wireless transmissions.
- Length of wire impacts the severity of attenuation.

Electromagnetic Interference (EMI):

- EMI is a disturbance generated by an external source that affects an electrical circuit.
- The disturbance may degrade the performance of the circuit or even stop it from functioning. In the case of a data path, these effects can range from an increase in error rate to a total loss of the data.
- EMI is caused by electrical storms or noisy electrical equipments (e.g. motors, fluorescent lighting, radio transmitters etc.)

Cross-Talks:

Crosstalk is electromagnetic interference from one unshielded twisted pair to another twisted pair, normally running in parallel.

Question, Answer & Explanation:

(1)An organization is considering type of transmission media which provide best security against unauthorized access. Which of the following provides best security?

A. Unshielded twisted pair
B. Shielded twisted pair
C. Fiber-optic cables
D.Coaxial cables

Answer: C. Fiber-optic cables

Explanation:
In fiber-optic cables, glass fibers are used to carry binary signals as flashes of light- Fiber-optic cables have proven to be more secure than the other media. They have very low transmission loss, not affected by EMI and preferred choice for high volumes and long distance calls.

(2)Which of the following transmission error can occur in wired as well as wireless communication?

A. Cross-talk
B. Attenuation
C. Sags, spikes and surges
D. Multipath interference

Answer: B. Attenuation

Explanation:
Attenuation is the weakening of signals during transmission. Attenuation can occur in both wired and wireless transmissions. Crosstalk can refer to electromagnetic interference from one unshielded twisted pair to another twisted pair, normally running in parallel. Cross-talk occurs only in wired communication. Multipath interference results in a direct signal coming with one or more reflected radio (wireless) signals.

(3)Which of the following transmission error can be caused by the length of cable if UTP is more than 100 meters long?

A. Electromagnetic interference (EMI)
B. Cross-talk
C. Attenuation
D. Sags, spikes and surges

Answer: C. Attenuation

Explanation:
Attenuation is the weakening of signals during transmission. Attenuation exists in both wired and wireless transmissions. Length of wire impacts the severity of attenuation. Electromagnetic interference (EMI) is caused by outside disturbance which is not the case here. Sags spikes & surges and cross-talk has nothing to do with the length of the UTP cable.

(4)To minimize the risk of data corruption, which of the following options can be effective?

A. Separate conduits for electrical and data cables.
B. Encryption
C.Check-digits
D. Hashing

Answer: A. Separate conduits for electrical and data cables.

Explanation:
Using separate conduits for data cables and electrical cables, minimizes the risk of data corruption due to an induced magnetic field created by electrical current. Other options will not prevent data from being corrupted. Data encryption minimizes the risk of data leakage & hashing ensures data integrity however they cannot prevent corruption. A check-digit will help detect the data corruption during communication, but will not prevent it.

(5)Which transmission method would provide best security?

A. Dedicated lines
B.Wireless Network
C.Dial-up
D.Broadband network

Answer: A. Dedicated lines

Explanation:
In computer networks and telecommunications, a dedicated line is a communications cable or other facility dedicated to a specific application, in contrast with a shared resource such as the telephone network or the Internet. Dedicated lines are most secured amongst the above options. Since there are no sharing of lines, data security can be assured.

Last Minute Revision:

Comparison

Basis of Difference	Fourth Preference UTP	Third Preference STP	Second Preference Co-axial	First Preference Fiber-Optic
Bandwidth	10 Mbps-100 Mbps	10 Mbps-100 Mbps	10 Mbps	100Mbps-1 Gbps
Length	500 meters	100 meters	185 m-500 m	2 km -above
Installation Cost	Least Expensive	Costlier than UTP	Costlier than twisted pair	More costly
Attenuation	Very high attenuation	High Attenuation	Low Attenuation	Very Low Attenuation
Interference	More affected by EMI	Lesser than UTP	Good resistance to EMI	Not Affected
Cross talk	More	Relatively Less	Minimum	No Affected

- In any given situation, fiber-optic cables have proven to be more secure than the other media. They have very low transmission loss, not affected by EMI and preferred choice for high volumes and long distance calls.
- When CISA question is about transmission error that can occur in wired as well as wireless communication, our answer should be attenuation.
- It is essential to understand the difference between diverse routing and alternate routing. The method of routing traffic through split-cable facilities or duplicate-cable facilities is called diverse routing. Whereas the method of routing information via an alternative medium, such as copper cable or fiber optics is called alternate routing.
- Also, CISA aspirant should be able to differentiate between last mile and long haul. Last mile provide redundancy for local loop whereas long haul provide redundancy for long distance availability.

What is alternate routing and diverse routing?

Alternate Routing:
Alternative routing is the method of routing information via an alternative medium, such as copper cable or fiber optics.

Alternate routing can be further bifurcated in two types:

Last mile circuit protection:
Last mile circuit protection provides redundancy for local communication loop.

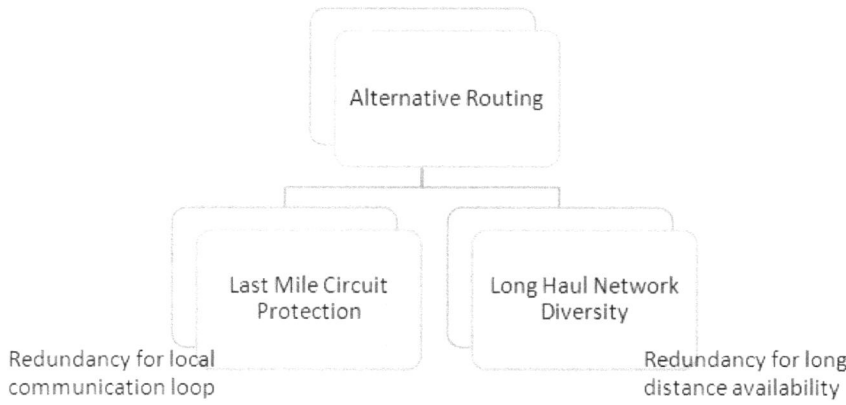

Long haul network diversity:
Long haul network diversity provides redundancy for long distance availability.

Diverse Routing:
Diverse routing is the method of routing traffic through split-cable facilities or duplicate cable facilities

Difference between alternate routing and diverse routing:

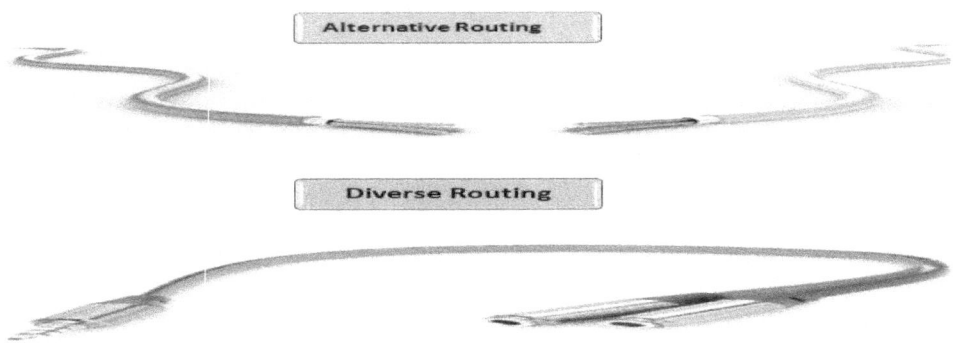

Question, Answer & Explanation:

(1)An organization is routing traffic through split -cable or duplicate-cable facilities. This arrangement is called:

A. Diverse routing
B. Alternate routing
C. Gateway
D.Bridge

Answer: A. Diverse routing

Explanation:
The method of routing traffic through split-cable facilities or duplicate-cable facilities is called diverse routing. Alternative routing is the method of routing information via an alternative medium, such as copper cable or fiber optics. Gateway and Bridge is used for network extension.

(2)Use of redundant combinations (local carrier lines, microwaves and/or coaxial cables) to access local communication loop is known as:

A.last-mile circuit protection
B.long-haul network diversity
C.diverse routing
D.alternative routing

Answer: A.last-mile circuit protection

Explanation:
Use of redundant combinations (local carrier lines, microwaves and/or coaxial cables) to access local communication loop is known as last mile circuit protection. The method of providing telecommunication continuity through the use of redundant combinations to access the local communication loop in the event of a disaster is called last-mile circuit protection. Long haul network diversity ensures long cistance availability. The method of routing traffic through split-cable facilities or duplicate cable facilities is called diverse routing. Alternative routing is the method of routing information via an alternative medium such as copper cable or fiber optics.

(3)Method of routing information via an alternative medium, such as copper cable or fiber optics is called:

A. Diverse routing
B. Alternate routing
C. Gateway
D. Bridge

Answer: B. Alternate routing

Explanation:
Alternative routing is the method of routing information via an alternative medium, such as copper cable or fiber optics. The method of routing traffic through split-cable facilities or duplicate-cable facilities is called diverse routing. Gateway and Bridge is used for network extension.

Last Minute Revision:

- It is essential to understand the difference between diverse routing and alternate routing. The method of routing traffic through split-cable facilities or duplicate-cable facilities is called diverse routing. Whereas the method of routing information via an alternative medium, such as copper cable or fiber optics is called alternate routing.
- Also, CISA aspirant should be able to differentiate between last mile and long haul. Last mile provide redundancy for local loop whereas long haul provide redundancy for long distance availability.

CRM covers following LAN components:

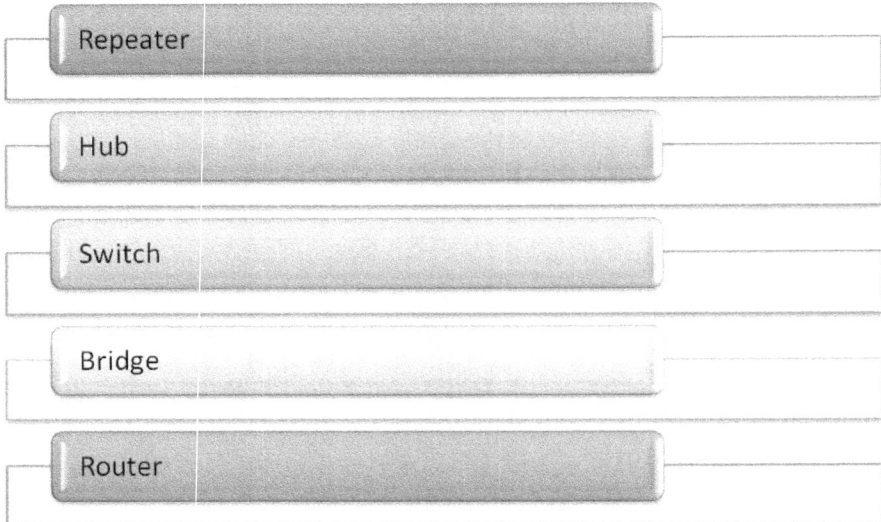

OSI Layer:

First very step is to understand OSI layer at which below devices operate. It must be noted that higher the layer, more intelligent the devices will be.

Higher the layer- More Intelligent the device will be

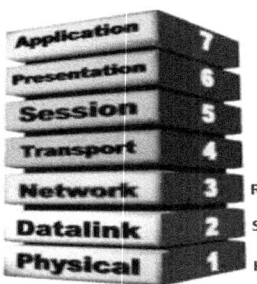

Router – More capability than Switch & Bridge

Switch & Bridge – More capability than Hub

Hub & Repeater – Dumb device

OSI Reference Model

CISA aspirant should be aware about layer of OSI at which below devices operate.

- Hub - Physical Layer (1st Layer)
- Switch – Data Link Layer (2nd Layer)
- Bridge – Data Link Layer (2nd Layer)
- Router – Network Layer (3rd Layer)
- Gateway-Application Layer (7th Layer)

Out of above Hub (layer 1) is dumbest device and Gateway (layer 7) is the most intelligent device.

Repeater:

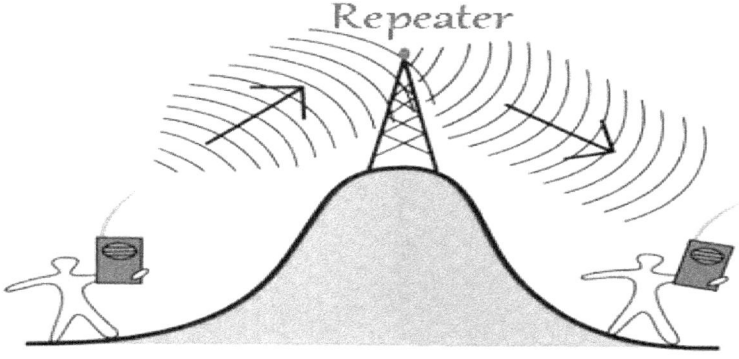

- Dictionary meaning of repeater is a person or thing that repeats something.
- In telecommunications, a repeater is an electronic device that receives a signal and retransmits it. Repeaters are used to extend transmissions so that the signal can cover longer distances or be received on the other side of an obstruction.
- They compensate for signals that are distorted due to a reduction of signal strength during transmission.

Hub & Switch:

Hub	Layer-2 Switch
Hub connects many devices together for exchange of data.	Switch is more advanced /intelligent version of a Hub.
Hub broadcast message to all the connected devices.	Switch send message to only required device.
Collusions occur commonly in setups using Hubs.	No collusion occurs in full duplex switch.
Hub cannot learn or store MAC address.	Switch stores MAC addresses in a look up table.
Hubs are classified as Layer 1 (Physical Layer) of OSI model.	Switches operate at Layer 2 (Data Link Layer) of OSI model.

Hub is a dumb device. It forwards message to all the connected computers irrespective of whether message is intended for them or not.

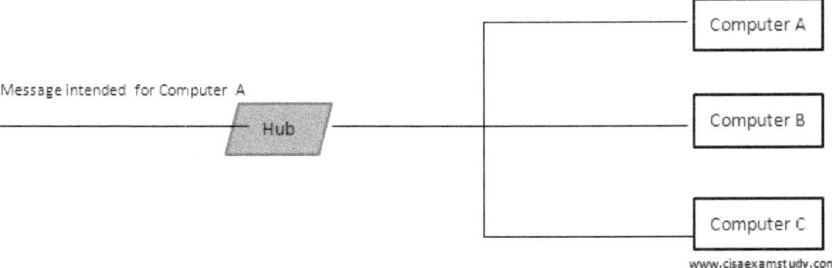

Switch is a smarter than Hub. It forwards message to only that computer for which message is intended.

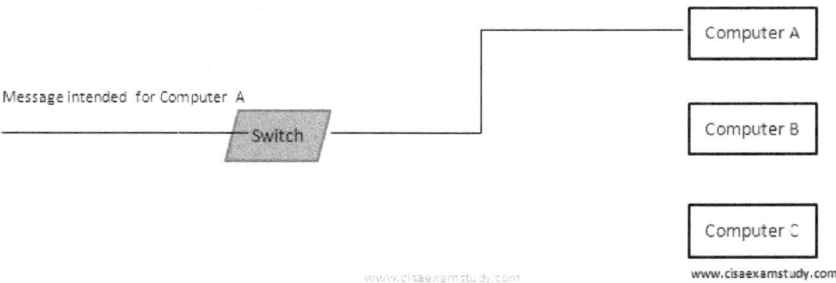

Bridge:
- Bridge works like Layer 2-Switch.
- Both Bridge & Switch works at layer 2 (Data Link Layer) of OSI Layers.
- By examining the MAC address, the bridge can make decisions to direct the packet to its destination.
- Bridge has the capacity to store frames and act as a storage and forward device

Difference between Bridge & Switch:

Bridge	Switch
Contains only few ports for LAN connectivity.	Contains many ports for LAN connectivity.

Router:
- Routers are more intelligent version of Switch.
- Routers operate at the network layer.
- By examining the IP address, the router can make intelligent decisions to direct the packet to its destination.
- The network segments linked by a router, however, remain logically separate and can function as independent networks.
- Router can block broadcast information, block traffic to unknown addresses, and filter traffic based on network or host information.

Difference between Router & Layer-2 Switch:

Router	Layer 2-Switch
Operates at Network Layer (layer 3) of OSI Model.	Operates at Data link Layer (layer 2)of OSI Model.
IP Address	MAC Address

Router connects two separate networks.

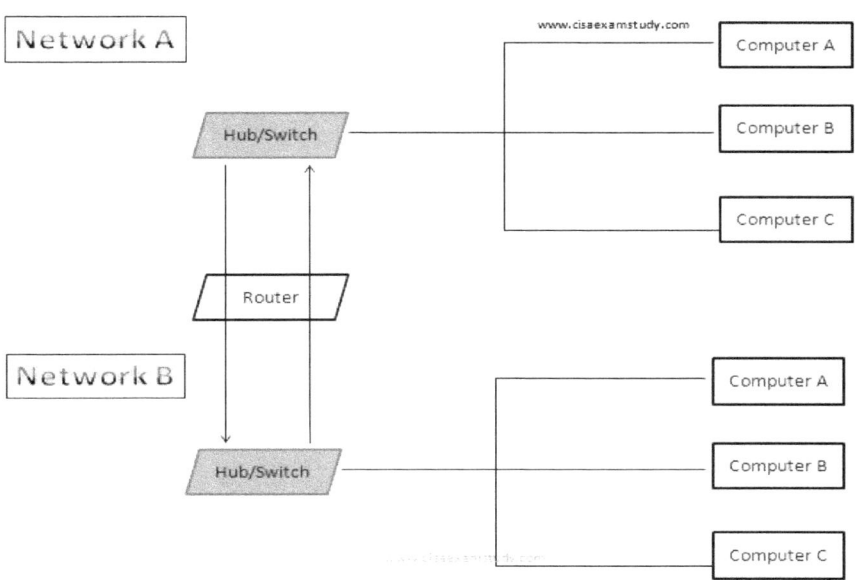

Question, Answer & Explanation:

(1) Which of the following devices has the capacity to store frames and act as a storage and forward device?

A. Hub
B. Bridge
C. Repeater
D. Router

Answer: B. Bridge

Explanation: Bridges act as store-and-forward devices in moving frames toward their destination. This is achieved by analyzing the MAC header of a data packet. By examining the MAC address, the bridge can make decisions to direct the packet to its destination. Bridge works like Layer 2-Switch. Both Bridge & Switch works at layer 2 (Data Link Layer) of OSI Layers.

(2) 'Hub' operates at which of the following OSI layer?
A. Data Link Layer
B.Physical Layer
C. Network Layer
D.Transport Layer

Answer: B.Physical Layer

Explanation: CISA aspirant should be aware about layer of OSI at which below devices operate.
Hub - Physical Layer (1st Layer)
Switch – Data Link Layer (2nd Layer)
Bridge – Data Link Layer (2nd Layer)
Router – Network Layer (3rd Layer)
Gateway-Application Layer (7th Layer)

It must be noted that higher the layer, more intelligent the devices will be. Out of above Hub (layer 1) is dumbest device and Gateway (layer 7) is the most intelligent device.

(3) 'Layer-2 Switch' operates at which of the following OSI layer?

A. Data Link Layer
B.Physical Layer
C. Network Layer
D.Transport Layer

Answer: A. Data Link Layer

Explanation: CISA aspirant should be aware about layer of OSI at which below devices operate.
Hub - Physical Layer (1st Layer)
Switch – Data Link Layer (2nd Layer)
Bridge – Data Link Layer (2nd Layer)
Router – Network Layer (3rd Layer)
Gateway-Application Layer (7th Layer)

It must be noted that higher the layer, more intelligent the devices will be. Out of above Hub (layer 1) is dumbest device and Gateway (layer 7) is the most intelligent device.

(4) 'Bridge' operates at which of the following OSI layer?

A. Data Link Layer
B. Physical Layer
C. Network Layer
D. Transport Layer

Answer: A. Data Link Layer

Explanation: CISA aspirant should be aware about layer of OSI at which below devices operate.
Hub - Physical Layer (1st Layer)
Switch – Data Link Layer (2nd Layer)
Bridge – Data Link Layer (2nd Layer)
Router – Network Layer (3rd Layer)
Gateway-Application Layer (7th Layer)

It must be noted that higher the layer, more intelligent the devices will be. Out of above Hub (layer 1) is dumbest device and Gateway (layer 7) is the most intelligent device.

(5) 'Router' operates at which of the following OSI layer?

A. Data Link Layer
B. Physical Layer
C. Network Layer
D. Transport Layer

Answer: C. Network Layer

Explanation: CISA aspirant should be aware about layer of OSI at which below devices operate.

Hub - Physical Layer (1st Layer)
Switch – Data Link Layer (2nd Layer)
Bridge – Data Link Layer (2nd Layer)
Router – Network Layer (3rd Layer)
Gateway-Application Layer (7th Layer)

It must be noted that higher the layer, more intelligent the devices will be. Out of above Hub (layer 1) is dumbest device and Gateway (layer 7) is the most intelligent device.

(6)Which of the following is the most intelligent device?

A. Hub
B. Switch
C. Bridge
D. Router

Answer: D. Router

Explanation: It must be noted that higher the layer at which device operates, more intelligent the devices will be. Out of above, Hub (layer 1) is dumbest device and Router (layer 3) is the most intelligent device. By examining the IP address, the router can make intelligent decisions to direct the packet to its destination. Router can block broadcast information, block traffic to unknown addresses, and filter traffic based on network or host information.

(7) By examining the IP address, which of the following device can make intelligent decisions to direct the packet to its destination?

A.Hub
B.Layer-2 Switch
C.Bridge
D.Router

Answer: D.Router

Explanation: Router operates at Network Layer (i.e. 3rd Layer) of OSI Model. By examining the IP address, the router can make intelligent decisions to direct the packet to its destination. Router can block broadcast information, block traffic to unknown addresses, and filter traffic based on network or host information.

Last Minute Revision:

Device	OSI Layer	MAC Address/IP Address	Functionality
Repeater	Physical Layer	-	Repeaters are used to extend transmissions so that the signal can cover longer distances or be received on the other side of an obstruction
Hub	Physical Layer	-	-Hub broadcast message to all the connected devices. -Dumb Device
Layer 2 Switch	Data Link Layer	MAC Address	-Switch send message to only required device. -MAC Address -More intelligent than Hub
Bridge	Data Link Layer	MAC Address	-Similar to Switch. -MAC Address -Bridge has the capacity to store frames and act as a storage and forward device
Router	Network Layer	IP Address	-More intelligent than all the above devices -By examining the IP address, the router can make intelligent decisions to direct the packet to its destination.

CRM covers following types of Backup Schemes:

(1)Backup of full database:

- Full Backup

(2)Backup of only changed database:

- Differential Backup
- Incremental Backup

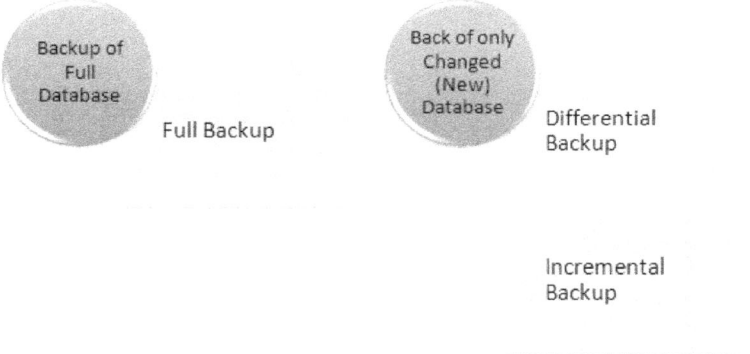

Full Backup

Differential Backup

Incremental Backup

CISA aspirants should understand various backup schemes as follow:

- Full Backup- Every time data backup is taken of full database irrespective of earlier backup.

- Differential Backup-Backup is taken only of data changed/modified since last full backup (last back to be full back-up only).

- Incremental Backup-Backup is taken only of data changed/modified since last backup (last backup can be either full backup or incremental backup).

How to differentiate between Incremental & Differential Backup:

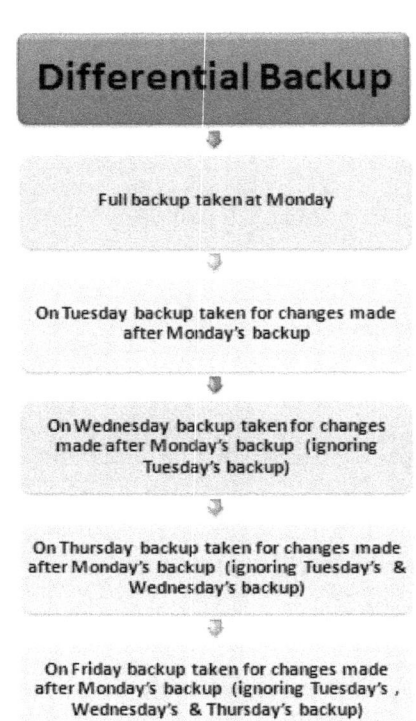

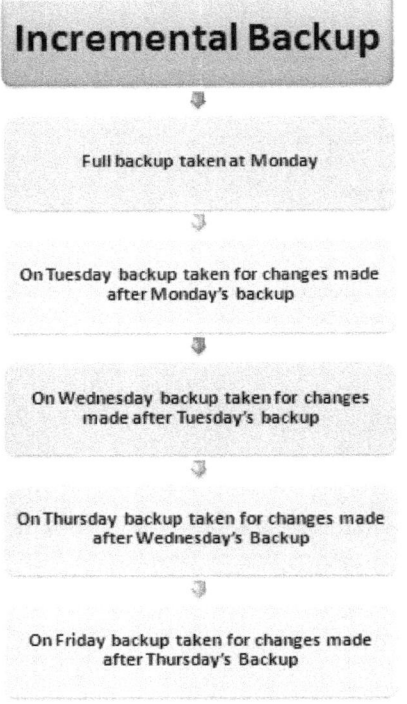

Storage Capacity for each backup Scheme: Let us understand the requirements for time and media capacity for various schemes for data storage:

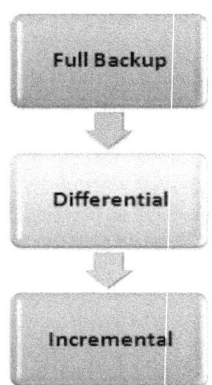

- Full Backup- Requires more time and storage capacity as compared to other two schemes.

- Differential- Requires less time and storage capacity as compared to full backup but more time and storage capacity as compared to Incremental.
- Incremental- Requires less time and storage capacity as compared to other two schemes.

Restoration Capability for each backup Scheme: Let us understand effectiveness of various schemes in case of data restoration:

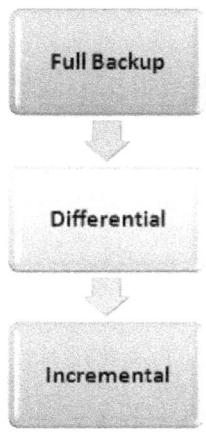

- Full Backup- Fastest of all three schemes.
- Differential- Slower than Full backup but faster than incremental.
- Incremental-Slowest of all three schemes.

Advantages & Disadvantages of each Scheme:

Full Backup	Incremental Backup	Differential Backup
• Advantage-Unique Repository in case of restoration • Disadvantage-Requires more time and capacity	• Advantage-Faster backup and less media capacity is required. • Disadvantage-Restoration requires more time.	• As compared to full backup, faster backup and requires less capacity. However more times requires for restoration. • As compared to incremental backup, more media capacity is required. However restoration is quicker.

Question, Answer & Explanation:

(1)Backup scheme wherein every time data backup is taken of full database irrespective of earlier backup availability is known as:

A. Incremental Backup
B. Differential Backup
C. Grandfather-father-son rotation
D. Full Backup

Answer: D. Full Backup

Explanation:
CISA aspirants should understand various backup schemes as follow:

- Full Backup- Every time data backup is taken of full database irrespective of earlier backup.
- Incremental Backup-Backup is taken only of data changed/modified since last backup (last backup can be either full backup or incremental backup).
- Differential Backup-Backup is taken only of data changed/modified since last full backup (last back to be full back-up only).
- Grandfather-father-son rotation - This is a method of media rotation and not backup scheme.

(2)Backup scheme wherein backup of data is taken only for data changed/modified either after full backup or incremental backup is known as:

A. Incremental Backup
B. Differential Backup
C. Grandfather-father-son rotation
D. Full Backup

Answer: A. Incremental Backup

Explanation:
CISA aspirants should understand various backup schemes as follow:

- Incremental Backup-Backup is taken only of data changed since last backup (last backup can be either full backup or incremental backup).
- Differential Backup-Backup is taken only of data changed since last full backup (last back to be full back-up only).
- Full Backup- Every time data backup is taken of full database irrespective of earlier backup.
- Grandfather-father-son rotation - This is a method of media rotation and not backup scheme.

(3)Backup scheme wherein backup of data is taken only for data changed after full backup (incremental backup is ignored) is known as:

A. Incremental Backup
B. Differential Backup
C. Grandfather-father-son rotation Backup
D. Full Backup

Answer: B. Differential Backup

Explanation:
CISA aspirants should understand various backup schemes as follow:

- Differential Backup-Backup is taken only of data changed since last full backup (last back to be full back-up only).
- Incremental Backup-Backup is taken only of data changed since last backup (last backup can be either full backup or incremental backup).
- Full Backup- Every time data backup is taken of full database irrespective of earlier backup.
- Grandfather-father-son rotation - This is a method of media rotation and not backup scheme.

(4)Which of the following backup scheme requires more time and media capacity for backup storage?

A. Incremental Backup
B. Differential Backup
C. Grandfather-father-son rotation Backup
D. Full Backup

Answer: D. Full Backup

Explanation: In full backup, every time data backup is taken of full database irrespective of earlier backup. However, full backup scheme requires more time and media capacity for backup Storage. Advantage of full backup scheme is easy restoration due to unique repository.

Let us understand requirement for time and media capacity for various schemes for data storage:

-Full Backup- Requires more time and storage capacity as compared to other two schemes.

-Differential- Requires less time and storage capacity as compared to full backup but more time and storage capacity as compared to Incremental.

-Incremental- Requires less time and storage capacity as compared to other two schemes.

(5)Which of the following backup scheme is more effective and faster for data restoration?

A. Incremental Backup
B. Differential Backup
C. Grandfather-father-son rotation Backup
D. Full Backup

Answer: D. Full Backup

Explanation: In full backup, every time data backup is taken of full database irrespective of earlier backup. Advantage of full backup scheme is easy restoration due to unique repository. However, full backup scheme requires more time and media capacity for backup Storage.

Let us understand effectiveness of various schemes in case of data restoration:

- Full Backup- Fastest of all three schemes.
- Differential- Slower than Full backup but faster than incremental.
- Incremental-Slowest of all three schemes.

Following are some of the security testing tools and techniques:

Control Areas	Techniques
Terminal Cards and Keys	• Check whether security administrator has followed up on any unauthorized attempt. • Take sample of these cards/keys and try to access beyond that which is authorized.
Terminal Identification	• Obtain a list of terminal addresses and locations. • Same can be used to identify incorrectly logged, missing or additional terminals. • Also to ensure that they are identified in the network diagram.
Logon IDs and Passwords	
Confidentiality	• To look for passwords taped to the side of terminals or the inside of desk drawers. • Attempt social engineering to validate user awareness. • Verify global configuration settings for password strength in the system application and compare this with the organization's security policy.
Encryption	• Check application logs and ensue that passwords and logon IDs are not captured in clear form. • With the help of security administrator, check internal password table to ensure that content should be unreadable.
Access Authorization	• Verify sample authorization forms and check whether the authorization was granted on a need-to-know basis. • Attempt to match access granted and current role of the employee on sample basis.
Periodic Password Change Requirements	• Interview a sample of users to determine if they are forced to change their password after the prescribed time interval. • Check the password rule defined in OS/access control software.
Disabling / deleting of inactive logon IDs and passwords	• Obtain a list of active logon IDs and match with current employees. • Logon IDs of existed employees should not be active.
Password Syntax	• Attempt to create an invalid password (too short, too long, repeated from the previous password, incorrect mix of alpha or numeric characters, or the use of inappropriate characters) to verify password syntax rules.
Automatic logoff	• Logon to few sample terminals and waits for the terminals to disconnect after the established time interval.
Automatic Deactivation	• Logon to few sample terminals and purposefully enter wrong password few times. • Logon ID should deactivate after the established number of invalid passwords has been entered. • Also to verify reactivation process followed by security

	administrator.
	• Security administrator should follow proper verification to identify the user.
Password Masking	• Logon to a terminal and observe if the password is displayed in plain text.
Logging and Reporting of Computer Access Violations	• Attempt to access unauthorized data. • Attempts should be unsuccessful and identified on security reports. • This test should be coordinated with the data owner and security administrator to avoid violation of security regulations.
Follow-up Access Violations	• To select a sample of security reports and look for evidence of follow-up and investigation of access violations.
Bypassing Security and Compensating Controls	• Being technical area of review auditor need to work with the system software analyst, network manager, operations manager and security administrator to determine ways to bypass security. • Areas to be reviewed includes bypass label processing, special system maintenance logon IDs, OS exits, installation utilities and input/output (I/O) devices. • Check whether access provided is on a need-to-know basis. • Check whether restrictions and procedures of monitoring access to computer features that bypass security is appropriate. **Bypass label processing (BLP):** BLP bypasses validation of existing file names/label. Most access control rules are based on file names (labels). **System exit:** This feature permits user to perform system maintenance. They often exist outside of the computer security system and, thus, are not restricted or reported in their use. **Special system logon IDs:** Some specific logon IDs are provided by manufacturer/vendor with default passwords. Auditor to ensure: • Deactivation of unused bypass security features. • Additional access controls for such bypass security features. • Process is place for logging and monitoring use of these features.

Network Penetration Tests

- In penetration testing, IS auditor uses the same techniques as used by hacker to gain access to critical system/data.
- Penetration test is an effective method of identifying the real-time risk to an information processing environment.

- Objective of penetration testing is to verify control environment of the organization and to take corrective action in case if deficiency is noted.
- During penetration testing, an auditor attempts to circumvent the security features of a system and exploits the vulnerabilities to gain access that would otherwise be unauthorized.
- Penetration testing should only be performed by experienced and qualified professionals.

Aspects to be covered in audit Scope:

From an audit risk perspective, following aspects to be covered in audit scope of Penetration Testing:

- Exact details of IP addresses to be included in scope of audit.
- Details of host not to be tested.
- Details of testing technique (i.e. SQL injection/DOS/DDOD/Social Engineering etc.)
- Day and Timing of the attack (i.e. either during office hours or after office hours)
- Nondisclosure agreement [NDA] with the penetration testing team members.
- Responsibility of penetration tester/auditor to provide appropriate warning before the simulation to avoid false alarms to law enforcement bodies.

Types of Penetration Tests

Penetration Tests	Description
External Testing	• Attacks on the target's network perimeter from outside the target's system (i.e. usually the Internet).
Internal Testing	• Attacks on the target from within the perimeter.
Blind Testing	• Attacks scenario wherein the penetration tester is provided with limited or no knowledge of the target's information systems. • Such testing is expensive because detailed study and research is required for attack.
Double blind Testing	• Extension of blind testing wherein administrator and security staff at the target are also not aware of the test. • This helps to evaluate the incident handling and response capability of the target.
Targeted Testing	• Attacks on the target where both the target's IT team and penetration testers are aware of the testing activities. • Relevant information related to target and network design is available with penetration testing.

Risks associated with Penetration Testing:

- Inappropriate test plan may trigger escalation procedures
- Disclosure of sensitive information to external tester may further increases target's exposure level. Information can be misused personal benefits.
- Inexperienced tester may damage the information assets.
- Attempt to break into a live production system may cause the system to fail.
- It is a simulation of a real attack and may be restricted by the law or regulations. Such attacks without appropriate approvals may have some adverse impact.

Threat Intelligence

- Threat intelligence is intelligent information about likely attacks.

- This information is organized and provided by the service providers and computer emergency response teams (CERTs).
- Threat intelligence is to help an organization understand common and severe external threats, such as zero-day threats, advanced persistent threats (APTs) and exploits
- Threat Intelligence helps the organization to protect itself from the attacks.

CISA aspirants should be aware of following controls for protection of wireless (Wi-Fi) security:

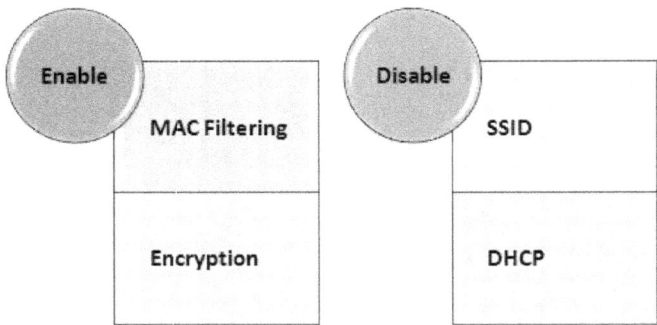

Enable MAC (Media Access Control) Filtering:

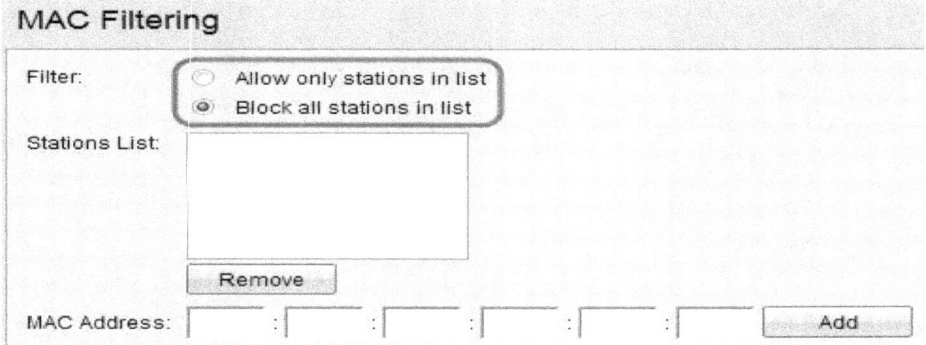

Every Machine (PC/Laptop/Mobiles) has a unique identification number. That is known as Media Access Control (MAC) address. So through this control, we allow access to only selected devices. Any other device trying to access the network will be rejected by router.

Also feature of black-list can be used to specifically reject some MAC addresses.

Enable Encryption:

Encryption helps to scrambles the information we send through wireless network into a code so that it's difficult for other to access. Using encryption is the effective way to secure your network from intruders. Two main types of encryption are available for this purpose: Wi-Fi Protected Access (WPA) and Wired Equivalent Privacy (WEP). WPA 2 is the strongest encryption standard for wireless connection as on today. It must be noted that these encryption techniques protects data in transit (and not on device).

Disable SSID (Service Set Identifier):

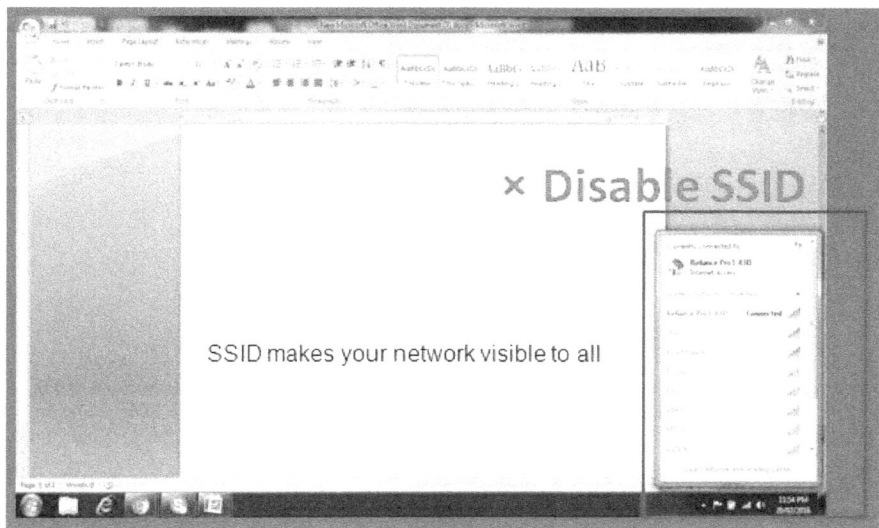

A Service Set Identifier (SSID) is the wireless network name broadcast by a router and it is visible for all wireless devices. When a wireless device searches the area for wireless networks it will detect the SSID.

There is no need for such open broadcast unless it is purposefully required to promote Wi-Fi (in case of hotel/restaurant/lounge/mall etc).

Disable DHCP:

Dynamic Host Configuration Protocol (DHCP) automatically assigns IP addresses to anyone connected to the network. With DHCP disabled, static IP addresses must be used which reduces the risk of unauthorised access.

Common attack methods and techniques for Wireless Network:

War Driving:

War driving is a term used to describe the process of a hacker who, armed with a laptop or other wireless device along with some hacking tools, travelling via a car, bus or other form of mechanized transport, goes around sniffing for wireless network. Same technique is used by IS auditor to test wireless security of an organization.

War Walking:

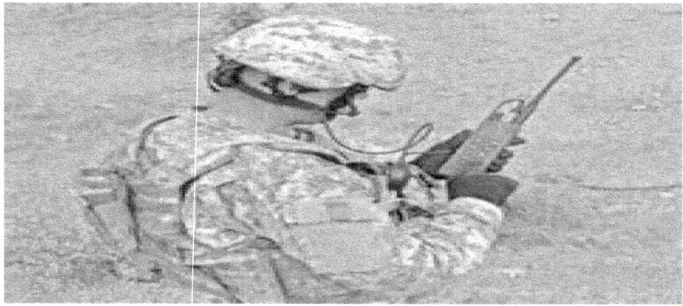

War *walking* refers to the same process, commonly in public areas like malls, hotels, or city streets, but walking with his devices instead of driving.

War Chalking:

War chalking is the drawing of symbols in public places to advertise an open Wi-Fi network. These symbols are subsequently used by others to exploit weak wireless networks.

Question, Answer & Explanation:

(1)Which of the following should be disabled to increase security of wireless network against unauthorized access?

A. MAC (Media Access Control) address filtering
B. Encryption
C. WPA-2 (Wi-Fi Protected Access Protocol)
D. SSID (service set identifier) broadcasting

Answer: D. SSID (service set identifier) broadcasting

Explanation:
A Service Set Identifier (SSID) is the network name broadcasted by a router and it is visible for all wireless devices. When a device searches the area for wireless networks it will detect the SSID. Disabling SSID broadcasting adds security by making it more difficult for unauthorized users to find the network. For better security controls, MAC filtering & WPA-2 should be enabled (and not disabled).

(2)Which of the following technique is more relevant to test wireless (Wi-Fi) security of an organization?

A. WPA-2
B. War dialling
C. War driving
D. Social Engineering

Answer: C. War driving

Explanation:
'War Driving' technique is used by hacker for unauthorised access to wireless infrastructure. War driving is a technique in which wireless equipped computer is used to locate and gain access to wireless networks. Same is done by driving or walking in and around building. 'War Driving' is also used by auditors to test wireless. WPA-2 is an encryption standard and not a technique to test the security. War dialling is a technique for gaining access to a computer or a network through the dialling of defined blocks of telephone numbers.

(3) Which of the following should be a concern to an IS auditor reviewing a wireless network?

A. System hardening of all wireless clients.
B. SSID (service set identifier) broadcasting has been enabled.
C. WPA-2 (Wi-Fi Protected Access Protocol) encryption is enabled.
D. DHCP (Dynamic Host Configuration Protocol) is disabled at all wireless access points.

Answer: B. SSID (Service Set IDentifier) broadcasting has been enabled.

Explanation:
Disabling SSID broadcasting adds security by making it more difficult for unauthorized users to find the network. In any given scenario, following are the best practises for wireless (wi-fi) security:
(a)Enable MAC (Media Access Control) address filtering.
(b)Enable Encryption to protect data in transit.
(c)Disable SSID (service set identifier) broadcasting.
(d)Disable DHCP (Dynamic Host Configuration Protocol).

(4)Dynamic Host Configuration Protocol (DHCP)is disabled at all wireless access points. Which of the following statement is true when DHCP is disabled for wireless networks?

A. increases the risk of unauthorized access to the network.
B. decreases the risk of unauthorized access to the network.
C. automatically provides an IP address to anyone.
D. it disables SSID (Service Set Identifier).

Answer: B. decreases the risk of unauthorized access to the network.
Explanation:
Dynamic Host Configuration Protocol (DHCP) automatically assigns IP addresses to anyone connected to the network. With DHCP disabled, static IP addresses must be used and hence risk of unauthorized access can be reduced. Option C is incorrect because DHCP does not provide IP addresses when disabled. Option D is incorrect because disabling of the DHCP will not automatically disables SSID.

(5) Best method to ensure confidentiality of the data transmitted in a wireless LAN is to:

A. restrict access to predefined MAC addresses.
B. protect the session by encrypting with use of static keys.
C. protect the session by encrypting with use dynamic keys.
D. initiate the session by encrypted device.

Answer: C. protect the session by encrypting with use dynamic keys.

Explanation:
In any given scenario, confidentiality of the data transmitted in a wireless LAN is BEST protected, if the session is encrypted using dynamic keys (as compared to static keys). When using dynamic keys, the encryption key is changed frequently, thus reducing the risk of the key being compromised and the message being decrypted. Option A & D will not ensure data confidentiality during transit. Encryption of the data on the connected device addresses the confidentiality of the data on the device, not the wireless session. When using dynamic keys, the encryption key is changed frequently, thus reducing the risk of the key being compromised and the message being decrypted. Limiting the number of devices that can access the network does not address the issue of encrypting the session.

(6)Usage of wireless infrastructure for use of mobile devices within the organization, increases risk of which of the following attacks?

A. Port scanning
B. Social Engineering
C. Piggybacking
D. War driving

Answer: D. War driving

Explanation:
'War Driving' technique is used by hacker for unauthorised access to wireless infrastructure. War driving is a technique in which wireless equipped computer is used to locate and gain access to wireless networks. Same is done by driving or walking in and around building. A war driving attack uses a wireless Ethernet card, set in promiscuous mode, and a powerful antenna to penetrate wireless systems from outside.

(7)For man-in-the-middle attack, which of the following encryption techniques will BEST protect a wireless network?

A. Wired equivalent privacy (WEP)
B. MAC-based pre-shared key (PSK)
C. Randomly generated pre-shared key (PSK)
D. Service set identifier (SSID)

Answer: Randomly generated pre-shared key (PSK)

Explanation:
SSID is not an encryption technique.MAC address of a computer is fixed and often accessible. A randomly generated PSK is stronger than a MAC-based PSK. WEP has been shown to be a very weak encryption technique and can be cracked within minutes. The SSID is broadcast on the wireless network in plaintext.

Last Minute Revision:

- In any given scenario, following are the best practices for Wireless (Wi-Fi) security:

    ➢ Enable MAC (Media Access Control) address filtering.
    ➢ Enable Encryption to protect data in transit.
    ➢ Disable SSID (service set identifier) broadcasting.
    ➢ Disable DHCP (Dynamic Host Configuration Protocol).

- In any given scenario, 'War Driving' technique is used by hacker for unauthorized access to wireless infrastructure. War driving is a technique in which wireless equipped computer is used to locate and gain access to wireless networks. Same is done by driving or walking in and around building. 'War Driving' is also used by auditors to test wireless networks.
- In any given scenario, WPA-2 (Wi-Fi Protected Access) is the strongest encryption standard for the wireless connection.
- In any given scenario, confidentiality of the data transmitted in a wireless LAN is BEST protected, if the session is encrypted using dynamic keys (as compared to static keys)

CMR covers following types and implementation of firewall:

Types of Firewall	Types Firewall Implementation
• Packet Filtering Router • Statefull Inspection • Circuit-Level • Application-Level	• Dual Homed Firewall • Screened Host Firewall • Screened Subnet Firewall (DMZ)

Types of Firewall:

Packet Filtering Router:
- Simplest & earliest kind of firewall.
- Allow or Deny action is done as per IP address and port number of source & destination of packets.
- Works at Network Layer of OSI.

Stateful Inspection:
- A statefull Inspection firewall keeps track of destination of each packet that leaves the internal network.
- It ensures that incoming message is in response to the request that went out of the organization.
- Works at Network Layer of OSI.

Circuit Level:
- Works on concept of bastion host and proxy server.
- Same Proxy for all services.
- Works at Session Layer of OSI.

Application Level:
- Works on concept of bastion host and proxy server.
- Separate Proxy for each application.
- Works at Application Layer of OSI.
- Controls application such as FTP and http.
- Out of above firewalls, Application level firewall is the most secured type of firewall.

What is bastion host?
- Both Application-Level Firewall as well as Circuit-Level Firewall works on concept of bastion hosting.
- On the Internet, a bastion host is the only host computer that a company allows to be addressed directly from the public network and that is designed to protect the rest of its network from exposure.
- Bastion host are heavily forfeited against attack.
- Common characteristics of a bastion host are as follows:

  ➢ Its Operating system is hardened, in the sense that only essential services are installed on it.

> System should have all the unnecessary services disabled, unneeded ports closed, unused applications removed, unnecessary administrative tools removed i.e. vulnerabilities to be removed to the extent possible.
> It is configured to require additional authentication before a user is granted access to proxy services.
> It is configured to access only specific hosts.

What is Proxy?

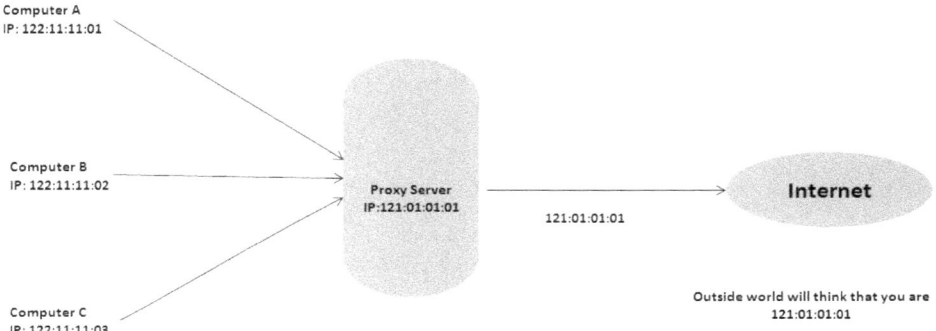

- A proxy is a middleman. Proxy stands between internal and external network.
- Proxy will not allow direct communication between two networks.
- Proxy technology can work at different layer of OSI model. A proxy based firewall that works at lower layer (session layer) is referred to as circuit-level proxy. A proxy based firewall that works at higher layer (application layer) is called as an application level proxy.

Types of Firewall Implementation:
Following three types of firewall implementation are relevant for CISA Exam:

Dual-Homed Firewall:

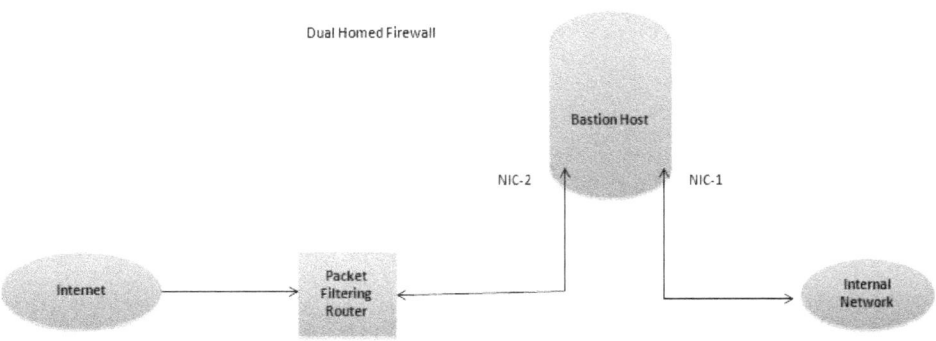

Characteristics:

- One Packet Filtering Router

- One bastion host with two NIC (Network Interface Card).

Screened Host Firewall:

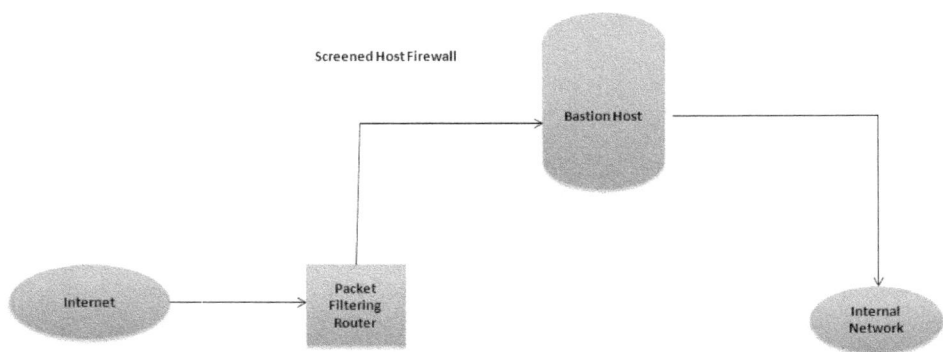

Characteristics:

- One Packet Filtering Router
- One Bastion Host

Screened Host Firewall (Demilitarized Zone):

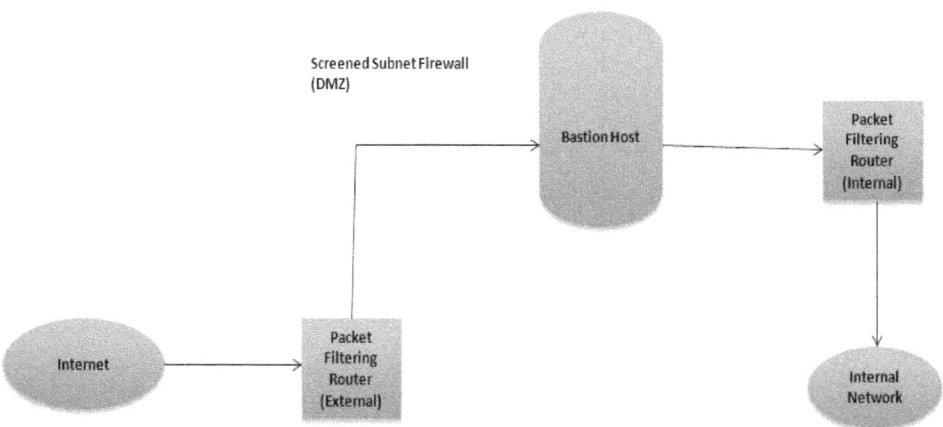

Characteristics:

- Two Packet Filtering Router
- One Bastion Host
- Out of above firewall implementations, Screen-Subnet Firewall (DMZ) is the mcst secured type of firewall implementation.

Last Minute Revision:

- Out of all types of firewall, Application-Level Firewall provides greatest security environment (as it works on application layer of OSI model).
- Out of all types of firewall implementation structures, Screened Subnet Firewall (DMZ) provides greatest security environment (as it implements 2 packet filtering router and 1 bastion host).
- In any given scenario, most robust configuration in firewall rule is 'deny all traffic and allow specific traffic' (as against 'allow all traffic and deny specific traffic').
- In any given scenario, Stateful Inspection Firewall allows traffic from outside only if it is in response to traffic from internal hosts.
- In any given scenario, following are the OSI layers at which various firewall operates:

Firewall	OSI Layer
Packet Filtering Firewall	Network Layer (3rd Layer)
Statefull Inspection Firewall	Network Layer (3rd Layer)
Circuit-Level Firewall	Session Layer (5th Layer)
Application-Level Firewall	Application Layer (7th Layer)

Question, Answer & Explanation on Firewall:

(1)The most robust configuration in firewall rule base is:

A. Allow all traffic and deny the specified traffic
B. Deny all traffic and allow the specified traffic
C. Dynamically decide based on traffic
D.Control traffic on the basis of discretion of network administrator.

Answer: B. Deny all traffic and allow the specified traffic

Explanation:
In any given scenario, most robust configuration in firewall rule is 'deny all traffic and allow specific traffic' (as against 'allow all traffic and deny specific traffic'). This will help to block unknown traffic to critical systems and servers.

(2)A packet filtering firewall operates on which layer of following OSI model?

A. Network layer
B. Application layer
C. Transport layer
D. Session layer

Answer: A. Network layer
Explanation:
In any given scenario, following are the OSI layers at which various firewall operates:

Firewall	OSI Layer
Packet Filtering Firewall	Network Layer (3rd Layer)
Statefull Inspection Firewall	Network Layer (3rd Layer)
Circuit-Level Firewall	Session Layer (5th Layer)
Application-Level Firewall	Application Layer (7th Layer)

(3)Which of the following would be the MOST secure firewall system implementation?

A. Screened-host firewall
B. Screened-subnet firewall
C. Dual-homed firewall
D. Stateful-inspection firewall

Answer: B. Screened-subnet firewall

Explanation:
Out of all types of firewall implementation structures, Screened Subnet Firewall provides greatest security environment (as it implements 2 packet filtering router and 1 bastion host). It acts as proxy and direct connection between internal network and external network is not allowed. A screened subnet firewall is also used as a demilitarized zone (DMZ). Difference between screened-subnet firewall and screened host firewall is that, screened-subnet firewall uses two packet filtering router whereas screened-host firewall uses only one packet-filtering firewall.

(4)Which of the following types of firewalls provide the MOST secured environment?

A. Stateful Inspection
B. Packet filter
C. Application gateway
D. Circuit gateway

Answer: C. Application gateway

Explanation:
Out of all types of firewall, Application-Level Firewall provides greatest security environment (as it works on application layer of OSI model).
Following is the major difference between application and circuit gateway:
- Application gateway works on application layer of OSI model and Circuit gateway works on session layer.
- Application gateway has different proxies for each service whereas Circuit gateway has single proxy for all services.
Therefore, application gateway works in a more detailed (granularity) way than the others.

(5)An organization wants to protect a network from Internet attack. Which of the following firewall structure would BEST ensure the protection?

A. Screened subnet firewall
B. Screened host firewall
C. Packet filtering router

D. Circuit-level gateway

Answer: A. Screened subnet firewall

Explanation:
Out of all types of firewall implementation structures, Screened Subnet Firewall provides greatest security environment (as it implements 2 packet filtering router and 1 bastion host). It acts as proxy and direct connection between internal network and external network is not allowed. A screened subnet firewall is also used as a demilitarized zone (DMZ).
Difference between screened-subnet firewall and screened host firewall is that, screened-subnet firewall uses two packet filtering router whereas screened-host firewall uses only one packet-filtering firewall. Both works on the concept of bastion host and proxy.

(6)The firewall that allows traffic from outside only if it is in response to traffic from internal hosts, is:

A. Application level gateway firewall
B. Stateful Inspection Firewall
C. Packet filtering Router
D. Circuit level gateway

Answer: B. Stateful Inspection Firewall

Explanation:
Stateful Inspection Firewall keeps track of the connection and ensures that incoming message is in response to the request that went out of the organization.

(7)An organization with the objective of preventing downward of file through FTP (File Transfer Protocol) should configure which of the firewall types ?

A. Stateful Inspection
B. Application gateway
C. Packet filter
D. Circuit gateway

Answer: B. Application gateway

Explanation:
Application gateway works on application layer of OSI model and effective in preventing applications, such as FTPs and https. A circuit gateway firewall is able to prevent paths or circuits, not applications, from entering the organization's network.

(8)An organization wants to connect a critical server to the internet. Which of the following would provide the BEST protection against hacking?

A. Stateful Inspection
B. A remote access server
C. Application-level gateway
D. Port scanning

Answer: C. Application-level gateway

Explanation:

Out of all types of firewall, Application-Level Firewall provides greatest security environment (as it works on application layer of OSI model).An application-level gateway is the best way to protect against hacking because it can define with detail rules that describe the type of user or connection that is or is not permitted. It analyze each package in detail at application level of OSI which means that it reviews the commands of each higher-level protocol such as HTTP, FTP etc.

(9)An IS auditor should be most concern about which of the following while reviewing a firewall?

A. Properly defined security policy
B Use of latest firewall structure with most secure algorithm.
C. The effectiveness of the firewall in enforcing the security policy.
D. Technical knowledge of users.

Answer: The effectiveness of the firewall in enforcing the security policy.

Explanation:
In absence of effective firewall implementation, other factors will not be effective. The existence of a good security policy is important, but if the firewall has not been implemented so as to effectively enforce the policy, then the policy is of little value.

(10)While implementing a firewall, the most likely error to occur is:

A. wrong configuration of the access lists.
B. compromise of the password due to shoulder surfing.
C. inadequate user training about firewall rules.
D. inadequate anti-virus updation.

Answer: A. wrong configuration of the access lists.

Explanation:
Updation of correct and current access list is a significant challenge and, therefore, has the greatest chance for errors at the time of the initial installation. Others are not an element in implementing a firewall.

(11)The first step in installing a Firewall in a large organization is:

A. Develop Security Policy
B. Review firewall settings
C. Prepare Access Control List
D. Configure the firewall

Answer: A. Develop Security Policy

Explanation:
First step is to develop security policy and on the basis of approved security policy other steps to be considered.

(12)Which of the following is the MOST critical function of a firewall?

A. to act as a special router that connects different network.
B. device for preventing authorized users from accessing the LAN.
C. device used to connect authorized users to trusted network resources.
D. proxy server to increase the speed of access to authorized users.

Answer: C. device used to connect authorized users to trusted network resources.

Explanation:
Main and critical function of a firewall is to prevent unauthorised access to server. A firewall is a set of related programs that protects the resources of a private network from users of other networks.

(13)Which of the following should be the GREATEST concern to an IS auditor reviewing the firewall security architecture?

A. Secure Sockets Layer (SSL) has been implemented.
B. Firewall policies are updated on the basis of changing requirements.
C. Inbound traffic is blocked unless the traffic type and connections have been specifically permitted.
D. The firewall is placed on top of the commercial operating system with all installation options.

Answer: D. The firewall is placed on top of the commercial operating system with all installation options.

Explanation:
Firewall Security can be compromised when all the installation options are kept open. Other choices are prudent options for better firewall security.

(14)An IS auditor is reviewing firewall security of the organization. Which of the following is the BEST audit procedure to determine if a firewall is configured as per security policy?

A. Review incident logs.
B. Review Access Control List.
C. Review the actual procedures.
D. Review the parameter settings.

Answer: D. Review the parameter settings.

Explanation:
A review of the parameter settings will provide a good basis for comparison of the actual configuration to the security policy and will provide audit evidence documentation. The other choices do not provide as strong audit evidence as choice A.

(15)Which of the following concerns would be addressed by a firewall?

A. Unauthorized access from external network
B. Unauthorized access from internal network
C. A delay in Internet connectivity
D. A delay in system processing

Answer: A. Unauthorized access from outside the organization

Explanation:
Firewalls are meant to prevent outsiders from gaining access to an organization's computer systems through the Internet gateway.

A CISA aspirant is expected to understand following norms for logical access:

- In information technology, logical access controls are tools and protocols used for identification, authentication, authorization, and accountability in computer information systems.
- There are two main types of access control: physical and logical. Physical access control limits access to campuses, buildings, rooms and physical IT assets. Logical access limits connections to computer networks, system files and data.
- The four main categories of access control are:

- Mandatory access control
- Discretionary access control
- Role-based access control
- Rule-based access control

- Mandatory Access Control: Mandatory Access Controls (MACs) are logical access control that cannot be controlled or modified by normal users or data owners.
- Discretionary Access Control: Discretionary Access Controls (DACs) are logical access control that may be activated or modified by the data owners at their discretion.
- In any given scenario, MACs are better choice in terms of data security as compared to DACs.
- In any given scenario, following are the steps for implementing logical access controls:

- Inventory of IS resources.
- Classification of IS resources.
- Grouping/labeling of IS resources.
- Creation of an access control list.

- In any given scenario, first step in data classification is to identify the owner of the data/application.
- In any given scenario, an automated password management tool works as best preventive control and ensures compliance with password management policy.
- Please note below access control best practices for wireless security. Invariably 2-3 questions will be there on this concept:

- Enable MAC address filtering: Every Machine (PC/Laptop/Mobiles) has a unique identification number. That is known as Media Access Control (MAC) address. So through this control, access is allowed to only selected devices. Any other device trying to access the network will be rejected by router.
- Disable SSID (Service set identifier) broadcasting: A Service Set Identifier (SSID) is the wireless network name broadcast by a router and it is visible for all wireless devices. When a wireless device searches the area for wireless networks it will detect the SSID.
- Enable WPA-2 (Wi-Fi protected access) protection: Encryption helps to scrambles the information we send through wireless network into a code so that it's difficult for other to access. Using encryption is the effective way to secure your network from intruders.
- Enable Encryption: Two main types of encryption are available for this purpose: Wi-Fi Protected Access (WPA) and Wired Equivalent Privacy (WEP). WPA 2 is the strongest encryption standard for wireless connection as on today.

- In any given scenario, preference to be given to preventive controls as compared to detective or deterrent controls.

- In any given scenario, preference to be given to automated controls as compared to manual controls.

- In any given scenario, default deny access control policy (i.e. deny all traffic except selected ones) is more robust and stringent access control policy as compared to default allow access control policy (i.e. allow all traffic except selected ones).

- Prime objective of review of logical access control is to ensure access have been assigned as per organization's authorization.

Question, Answer & Explanation:

(1)The IS auditor reviews logical access control with a primary objective to:

A. Access control software is working properly.
B. ensures access is granted as per the approved structure.
C. to protect computer software.
D. to protect computer hardware.

Answer: B. ensures access is granted as per the approved structure.

Explanation:
The scope of a logical access control review is primarily to determine whether or not access is granted per the organization's authorizations. Choices A and C relate to procedures of a logical access control review, rather than objectives. Choice D is relevant to a physical access control review.

(2)During review of critical application system, the IS auditor observes that user accounts are shared. The Major risk resulting from this situation is that:

A. passwords are changed frequently.
B. Outsider can gain access to the system.
C. passwords are easily guessed.
D. user accountability may not be established.

Answer: D. user accountability may not be established.

Explanation:
If same user accounts are shared with multiple employees, it will be difficult to trace the particular employee during audit trail. User accountability may not be established is such scenario.

(3)Which of the following is the best technique for protecting critical data inside the server?

A. Security awareness
B. Reading the security policy
C. Security committee
D. Logical access controls

Answer: D. Logical access controls

Explanation:
(1) In any given scenario, preference to be given to preventive controls as compared to detective or deterrent controls. Logical access controls are best preventive controls to ensure data integrity and confidentiality.
(2) Awareness itself does not protect against unauthorized access or disclosure of information.
(3)Knowledge of an information systems security policy which should be known by the organizations employees, would help to protect information, but would not prevent the unauthorized access of information.

(4)A security committee is key to the protection of information assets, but would address security issues within a broader perspective.

(4)Which of the following BEST logical control mechanism to ensure that access allowed to users to only those functions needed to perform their duties?

A. Application level access control
B. Data encryption
C. HTTPs protocol
D. Network monitoring device

Answer: A. Application level access control

Explanation:
The use of application-level access control programs is a management control that restricts access by limiting users to only those functions needed to perform their duties.

(5)Which of the following is the MOST important objective of data protection?

A. current technology trend
B. Ensuring the confidentiality & integrity of information
C. Denying or authorizing access to the IS system
D. internal processing efficiency.

Answer. Ensuring the confidentiality of information

Explanation:
Maintaining data confidentiality and integrity is the most important objective of data security. This is a basic requirement if an organization is to continue as a viable and successful enterprise.

(6) The FIRST step in data classification is to:

A. identify data owners.
B. perform a criticality analysis.
C. define access rules.
D. define firewall rules.

Answer: A. identify data owners.

Explanation:
Data classification is necessary to define access rules based on a need-to-do and need-to know basis. The data owner is responsible for defining the access rules; hence, establishing ownership is the first step in data classification.

(7)IS auditor is reviewing an organization's logical access security. He should be most concerned if:

A. Passwords are shared.
B. Password files are not protected.
C. Resigned employees' logon IDs are not deleted immediately.
D. Logon IDs are issued centrally.

Answer: B. Password files are not protected.

Explanation:
Unprotected passwords files represent the greatest risk. Such files should be stored in an encrypted manner. Other options are also essential but they are less important than ensuring that the password files are encrypted.

(8)IS auditor is evaluating database-level access control functions. Which of the following access control function will not be in his scope?

A. Creating database profiles for monitoring
B. authorization user at field level.
C. establishing individual accountability
D. Logging database access activities for monitoring access violation

Answer: establishing individual accountability

Explanation:
Establishing individual accountability is the function of the general operating system. Creating database profiles, verifying user authorization at a field level and logging database access activities for monitoring access violations are all database-level access control functions.

(9)IS auditor observed that even though password policy requires passwords to be a combination of letters, numbers and special characters, users are not following the same rigorously. To ensure compliance within security policy, the IS auditor should recommend that:

A. password policy to be simplified.
B. password policy to be sent to all users every month.
C. usage of automated password management tool
D. monthly security awareness training to be delivered.

Answer: C. usage of automated password management tool

Explanation:
Among the choices given, use of an automated password management tool is a best preventive control measure. The software would prevent usage of passwords which are not allowed as per policy. It would also provide a method for ensuring frequent changes and would prevent the same user from reusing his/her old password for a designated period of time. Choices A, B and D do not enforce compliance.

(10) An IS auditor observes that default printing options are enabled for all users. In this situation, the IS auditor is MOST likely to conclude that:

A. risk of data confidentially increases.
B. risk if data integrity increases.
C. it improvises the productivity of employees.
D. it ensures smooth flow of information among users.

Answer: A. risk of data confidentially increases.

Explanation:
Risk of data confidentiality increases as any user can print documents. Print option will not impact data integrity as data integrity can be impacted by write/delete access for user.

(11)IS Auditor is reviewing wireless network security policy of the organization. Which of the following action would make the wireless network more secure?

A. Disabling MAC (Media Access Control) address filtering
B. Disabling WPA (Wi-Fi Protected Access Protocol)
C. Enabling SSID (service set identifier) broadcasting
D. Disabling SSID (service set identifier) broadcasting

Answer: D. Disabling SSID (service set identifier) broadcasting

Explanation:
Disabling SSID broadcasting adds security by making it more difficult for unauthorized users to find the name of the access point. Opting other options will infact reduces the security of network.

(12)Auditor is reviewing wireless network security of the organization. Which of the following should be a concern to an IS auditor?

A. 128-bit-static-key WEP (Wired Equivalent Privacy) encryption is enabled.
B. SSID (Service Set IDentifier) broadcasting has been enabled.
C. Antivirus software has been installed in all wireless clients.
D. MAC (Media Access Control) access control filtering has been deployed.

Answer. B.SSID (Service Set IDentifier) broadcasting has been enabled.

Explanation:
Enabling SSID broadcasting reduces the security by making it easier for unauthorized users to find the name of the access point. Opting other options will strengthen the security of network.

(13)IS auditor is evaluating general operating system access control functions. Which of the following access control function will be in his scope?

A. Logging user activities
B. Logging data communication access activities
C. Verifying user authorization at the field level
D. Changing data files

Answer: A. Logging user activities

Explanation:
General operating system access control functions include log user activities, log events, etc. Choice B is a network control feature. Choices C and D are database- and/or application level access control functions.

(14)An IS auditor reviewing system controls should be most concerned that:

A. security and performance requirements are considered.
B. changes are recorded in log.
C. process for change authorization is in place.
D. restricted access for system parameters is in place.

Answer: A. security and performance requirements are considered.

Explanation:
The primary concern is to ensure that security as well as performance aspects have been considered. This helps to ensure that control objectives are aligned with business objectives. Log maintenance and change

authorization are also important but in absence of proper security and performance requirements same may not be effective.

(15)Most effective transmission media in terms of security against unauthorized access is:

A. Copper wire
B. Twisted pair
C. Fiber-optic cables
D. Coaxial cables

Answer: C. Fiber-optic cables

Explanation:
Fiber-optic cables are more secure than the other media. Other media can be compromised easily as compared to fiber-optic.

(16)Mechanism that checks each request by a subject to access and use an object is as per security policy is known as:

A. Address Resolution Protocol
B. Access control analyzer
C. Reference monitor
D. Reverse Address Resolution Protocol

Answer: C. Reference monitor

Explanation:
(1)In operating systems architecture a reference monitor concept defines a set of design requirements on a reference validation mechanism, which enforces an access control policy over subjects' (e.g., processes and users) ability to perform operations (e.g., read and write) on objects (e.g., files and sockets) on a system. A reference monitor is implemented via a security kernel, which is a hardware/software/firmware mechanism.

(2)Address Resolution Protocol is a network layer protocol used to convert an IP address into a physical address such as an Ethernet address. A host wishing to obtain a physical address broadcasts an ARP request onto the TCP/IP network. The host on the network that has the IP address in the request then replies with its physical hardware address.

(3) An access control analyzer is an audit utility for analyzing how well access controls have been implemented and maintained within an access control package.

(4) Reverse ARP (RARP) can be used by a host to discover its IP address. In this case, the host broadcasts its physical address and a RARP server replies with the host's IP address.

(17) IS auditor is reviewing level of access available for different user. To determine the same, which of the following should an IS auditor review?

A. Log file maintained for system access
B. Job descriptions of users.
C. Logs maintained for access control violation.
D. System configuration files for control options used

Answer: D. System configuration files for control options used

Explanation:
A review of system configuration files for control options used would show level of access available for different user. Both log files are detective in nature. Job descriptions of users will not provide details about access level.

(18) Read Only option is always recommended for:

A. access control matrix/rule.
B. log files for suspected transactions.
C. logging rules
D. user profiles.

Answer: B. log files for suspected transactions.
.

Explanation:
Security administration procedures require read-only access to security log files to ensure that, once generated, the logs are not modified. Logs provide evidence and track suspicious transactions and activities. Other options may require modification and hence write access can also be provided.

(19) An IS auditor performing a telecommunication access control review should be concerned PRIMARILY with the:

A. regular updation of logs files of usage of various system resources.
B. authorization and authentication mechanism for allowing access only to authorized user.
C. Encryption mechanism for data protection.
D. mechanism to control remote access.

Answer: B. authorization and authentication mechanism for allowing access only to authorized user.

Explanation:
Unless and until proper authorization and authentication process is not established, other controls may not serve the purpose. This is a preventive control. The authorization and authentication of users is the most significant aspect. Other options will serve the purpose only if authorized users are allowed the access.

(20) Discretionary Access Control will be more effective if they:

A. are placed in accordance with mandatory access controls.
B. are placed independently of mandatory access controls.
C. allow enable users to bypass mandatory access controls as and when required.
D. are allowed by security policy.

Answer: A. are placed in accordance with mandatory access controls.

Explanation:
Mandatory Access Controls (MACs) are logical access control that cannot be controlled or modified by normal users or data owners. Discretionary Access Controls (DACs) are logical access control that may be activated or modified by the data owners at their discretion. DACs to be more effective have to be designed in accordance with MACs. Mandatory access controls are prohibitive, anything that is not expressly permitted is forbidden. Only within this context do discretionary controls operate, prohibiting still more access with the same exclusionary principle.

(21)Best method to remove confidential data from computer storage is:

A. hard disk should be demagnetized.
B. hard disk should be formatted.
C. data on the hard disk should be deleted.
D. data on the hard disk should be defragmented.

Answer: A. hard disk should be demagnetized.

Explanation:
The hard disk should be demagnetized, since this will cause all of the bits to be set to zero, eliminating any chance of retrieving information that was previously stored on the disk. Other options may not be that effective.

(22)Appropriateness of router setting is to be reviewed during:

A. Physical access review.
B. Network security review.
C. Data centre security review.
D. Data back-up review.

Answer: B. Network security review.

Explanation:
Network security reviews include reviewing router access control lists, port scanning, internal and external connections to the system, etc.

(23)IS auditor is reviewing physical controls for data centre. For visitor access to data centre, most effective control he should recommend is that:

A. Escort policy for every visitor.
B. Issuance of visitor badge
C. Proper sign in procedure for visitors.
D. Security Checks procedure for every visitor.

Answer: Escort policy for every visitor.

Explanation:
Escorting visitors will provide the best assurance that visitors have permission to access the data processing facility. Other controls are not as reliable as escort policy.

(24) The major risk for lack of an authorization process for users of an application would be:

A. many users can claim to be a specific user.
B. there is no way to limit role based access.
C. Sharing of user accounts.
D. principle of least privilege can be assured. .

Answer: B. there is no way to limit role based access.

Explanation:
(1) Without an appropriate authorization process, it will be impossible to establish functional limits and accountability. Hence correct option is option B i.e. there is no way to limit role based access.
(2) The risk that many users can claim to be a specific user can be better addressed by proper authentication process rather than authorization.

(3)Authorization process will not directly impact sharing user accounts. Other controls are required to prevent sharing of user accounts.

(4)In absence of proper authorization process principle of least privilege cannot be assured.

(25) An IS auditor has been asked to recommend effective control for providing temporary access rights to outsourced vendors. Which of the following is the MOST effective control?

A. Penalty clause in service level agreement (SLA).

B User accounts are created as per defined role (least privilege) with expiration dates.

C. Full access is provided for a limited period.

D. Vendor Management to be given right to delete Ids when work is completed.

Answer: B. User accounts are created as per defined role (least privilege) with expiration dates

Explanation:

(1)Creation of need based user ID and automated revocation of IDs as per expiration date will serve as most effective control under the given scenario and options.

(2)Penalty clause in SLA may act as a deterrent control but automated revocations of Ids are more effective method of control.

(3)Providing full access is a risky affair.

(4)Control in terms of providing rights to vendor management for deletion of IDs may not be reliable.

(26)For effective access control, proper naming conventions for system resources are essential because they:

A. ensures that resource names are as per their utility.

B. access rules can be structured and better managed.

C. ensures that user access to resources is clearly identified.

D. ensures that international standard for naming is maintained.

Answer: B. access rules can be structured and better managed.

Explanation:

(1)Naming conventions helps for efficient management of access rules. It helps for defining structured access rules. The conventions can be structured, so resources beginning with the same high level qualifier can be governed by one or more generic rules. This reduces the number of rules required to adequately protect resources, which in turn facilitates security administration and maintenance efforts.

(2)Though as a generic rule, naming conventions ensures that names represent the utility, it will not impact access controls.

(3) Naming convention in itself do not ensure that user access to resource is clearly identified. Ensuring the clear and unique identification of user access to resources is handled by access control rules and not naming conventions.

(4)Each organization has its own standard for naming convention. Internationally recognized names are not required to control access to resources.

(27)IS auditor is reviewing security of a payroll application. Which of the following should concern him?

A. Role-based access to users.

B. Hardening of systems where application runs.

C. The ability of users to access and modify the database directly.

D. Two factor authentication for access.

Answer: C. The ability of users to access and modify the database directly.

Explanation:
The ability of users to directly modify the database can affect the integrity of the data. Only DBA should be allowed for any backend changes to database. Other factors like role-based access, hardening of system and two factor authentication are good practices for IT security. Hardening of system involves disabling all functions such as disk driver, USB and other ports which can affect data security.

(28)Which among the below is the First step in implementation of access control list:

A. a categorization of IS resources.
B. the grouping of IS resources.
C. implementation of access control rules.
D. creating inventory of available IS resources.

Answer: D. creating inventory of available IS resources.

Explanation:
In any given scenario, following are the steps for implementing logical access controls:
(a) Inventory of IS resources.
(b) Classification of IS resources.
(c) Grouping/labelling of IS resources.
(d) Creation of an access control list.
Thus the first step in implementing access controls is an inventory of IS resources, which is the basis for classification. Grouping of resources cannot be done without first determining the resources' classifications.

(29)IS auditor is reviewing general IT controls of an organization. Which of the following should concern him?

A. LAN connections are easily in the facility to connect laptops to the network.
B. Two factor authentication is mandatory of access of critical applications.
C. Stand-alone terminals with password protection are located in insecure locations.
D. Terminals are located within the facility in small clusters under the supervision of an administrator.

Answer: A. LAN connections are easily in the facility to connect laptops to the network.

Explanation:
(1)Gaining access to network by an unauthorized person is the major risk in the given situation. Any person with wrongful intentions can connect a laptop to the network. The insecure connecting points make unauthorized access possible if the individual has knowledge of a valid user id and password.
(2)Two factor authentication is a good IS policy. Intruders will find it difficult to access the applications.
(3)Access to stand alone terminal is not as risky as access to full network. Hence in the given scenario, correct option would be easy availability of LAN connection.

(30)To prevent unauthorized entry to database of critical application, an IS auditor should recommend:

A. Online terminals are placed in restricted areas.
B. CCTV camera to be placed above terminals.
C. ID cards are required to gain access to online terminals.
D. Online access to be blocked after a specified number of unsuccessful attempts.

Answer: D. online access to be blocked after a specified number of unsuccessful attempts.

Explanation:

(1) In any given scenario, preference to be given to preventive controls as compared to detective or deterrent controls. The most appropriate control to prevent unauthorized entry is to terminate connection after a specified number of attempts. This will deter access through the guessing of ids and passwords.

(2)Other controls cannot prevent remote access by intruders. The other choices are physical controls, which are desirable but less effective as compared to blocking of access.

(31)The most robust access control policy is the Default Deny Access Control Policy. This policy:

A. Allows selected traffic and denies rest all traffic.
B. Denies selected traffic and allows rest all traffic.
C. Is frequently used for granting access from a trusted network to an external Systems.
D. Traffic is allowed as per discretion of application owner.

Answer: A. Allows selected traffic and denies rest all traffic.

Explanation:
Default Deny Access Control Policy envisages denial of all traffic by default and selectively allowing certain traffic alone through the firewall. It is frequently used for granting access from an un-trusted source to a protected system. It is also called Mandatory Access Control Policy.

(32)The Allow All Access Control Policy:

A. Allows selected traffic and denies rest all traffic.
B. Denies selected traffic and allows rest all traffic.
C. Is frequently used for granting access from un- trusted network to an external System.
D. Traffic is allowed as per discretion of application owner.

Answer: B. Denies selected traffic and allows rest all traffic.

Explanation:
The Allow All Access Control Policy envisages allowing of all traffic by default and selectively denying certain traffic alone through the firewall. It is frequently used for granting access from a trusted network to external systems like the Internet. It is also called Discretionary Access Control Policy.

Following are the objectives/benefits for Data Classification:

To reduce risk of under protection of Information Assets

To reduce cost of over protection of Information Assets

Following are the logical steps to be followed for Data Classification:

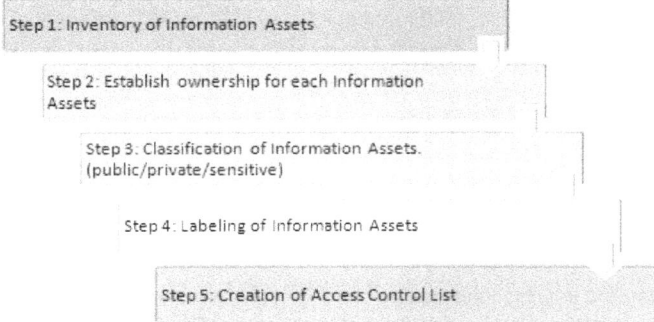

Step 1: Inventory of Information Assets

Step 2: Establish ownership for each Information Assets

Step 3: Classification of Information Assets. (public/private/sensitive)

Step 4: Labeling of Information Assets

Step 5: Creation of Access Control List

Other Important Points:

- Accountability for the maintenance of proper security controls over information assets resides with the data owner/system owner.
- Data owner/system owner is ultimately responsible for defining the access rules.
- Data classification must take into account following requirements:

- Legal/Regulatory/Contractual
- Confidential
- Integrity
- Availability

- It is very important for data owner and data custodian to have knowledge and awareness about data classification policy of the company. This ensures proper classification of data as per organizational requirement.

Question, Answer & Explanation:

(1)Responsibility for the maintenance of proper control measures over information resources resides with the:
A. database administrator
B. security administrator

C. data and systems owners
D. systems operations group

Answer: C. data and systems owners

Explanation:
In any given scenario, accountability for the maintenance of security controls over information assets resides with the data owner/system owner. Even though owner may delegate responsibilities to other specialized functions, owners remain accountable for the maintenance of appropriate security measures. Management should ensure that all information resources to have an appointed owner who makes decisions about classification and access rights.

(2)An IS auditor is evaluating data classification policy of an organization. The FIRST step in data classification is to:

A. the labelling of IS resources
B. establish ownership
C. perform a impact analysis
D. define access control rules

Answer: B. establish ownership
Explanation:
In any given scenario, following are the logical steps for data classification:
-First step is to have inventory of IS resources
-Second step is to establish ownership
-Third step is classification of IS resources
-Fourth step is labelling of IS resources
-Fifth step is creation of access control list
In the above question, step with respect to inventory of IS resource is not in option. Hence second logical step i.e. establishing ownership will be our answer. The data owner is responsible for defining the access rules; hence, establishing ownership is very critical.

(3)An IS auditor is evaluating access control policy of an organization. The implementation of access controls FIRST requires:

A. creation of an access control list
B. an inventory of IS resources
C. perform a impact analysis
D. labelling of IS resources

Answer: B. an inventory of IS resources

Explanation:
In any given scenario, following are the logical steps for data classification and implementation of access control:
-First step is to have inventory of IS resources
-Second step is to establish ownership
-Third step is classification of IS resources
-Fourth step is labelling of IS resources
-Fifth step is creation of access control list
The first step in implementing access controls is an inventory of IS resources.
(4)Which of the following is the MOST important objective of data protection?

A. creation of an access control list
B. ensuring the integrity of information
C. reduction in cost of control
D. to comply with risk management policy

Answer: B. ensuring the integrity of information

Explanation:
In any given scenario, most important objective of data protection is to ensure integrity/confidentiality of data.

(5)Proper classification and labelling for system resources are important for access control because they:

A. help to avoid ambiguous resource names
B. reduce the number of rules required to adequately protect resources
C. serve as stringent access control
D. ensure that internationally recognized names are used to protect resources

Answer:B. reduce the number of rules required to adequately protect resources.

Explanation:
Proper classification and labelling for system resources are important for the efficient administration of security controls. Proper labelling reduces the number of rules required to adequately protect resources, which in turn facilitates security administration and maintenance efforts. Reducing the number of rules makes it easier to provide access. Proper classification and labelling does not necessarily ensures option A, C and D.

(6)In co-ordination with database administrator, granting access to data is the responsibility of:

A. data owners
B. system engineer
C. security officer
D. librarians

Explanation: A. data owners

Explanation:
In any given scenario, accountability for the maintenance of proper security controls over information assets resides with the data owner/system owner. Data owners are responsible for the use of data. Written authorization for users to gain access to computerized information should be provided by the data owners.

(7)An IS auditor is reviewing data classification policy of an organization. From a control perspective, the PRIMARY objective of classifying information assets is to:

A. ensure that all assets are insured against losses.
B. to assist in risk assessment
C. establish appropriate access control guidelines
D. ensure all information assets have access controls

Answer: C. establish appropriate access control guidelines
Explanation:
First step of establishing access control is to ensure well defined information assets classification policy. By assigning levels of criticality to information resources, management can establish guidelines for the level of access controls that should be assigned. Hence from control perspective, primary objective of classification is

to establish appropriate access control guidelines. All assets are not required to be insured. Also access control may not be required for all assets. Classification helps in risk assessment however same is not prime objective.

(8)From control perspective, access to application data should be given by:

A. database administrator
B. data custodian
C. data owner
D. security administrator

Answer: C. data owner

Explanation:
In any given scenario, accountability for the maintenance of proper security controls over information assets resides with the data owner/system owner. The ultimate responsibility for data resides with the data owner. Data owners should have the authority and responsibility for granting access to the data and applications for which they are responsible. Data custodians are responsible only for storing and safeguarding the data. The DBA is responsible for managing the database.

(9)An IS auditor is reviewing access control policy of an organization. Which of the following is responsible for authorizing access rights to production data and systems?

A. Process owner
B. Data owner
C. Data custodian
D. security administrator

Answer: B. Data owner

Explanation:
In any given scenario, accountability for the maintenance of proper security controls over information assets resides with the data owner/system owner. The ultimate responsibility for data resides with the data owner. Data owners should have the authority and responsibility for granting access to the data and applications for which they are responsible. Data custodians are responsible only for storing and safeguarding the data. Process owners have greater knowledge of the process objectives; however, they are not the best suited to authorize access to specific data.

(10)An IS auditor is reviewing access control policy of an organization. Which of the following is the BEST basis for determining the appropriate levels of information resource protection?

A. Classification of Information Assets
B. Data owner
C. Threat Assessment
D. Cost of Information Assets

Answer: A. Classification of Information Assets

Explanation:
Classification of Information Asset on the basis of criticality and sensitivity provides the best basis for assigning levels of information resource protection. Threat assessment alone does not take into account criticality or sensitivity, which is the basis for assigning levels of information resource protection. Cost of assets is not an adequate basis for determining the needed level of protection. An asset can be negligible from a cost standpoint, but extremely critical to operations or sensitive if exposed.

(11)The MOST important benefit of having data classification policy is:

A. data classification ensures accurate inventory of information assets.
B.data classification helps to decrease cost of controls.
C.data classification helps in vulnerability assessment.
D.data classification helps in appropriate alignment with data owners.

Answer: B.data classification helps to decrease cost of controls.

Explanation:
In any given scenario, greatest benefit of well-defined data classification policy is decreased cost of control. Other choices are direct or indirect benefits of well-defined data classification policy but greatest benefit will be reduction of cost.

(12)For appropriate data classification, the MOST important requirement is:

A.Knowledge of technical controls for protection of data.
B.Awareness and training about organizational polices and standards.
C.Use of automatic data control tools.
D.Understanding the requirements of data user.

Answer: B.Awareness and training about organizational polices and standards.

Last Minute Revision:

Following table summarize the above provisions:

CISA Question	Our Answer
Ultimate responsibility for defining access rule .	Data owner/System owner
Accountability for maintenance of proper security controls over information assets.	Data owner/System owner
Benefits of data classification policy	(i)Reduce risk of under protection of information assets. (ii) Reduce cost of over protection of information assets.
First step in classification of information assets.	Inventory of information assets.

What is Digital Signature?

Digital Signature is a process wherein a digital code is attached to an electronically transmitted document to verify its contents and the sender's identity.

Digital Signature is created in below two steps:

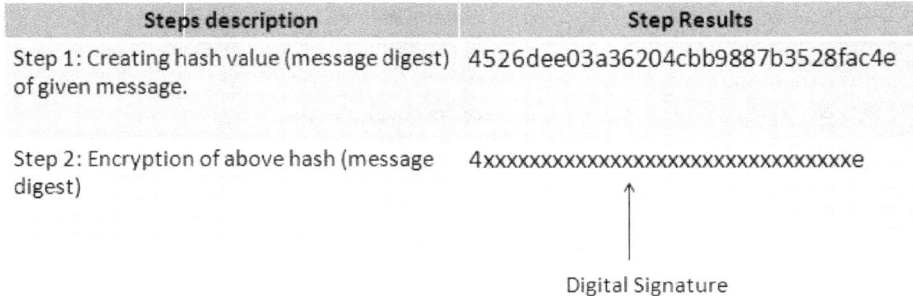

Steps description	Step Results
Step 1: Creating hash value (message digest) of given message.	4526dee03a36204cbb9887b3528fac4e
Step 2: Encryption of above hash (message digest)	4xxxxxxxxxxxxxxxxxxxxxxxxxxxxxxxxxxxe

Digital Signature

Step 1: Create Hash (Message digest) of the message.
Step 2: Encrypt the hash (as derived above) with private key of the sender.

What is hash or messages digest?
A hash function is mathematical algorithm which gives unique fixed string for any given message. It must be noted that the hash value will be unique for each message.

Message	Hash Value
Meeting at 8 AM	4526dee03a36204cbb9887b3528fac4e
Meeting at 8 PM	10ca8c76ec6b2b34a9a06505da298ed8

Software showing hash value of the message "Meeting at 8 AM"

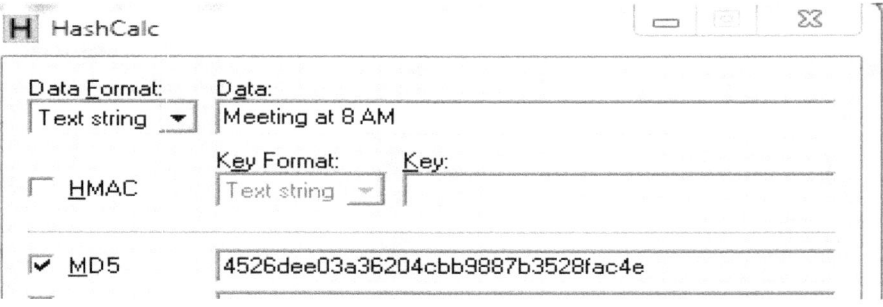

Software showing hash value of the message "Meeting at 8 PM"

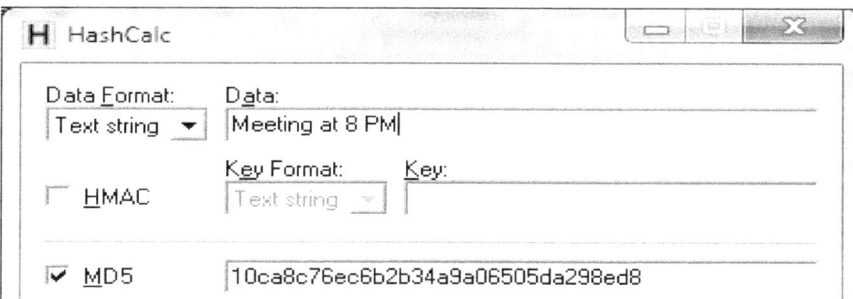

Hash value of first message is for 8 AM and second is for 8 PM. If you note above, hash value has changed even there is change in one alphabet.

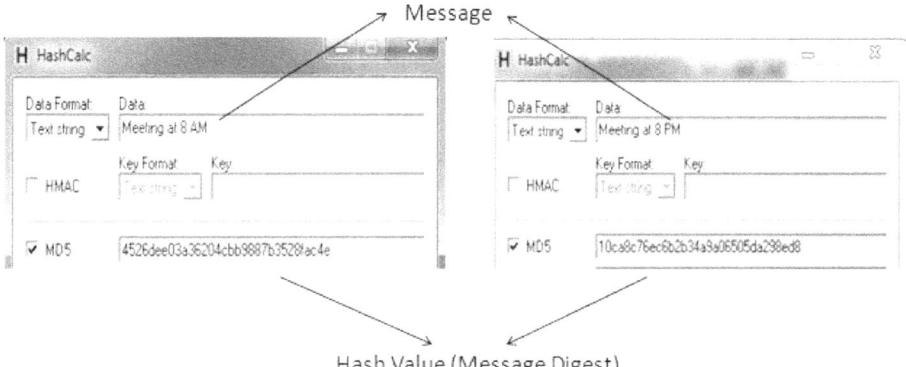

Hash Value (Message Digest)

Hash Value changes even with slightest change in message

Thus it helps in validating integrity of the message

Let us understand how message flows from sender A to recipient B:

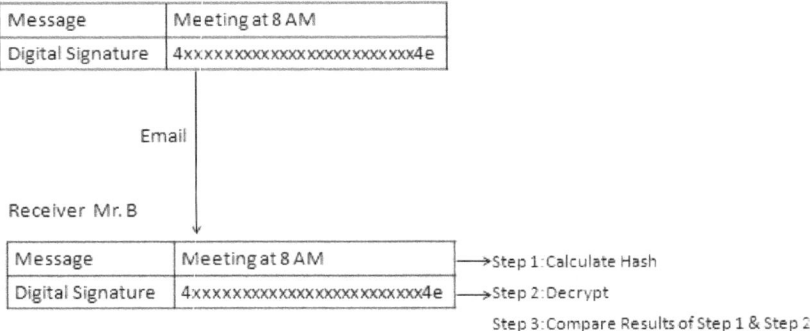

Receiver Mr. will perform following steps:

(i)He will independently calculate hash value of the message "Meeting at 8 AM". Hash value comes to 4526dee03a36204cbb9887b3528fac4e.

(ii)Then he will decrypt the digital signature i.e. 4xxxxxxxxxxxxxxxxxxxxxxxxxx4e using public key of sender Mr. A. (This proves authentication and non-repudiation).

(iii)Now, he will compare value derived under step (i) with value derived under step (ii) If both tallies, it proves integrity of the message.

Thus, Digital Signature ensures:

(1)Integrity (i.e. message has not been tampered)

(2)Authentication (i.e. message has been actually sent by sender)

(3)Non-repudiation (i.e. sender cannot later deny about sending the message)

But, digital signature does not provide:

× Confidentiality

It must be noted that digital signature does not provide confidentiality of the message.

Question, Answer & Explanation:

(1)Hash function will address which of the concerns about electronic message:

A. Message confidentiality
B. Message integrity
C. Message availability.
D. Message compression

Answer: B. Message integrity

Digital signature provides integrity, authentication and non-repudiation for electronic message. It does not ensure message confidentiality. A digital signature includes an encrypted hash total of the message. This hash would no longer be accurate if the message was subsequently altered, thus indicating that the alteration had occurred. Hence, it helps to ensure message integrity. Digital signatures will not identify or prevent any of the other options.

(2) Digital signature will address which of the concerns about electronic message:

A. Authentication and integrity of data
B. Authentication and confidentiality of data
C. Confidentiality and integrity of data
D. Authentication and availability of data

Answer: A. Authentication and integrity of data

Explanation:
Digital signature provides integrity, authentication and non-repudiation for electronic message. It does not ensure message confidentiality or availability of data. Digital Signature is created in below two steps:

Step 1: Create Hash (Message digest) of the message.
Step 2: Encrypt the hash (as derived above) with private key of the sender.

(3) A digital signature is created by the sender to prove message integrity by :

A. encrypting the message with the sender's private key. Upon receiving the data, the recipient can decrypt the data using the sender's public key.
B. encrypting the message with the recipient's public key. Upon receiving the data, the recipient can decrypt the data using the recipient's public key.
C. initially using a hashing algorithm to produce a hash value or message digest from the entire message contents. Upon receiving the data, the recipient can independently create it.
D.encrypting the message with the sender's public key. Upon receiving the data, the recipient can decrypt the data using the recipient's private key.

Answer: C. initially using a hashing algorithm to produce a hash value or message digest from the entire message contents. Upon receiving the data, the recipient can independently create it.

Explanation:
Digital Signature is created in below two steps:

Step 1: Create Hash (Message digest) of the message.

Step 2: Encrypt the hash (as derived above) with private key of the sender.

Upon receiving the message, recipient will perform following functions:

Step 1: He will independently calculate hash value of the message.

Step 2: Then he will decrypt the digital signature using public key of sender.

Step 3: Now, recipient will compare value derived under step (1) with value derived under step (2). If both tallies, it proves integrity of the message.

Option A, B and D are incorrect because digital signature will not encrypt the message itself, however it encrypts the hash of the message.

(4)Digital signature addresses which of the following concerns about electronic message?

A. Unauthorized archiving
B. Confidentiality
C. Unauthorized copying
D. Alteration

Answer: D. Alteration

Explanation:
A digital signature includes an encrypted hash total of the size of the message as it was transmitted by its originator. This hash would no longer be accurate if the message was subsequently altered, thus indicating that the alteration had occurred. Digital signatures will not identify or prevent any of the other options. Digital signature will not address other concerns.

(5)Which of the following is used to address the risk of hash being compromised ?

A. Digital signatures
B. Message encryption
C. Email password
D. Disabling SSID broadcast.

Answer: A. Digital signature

Explanation:
Digital signature is created by encrypting hash of the message. Encrypted hash cannot be altered without knowing public key of sender.

(6)Digital signature provides which of the following?

A. Non-repudiation, confidentiality and integrity
B. Integrity, privacy and non-repudiation
C. Integrity, authentication and non-repudiation
D. Confidentiality , privacy and non-repudiation

Answer: C. Integrity, authentication and non-repudiation

Explanation:
Digital signature provides integrity, authentication and non-repudiation for electronic message. It does not ensure message confidentiality or availability of data.

(7) The MAIN reason for using digital signatures is to ensure data:

A. privacy.
B. integrity.
C. availability.
D. confidentiality

Answer: B. integrity.

Explanation:
Digital signatures provide integrity because hash of the message changes in case of any unauthorized changes in the data (file, mail, document, etc.) thus ensuring data integrity.

(8)Which of the following message services provides the strongest evidence that a specific action has occurred?

A. Proof of delivery
B. Non-repudiation
C. Proof of submission
D. Authorization

Answer: B. Non-repudiation

Explanation:
Non-repudiation is the assurance that someone cannot deny something. Non-repudiation services provide evidence that a specific action occurred Typically, non-repudiation refers to the ability to ensure that a party to a contract or a communication cannot deny the authenticity of their signature on a document or the sending of a message that they originated.. Digital signatures are used to provide non-repudiation.

(9) Which of the following ensures a sender's authenticity?

A. Encrypting the hash of the message with the sender's private key
B. Encrypting the message with the receiver's Public key
C. Encrypting the hash of the message with the sender's public
D. Encrypting the message with the receiver's private key

Answer: A. Encrypting the hash of the message with the sender's private key

Explanation:
Sender encrypts the hash of the message using his private key. The receiver can decrypt the same with the public key of the sender, ensuring authenticity of the message. If recipient is able to decrypt the message successfully with public key of sender, then it proves authentication i.e. message is infact sent from the sender. It ensures non-repudiation i.e. sender cannot repudiate having sent the message.

(10) An organization states that digital signatures are used when receiving communications from customers. This is done by :

A. A hash of the data that is transmitted and encrypted with the organization's private key
B. A hash of the data that is transmitted and encrypted with the customer's private key
C. A hash of the data that is transmitted and encrypted with the customer's public key
D. A hash of the data that is transmitted and encrypted with the organization's public key

Answer : B. A hash of the data that is transmitted and encrypted with the customer's private key

Explanation:
Digital Signature is created in below two steps:
Step 1: Create Hash (Message digest) of the message.
Step 2: Encrypt the hash (as derived above) with private key of the sender.
In above scenario, sender is customer. Hence hash to be encrypted by using customer's (sender's) private key.

(11) Digital signatures helps to:

A. help detect spam.
B. provide confidentiality.
C. add to the workload of gateway servers.
D. decreases available bandwidth.

Answer: A. help detect spam.

Explanation:
Using strong signatures in email traffic, authentication and nonrepudiation can be assured and a sender can be tracked. The recipient can configure their e-mail server or client to automatically delete mails from specific senders
Digital signatures are only a few bytes in size and will not slash bandwidth. There will be no major impact to the workload of gateway servers.

(12)Basic difference between hashing & encryption is that hashing:

A. cannot be reversed.
B. can be reversed.
C. is concerned with integrity and security.
D. creates output of bigger length than original message.

Answer: A. cannot be reversed

Explanation:
Let us understand outcome of hashing as well as encryption:

For the message "Meeting at 8 AM" hash value comes to 4526dee03a36204cbb9887b3528fac4e

For the message "Meeting at 8 AM" encryption results comes to "Mxxxxxx xx x xM"

Now, from hash value 4526dee03a36204cbb9887b3528fac4e we cannot derive the message but from "Mxxxxxx xx x xM" we can derive the original message by decryption.

Hashing works one way. By applying a hashing algorithm to a message, a message hash/digest is created. If the same hashing algorithm is applied to the message digest, it will not result in the original message. As such, hashing is irreversible, while encryption is reversible. This is the basic difference between hashing and encryption.

(13)An organization is sharing critical information to vendors through email. Organization can ensure that the recipients of e-mails (i.e. vendors) can authenticate the identity of the sender (i.e. employees) by:

A. employees digitally signs their email messages.
B. employees encrypting their email messages.

C. employees compressing their email messages.
D. password protecting all e-mail messages.

Answer: A. employees digitally signs their email messages.

Explanation:
By digitally signing all e-mail messages, the receiver will be able to validate the authenticity of the sender. Encrypting all e-mail messages would not ensure the authenticity of the sender.

(14)Digital signature ensures that the sender cannot later deny generating and sending the message. This is known as:

A. Integrity.
B. authentication.
C. non-repudiation.
D. security.

Answer: C. non-repudiation.
Explanation:
Non-repudiation ensures that the claimed sender cannot later deny generating and sending the message.

(15)In an e-commerce application, which of the following should be rely on to prove that the transactions were actually made?

A. Proof of delivery
B. Authentication
C. Encryption
D. Non-repudiation

Answer: D. Non-repudiation

Explanation:
Non-repudiation ensures that a transaction is enforceable. Non-repudiation ensures that the claimed sender cannot later deny generating and sending the message.

(16)Mr. A has sent a message along with encrypted (by A's private key) hash of the message to Mr. B. This will ensure:

A. authenticity and integrity.
B. authenticity and confidentiality.
C. integrity and privacy.
D. privacy and non-repudiation.

Answer: A. authenticity and integrity.

Explanation: In the above case, message is not encrypted (only hash is encrypted) and hence it will not ensure privacy or confidentiality. Encryption of the hash will ensure authenticity and integrity.

(17) Digital signatures require the:

A. signer to have a public key of sender and the receiver to have a private key of the sender.
B. signer to have a private key of the sender and the receiver to have a public key of the sender.
C. signer and receiver to have a public key.

D. signer and receiver to have a private key.

Answer: B. signer to have a private key of the sender and the receiver to have a public key of the sender.

Explanation:
Digital Signature is created in below two steps:
Step 1: Create Hash (Message digest) of the message.
Step 2: Encrypt the hash (as derived above) with private key of the sender.
At the recipient end, hash is decrypted by using public key of the sender.

(18)A digital signature contains a hash value (message digest) to:

A. ensure message integrity.
B. define the encryption algorithm.
C. confirm the identity of the originator.
D. compress the message.

Answer: A. ensure message integrity.

Explanation:
The message digest is calculated and included in a digital signature to prove that the message has not been altered. It should be the same value as a recalculation performed upon receipt. Hence it helps to ensure message integrity.

Last Minute Revision:

- In any given scenario, digital signature provide assurance with respect to integrity of the message (i.e. message is not altered), authentication of message (i.e. message is infact sent by sender) and non-repudiation (i.e. sender cannot deny having sent the message in court of law).
- In any given scenario, digital signature encrypts the hash of the message (and not the message). Hence digital signature does not provide confidentiality or privacy.
- In any given scenario, for encryption of the hash of the message, private key of the sender is to be used.
- In any given scenario, non-repudiation provides the strongest evidence that a specific transaction/action has occurred. No one can deny about the transaction/action.

Let us understand difference between Symmetric Encryption vis-a-vis Asymmetric Encryption:

Symmetric Encryption	Asymmetric Encryption
Single key is used to encrypt & decrypt messages.	Asymmetric set includes 2 keys i.e. Private Key and Public Key.
Key is said to be symmetric because the encryption key is same as the decryption key.	Message encrypted by private key can be decrypted only by corresponding public key.
	Similarly, message encrypted by public key can only be decrypted by corresponding private key.
Faster computation & processing.	Slower computation & processing
Inexpensive as compared to asymmetric.	Expensive as compared to symmetric.
Major disadvantage is challenge of sharing key with other party.	No such challenge as 2 different keys are required.

Accessibility of Keys-Asymmetric Encryption:

Key	Availability
Sender's Private Key.	Key is available only with sender.
Sender's Public Key.	Available in public domain. Public key can be accessed by anyone.
Receiver's Private Key.	Key is available only with receiver.
Receiver's Public Key.	Available in public domain. Public key can be accessed by anyone.

Use of keys for different objectives:

It must be noted t keys are used to achieve following objectives:

- Confidentiality
- Authentication (and Non-Repudiation)
- Integrity

Use of key when objective is to maintain Confidentiality:
In any given scenario, when objective is to ensure 'confidentiality', message has to be encrypted using receiver's public key

183

Use of key when objective is to ensure Authentication/Non-repudiation:
In any given scenario, when objective is to ensure authentication and/or non-repudiation following steps to be performed:

- hash (message digest) of the message has to be created
- and hash to be encrypted using sender's private key.

Use of key when objective is to ensure Integrity:

In any given scenario, when objective is to ensure 'Integrity' following steps to be performed:
- hash (message digest) of the message has to be created
- and hash to be encrypted using sender's private key.

Use of keys when objective is to ensure Confidentiality & Authentication:
In any given scenario, when objective is to ensure 'confidentiality & authentication', following treatment is required:

- message to be encrypted using receiver's public key (to ensure confidentiality).
- hash of the message to be encrypted using sender's private key (to ensure authentication/non-repudiation).

Use of keys when objective is to ensure Confidentiality & Authentication & Integrity:
In any given scenario, when objective is to ensure 'confidentiality & authentication & integrity', following treatment is required:

- message to be encrypted using receiver's public key (to ensure confidentiality)
- hash of the message to be encrypted using sender's private key (to ensure authentication/non-repudiation and integrity)

Question, Answer & Explanation:

(1)In public key encryption (asymmetric encryption) to secure message confidentiality:

A. encryption is done by private key and decryption is done by public key.
B. encryption is done by public key and decryption is done by private key.
C. both the key used to encrypt and decrypt the data are public.
D. both the key used to encrypt and decrypt the data are private.

Answer: B. encryption is done by public key and decryption is done by private key.

Explanation:
In any given scenario, when objective is to ensure 'confidentiality', message has to be encrypted using receiver's public key and decrypted using receiver's private key.
Option-wise explanation is given as below:
A. encryption is done by private key and decryption is done by public key (public is easily accessible by everyone and hence confidentiality cannot be ensured).
B. encryption is done by public key and decryption is done by private key (private key is accessible only with owner and this ensures confidentiality).
C. both the key used to encrypt and decrypt the data are public. (anything encrypted by public key can be decrypted only by corresponding private key).

D. both the key used to encrypt and decrypt the data are private. (anything encrypted by private key can be decrypted only by corresponding public key).

(2)In public key encryption (asymmetric encryption) to authenticate the sender of the message:

A. hash of the message to be encrypted by sender's private key and decryption is done by sender's public key.
B. hash of the message to be encrypted by sender's public key and decryption is done by sender's private key.
C. hash of the message to be encrypted by receiver's private key and decryption is done by receiver's public key.
D. hash of the message to be encrypted by receiver's public key and decryption is done by receiver's private key.

Answer: A. hash of the message to be encrypted by sender's private key and decryption is done by sender's public key.

Explanation:
In any given scenario, when objective is to ensure 'authentication', hash (message digest) of the message has to be created and hash to be encrypted using sender's private key and decrypted using sender's public key.
Option-wise explanation is given as below:
A. hash of the message to be encrypted by sender's private key and decryption is done by sender's public key (to ensure authentication, sender should have something unique which is not accessible by anyone else. Sender's private key is available only with sender and this ensures authentication).
B. hash of the message to be encrypted by sender's public key and decryption is done by sender's private key. (to ensure authentication, sender should have something unique which is not accessible by anyone else. Sender's public key is available publicly and hence cannot ensure authentication).
C. hash of the message to be encrypted by receiver's private key and decryption is done by receiver's public key.(sender will not have access to receiver's private key).
D. hash of the message to be encrypted by receiver's public key and decryption is done by receiver's private key. (to ensure authentication, sender should have something unique which is not accessible by anyone else. Receiver's public key is available publicly and hence cannot ensure authentication).

(3)In public key encryption (asymmetric encryption) to ensure integrity of the message:

A. hash of the message to be encrypted by sender's private key and decryption is done by sender's public key.
B. hash of the message to be encrypted by sender's public key and decryption is done by sender's private key.
C. hash of the message to be encrypted by receiver's private key and decryption is done by receiver's public key.
D. hash of the message to be encrypted by receiver's public key and decryption is done by receiver's private key.

Answer: A. hash of the message to be encrypted by sender's private key and decryption is done by sender's public key.

Explanation:
In any given scenario, when objective is to ensure 'integrity of the message', hash (message digest) of the message has to be created and hash to be encrypted using sender's private key. Sender will send (i) message and (ii) encrypted hash to receiver.

Receiver will (i) decrypt the received hash by using public key of sender and (ii) re-compute the hash of the message and if the two hashes are equal, then it proves that message integrity is not tampered with.

(4)Which of the following ensures confidentiality of the message & also authenticity of the sender of the message?

A. Encrypting the hash of the message with the sender's private key and thereafter encrypting the message with the receiver's public key.
B. Encrypting the hash of message with the sender's private key and thereafter encrypting the message with the receiver's private key.
C. Encrypting the hash of the message with the receiver's public key and thereafter encrypting the message with the sender's private key.
D. Encrypting the hash of the message with the receiver's public key and thereafter encrypting the message with the sender's public key.

Answer: A. Encrypting the hash of the message with the sender's private key and thereafter encrypting the message with the receiver's public key.

Explanation:
In the above question, objective is to ensure confidentiality & authenticity. In any given scenario, when objective is to ensure 'confidentiality & authentication', following treatment is required:

-Hash of the message to be encrypted using sender's private key (to ensure authentication/non-repudiation).
-Message to be encrypted using receiver's public key (to ensure confidentiality).

Encryption of hash of the message by sender's private key proves that sender himself is the sender of the message as his private key can be accessed by him only.
Encryption of the message using receiver's public key ensures confidentiality as only receiver can decrypt the message using his private key.

(5)Message authenticity and confidentiality is BEST achieved by encrypting hash of the message using the:

A. sender's private key and encrypting the message using the receiver's public key.
B. sender's public key and encrypting the message using the receiver's private key.
C. receiver's private key and encrypting the message using the sender's public key.
D. receiver's public key and encrypting the message using the sender's private key.

Answer: A. sender's private key and encrypting the message using the receiver's public key.

Explanation:
In the above question, objective is to ensure confidentiality & authenticity. In any given scenario, when objective is to ensure 'confidentiality & authentication', following treatment is required:

-Hash of the message to be encrypted using sender's private key (to ensure authentication/non-repudiation)
-Message to be encrypted using receiver's public key (to ensure confidentiality)

Encryption of hash of the message by sender's private key proves that sender himself is the sender of the message as his private key can be accessed by him only.

Encryption of the message using receiver's public key ensures confidentiality as only receiver can decrypt the message using his private key.

(6)Greatest assurance about E-mail authenticity can be ensured by which of the following?

A. The prehash code is encrypted using sender's public key.
B. The prehash code is encrypted using the sender's private key.

C. The prehash code is encrypted using the receiver's public key.
D. The prehash code is encrypted using the receiver's private key.

Answer: B. The prehash code is encrypted using the sender's private key.

Explanation:
In the above question, objective is to ensure authenticity. In any given scenario, when objective is to ensure 'authentication', HASH of the message has to be created and HASH to be encrypted using sender's private key. Encryption of hash of the message by sender's private key proves that sender himself is the sender of the message as his private key can be accessed by him only.

(7)A message and message hash is encrypted by the sender's private key. This will ensure:

A. authenticity and integrity.
B. authenticity and confidential.
C. integrity and privacy.
D. confidential and non-repudiation.

Answer: A. authenticity and integrity.

Explanation:
In any given scenario, when objective is to ensure 'authentication & integrity', hash (message digest) of the message has to be created and hash to be encrypted using sender's private key. Sender will send (i) message and (ii) encrypted hash to receiver.

Receiver will (i) decrypt the received hash by using public key of sender and (ii) re-compute the hash of the message and if the two hashes are equal, then it proves that message integrity is not tampered with.

(8)A stock broking firm sends invoices to clients through email and wants reasonable assurance that no one has modified the newsletter. This objective can be achieved by:

A. encrypting the hash of the invoice using the firm's private key.
B. encrypting the hash of the invoice using the firm's public key.
C. encrypting invoice using firm's private key.
D. encrypting invoice using firm's public key.

Answer: A. encrypting the hash of the invoice using the firm's private key.

Explanation:
In the above question, objective is to ensure integrity of invoices. In any given scenario, when objective is to ensure 'integrity', HASH (message digest) of the message has to be created and HASH to be encrypted using sender's private key.
Clients can open the invoice, re-compute the hash, decrypt the received hash using the firm's public key and, if the two hashes are equal, the invoice was not modified in transit.

(9) A commercial website uses asymmetric encryption where there is one private key for the server and corresponding public key is made available to the customers. This ensures:

A. authenticity of the customer.
B. authenticity of the website.
C. confidentiality of messages from the website hosting organization to customer.
D. Non-repudiation from customer.

Answer: B. authenticity of the website.

Explanation:
If customer can able to decrypt the message using public key of the website, then it ensures that message has been sent from authentic website. Any false site will not be able to encrypt using the private key of the real site, so the customer would not be able to decrypt the message using the public key. Public key is widely distributed and hence authenticity of customer cannot be ensured. Also confidentiality of messages cannot be ensured many people have access to the public key and can decrypt the messages from the hosting website.

(10)Which of the following options increases the cost of cryptography?

A. Use of symmetric technique rather than asymmetric.
B. Use of long asymmetric key rather than short.
C. Only hash is encrypted rather than full message.
D. Use of short asymmetric key rather than long.

Answer: B. Use of long asymmetric key rather than short.

Explanation:
A. Use of symmetric technique rather than asymmetric-This will actually decrease the cost. Symmetric technique is faster and inexpensive as compared to asymmetric technique.
B. Use of long asymmetric key rather than short- Computer processing time is increased for longer asymmetric encryption keys and also cost associated with the same will increase.
C. Only hash is encrypted rather than full message- A hash is shorter than the original message; hence, a smaller overhead is required if the hash is encrypted rather than the message.
D. Use of short asymmetric key rather than long-This will decrease the cost.

(11)Encryption of which of the following can be considered as an efficient use of PKI:

A. sender's private key
B. sender's public key
C. entire message
D. symmetric session key

Answer: D. symmetric session key

Explanation:
Best use of PKI is to combine the best feature of symmetric as well as asymmetric encryption technique. Asymmetric encryption involves intensive and time-consuming computations. In comparison, symmetric encryption is considerably faster, yet faces the challenge of sharing the symmetric key to other party. To enjoy the benefits of both systems, following process is used:

Step No.	Objective	Step Description	Rationale for the step
1	Confidentiality of the message	Encrypt the message by symmetric key	Encryption of entire message through asymmetric encryption would be time-consuming and expensive. Hence message is encrypted using symmetric key.
2	Confidentiality of symmetric key	Encrypt above 'symmetric key' using public key of receiver	Only receiver can encrypt the 'symmetric key' using private key of receiver. This ensures confidentiality of 'symmetric key'
3	Sending encrypted message and symmetric key.	Encrypted Message (as created in step 1) & Encrypted 'symmetric key' (as created in step 2) to send to receiver.	-
4	Decryption of symmetric key.	Receiver will decrypt 'symmetric key' using private key of receiver.	-
5	Decryption of entire message	With the help of above symmetric key, receiver can decrypt the message.	-

(12)When objective is to ensure message integrity, confidentiality and non-repudiation, the MOST effective method would be to create a message digest and encrypt the message digest:

A. using the sender's private key, encrypting the message with a symmetric key and encrypting the symmetric key by using the receiver's public key.
B. using the sender's private key, encrypting the message with a symmetric key and encrypting the symmetric key by using the receiver's private key.
C. using the sender's private key, encrypting the message with a symmetric key and encrypting the symmetric key by using the sender's private key.
D. using the sender's private key, encrypting the message with a symmetric key and encrypting the symmetric key by using the sender's public key.

Answer: A. using the sender's private key, encrypting the message with a symmetric key and encrypting the symmetric key by using the receiver's public key.

Explanation:
Above question in based on the concept of combining best features of symmetric as well as asymmetric encryption technique. Following are the steps:

Step No.	Objective	Step Description	Rationale for the step
1	Confidentiality of the message	Encrypt the message by symmetric key	Encryption of entire message through asymmetric encryption would be time-consuming and expensive. Hence message is encrypted using symmetric key.
2	Confidentiality of symmetric key	Encrypt above 'symmetric key' using public key of receiver	Only receiver can encrypt the 'symmetric key' using private key of receiver. This ensures confidentiality of 'symmetric key'
3	Integrity of the message	(1)Create hash(message digest) of the message (2)Encrypt above hash (message digest)using private key of the sender	In any given scenario, when objective is to ensure 'integrity of the message', hash (message digest) of the message has to be created and hash to be encrypted using sender's private key. Sender will send (i) message and (ii) encrypted hash to receiver. Receiver will (i) decrypt the received hash by using public key of sender and (ii) re-compute the hash of the message received and if the two hashes are equal, then it proves that message integrity is not tampered with.
4	Non-Repudiation		Sender encrypts the hash (message digest) using his private key (which is accessible by him only). Later he cannot repudiate about sending the message

Same process is involved in digital envelope.

Last Minute Revision:

CISA Question Objective	Your Answer
Confidentiality of the message	Encrypt using receiver's public key
Authentication of the message	Create hash of the message and encrypt the hash using sender's private key
Integrity of the message	Create hash of the message and encrypt the hash using sender's private key
Confidentiality & Authentication of the message	Hash-Encrypt using sender's private key Message-Encrypt using receiver's public key
Confidentiality & Authentication & Integrity of the message	Hash-Encrypt using sender's private key Message-Encrypt using receiver's public key

What is PKI?

Public key Infrastructure (PKI) is a framework to issue, maintain and revoke public key certificates by a trusted third party known as Certifying Authority (CA).

Process involved in PKI:

- Applicant will apply for digital certificate from Certifying Authority (CA).
- Certifying Authority (CA) delegates the process for verification of information (as supplied by applicant) to Registration Authority (RA).
- Registration Authority (RA) validates the information and if information is correct, tells Certifying Authority (CA) to issue the certificate.
- Certifying Authority issues the certificate and manages the same through its life cycle.
- Certifying Authority (CA) maintains a list of certificates which have been revoked/terminated before its expiry date. This list is known as certificate revocation list (CRL).
- Certifying Authority (CA) will also have Certification Practice Statement (CPS) in which standard operating procedure (SOP) for issuance of certificate and other relevant details are documented.

Certifying Authority (CA) vis-a-vis Registration Authority (RA):

Certifying Authority (CA)	Registration Authority (RA)
CA issues & manages digital certificates.	RA verifies the information provided by applicant of digital certificate and tells CA to issue certificate.
CA is solely responsible for issuance of digital certificate	-
CA is responsible for managing the certificate throughout its life cycle.	-
CA delegates to RA some of the administrative function like verification of information needed to issue certificates.	-
CA delegates to RA some of the administrative function like verification of information needed to issue certificates.	-
CA validates and authenticates the holder of certificate after issuance of certificate.	RA validates and authenticates information of the applicant before issuance of certificate.

Functions of Registration Authority:

- Verifying information supplied by the applicant.
- Verifying that the applicant actually possesses the private key being registered and that is matches public key requested for certificate. This is generally referred to proof of possession (POP).
- Distributing the physical tokens containing the private keys.
- Generating shared secrets key for use during initialization and certificate pick-up phases of registration.

Certificate Revocation List (CRL) vis-a-vis Certificate Practice Statement (CPS):

Certificate Revocation List(CRL)	Certification Practice Statement (CPS)
CRL is a list of certificates that have been revoked before their scheduled expiration date.	CPS is a detailed set of rules and processes of Certifying Authority's (CA) operations.
CRL is maintained by CA.	It contains (i) controls that CA observes (ii) method it uses to validate the authenticity of applicants (iii) CA's expectations of how its certificate may be used.
-	It provides value and trustworthiness of certificates issued by that CA.

Question, Answer & Explanation:

(1)Authority that manages the certificate life cycle is the:

A. certificate authority (CA)
B. certificate revocation list (CRL)
C. certification practice statement (CPS)
D. registration authority (RA)

Answer: A. certificate authority (CA)

Explanation:
In any given scenario, certifying authority (CA) is solely responsible for issuance of digital certificate and managing the certificate throughout its life cycle. Registration authority performs the process of identification and authentication by establishing a link between the identity of the requesting person or organization and the public key. In short, a CA manages and issues certificates, whereas a RA is responsible for identifying and authenticating the information provided by subscribers, but does not sign or issue certificates. CRL is a list of certificates that have been revoked before their scheduled expiration date. CPS is a detailed set of rules and processes of Certifying Authority's (CA) operations.

(2)In a public key infrastructure, role of a registration authority is to:

A. issue the certificate to subscriber.
B. manage certificate throughout its life cycle.
C. maintain list of revoked list.
D. validate the information provided by the subscriber requesting a certificate.

Answer: D. validate the information provided by the subscriber requesting a certificate.

Explanation:
In any given scenario, registration authority (RA) is responsible for identifying and authenticating subscribers, but does not sign or issue certificates. Certifying authority (CA) is solely responsible for issuance of digital certificate, managing the certificate throughout its life cycle and maintaining list of revoked certificates.

(3)Which of the following PKI element control and manage the digital certificate life cycle to ensure proper security exist in digital signature applications?

A. Certification revocation list
B. Registration authority (RA)
C. Certificate authority (CA)
D. Certification practice statement

Answer: C. Certificate authority (CA)

Explanation:
In any given scenario, certifying authority (CA) is solely responsible for issuance of digital certificate and managing the certificate throughout its life cycle. Registration authority is an optional entity that is responsible for the administrative tasks like identifying and authenticating the information provided by applicants. Choice A is incorrect since a CRL is a list of certificates that have been revoked before their scheduled expiration date. Choice D is incorrect because a certification practice statement is a detailed set of rules governing the certificate authority's operations.

(4)Which of the following processes can be delegated by a certificate authority (CA)?

A. issuance of digital certificates.
B. managing the certificate throughout its life cycle.
C. establishing a link between the requesting entity and its public key.
D. maintain list of revoked list.

Answer: C. establishing a link between the requesting entity and its public key.

Explanation:
Establishing a link between the requesting entity and its public key is a function of a registration authority. This function can be delegated to RA. Other functions have to be managed by CA only.

(5) In public key infrastructure, which of the following would ban IS auditor consider a weakness?

A. Certificate authorities are centrally located however customers are widely dispersed geographically.
B.Transactions can be made from any computer or mobile device.
C The certificate authority has multiple data processing centers to manage the certificates.
D.The organization is the owner of the certificate authority.

Answer: D. The organization is the owner of the certificate authority.

Explanation:
If organization is the owner of the certificate authority, this would generate a conflict of interest. Independence of certifying authority will not be there in such cases and third party may repudiate the transactions. The other options are not weaknesses.

(6)In a public key infrastructure, a registration authority:

A. issues the certificate.
B. verifies information supplied by the subject requesting a certificate.
C. signs the certificate to achieve authentication and non-repudiation.
D. managing the certificate throughout its life cycle.

Answer: B. verifies information supplied by the subject requesting a certificate.

Explanation:
In any given scenario, registration authority (RA) is responsible for identifying and authenticating subscribers, but does not sign or issue certificates. A registration authority is responsible for verifying information supplied by the subject requesting a certificate. Option A & Option D are the functions of CA. Option C is not the task performed by RA. . On the other hand, the sender who has control of his/her private key, signs the message, not the registration authority.

(7)Detailed descriptions for dealing with a compromised private key is provided in which of the following public key infrastructure (PKI) elements?

A. Certificate policy (CP)
B. Certificate revocation list (CRL)
C. Certification practice statement (CPS)
D. PKI disclosure statement (PDS)

Answer: C. Certification practice statement (CPS)

Explanation:
Certification practice statement (CPS) is a detailed set of rules and processes of Certifying Authority's (CA) operations. Certification Practice Statement (CPS) is a document in which standard operating procedure (SOP) for issuance of certificate and other relevant details are documented. The CPS is the how-to part in policy-based PKI. CRL is a list of certificates that have been revoked before their scheduled expiration date. The PDS covers critical items, such as the warranties, limitations and obligations that legally bind each party.

(8) In a public key infrastructure, role of a certificate authority is to:

A. ensure secured communication and secured network services based on certificates.
B. validate the identity and authenticity of the entity owning the certificate and integrity of the certificate issued by that CA.
C. ensure secured communication infrastructure between parties.
D. hosting of private keys of subscribers in public domain.

Answer: B. validate the identity and authenticity of the entity owning the certificate and integrity of the certificate issued by that CA.

Explanation:
The primary activity of a CA is to issue certificates and to validate the identity and authenticity of the entity owning the certificate and integrity of the certificate issued by that CA. CAs are not responsible of secured communication channel. Private keys are not made available in public domain.

Last Minute Revision:

- In any given scenario, certifying authority (CA) is solely responsible for issuance of digital certificate and managing the certificate throughout its life cycle.
- In any given scenario, registration authority (RA) is responsible for identifying and authenticating subscribers, but does not sign or issue certificates.
- In any given scenario, a digital certificate is composed of public key and information about the owner of public key.
- In any given scenario, time gap between update of CRL (certificate revocation list) is critical and is also posses risk in certification verification.

What is Biometric?

- Biometrics refers to metrics related to human characteristics.
- Biometric verification is any means by which a person can be uniquely identified by evaluating one or more distinguishing biological features.
- Unique identifiers include palm, hand geometry, fingerprints, retina and iris patterns, voice waves and DNA.

Accuracy measures for Biometrics:

Measure	What is means	Example
False Acceptance Rate	Rate of acceptance of unauthorized person(s) i.e. biometric will allow unauthorized person to access the system.	Mr. A is the only authorized person to access the system. However, if biometric allows access to Mr. B, then same is false acceptance.
False Rejection Rate	Rate of rejection of authorized person(s) i.e. biometric will reject even though person is authorized to access the system.	Mr. A is the only authorized person to access the system. However, if biometric does not allow access to Mr. A, then same is false rejection.
Cross Error Rate (CER) or Equal Error Rate (EER)	CER or EER is a rate at which FAR and FRR is equal. The most effective biometric system is the one with lowest CER or EER. The biometric which has highest CER or EER is the most ineffective.	-

Biometrics-Attacks:

Attacks	What it means
Replay	In Replay attack, a residual biometric characteristic (example-such as fingerprints left on a biometric device) is used by an attacker to gain unauthorized access.
Brute-Force	A brute-force attack involves sending the numerous different biometric samples to a biometric device.
Cryptographic	A cryptographic attack targets the algorithm or the encrypted data transmitted between biometric device and access control system.
Mimic	In a mimic attack, the attacker attempts to fake the biometric characteristics similar to those of the enrolled user (such as imitating a voice).

Last Minute Revision:

- Three main accuracy measures used for a biometric solution are:

  - False-Acceptance Rate (FAR) (i.e. access given to unauthorized person)
  - False-Rejection Rate (FRR), (i.e. access rejected to authorised person)
  - Cross-Error Rate (CER) or Equal-Error Rate (EER) (i.e. rate at which FAR is equal to FRR)

- Both FAR & FRR are inversely proportionate. As a general rule when FAR decreases, FRR increases and vice versa. Similarly if FRR decreases, FAR increases and vice versa. Adjustment point where both errors are equal is known as cross-error rate or equal-error rate.
- In any given scenario, most important performance indicator for biometric system is false-acceptance rate (FAR).
- In any given scenario, most important **overall** quantitative performance indicator for biometric system is CER or EER.
- In any given scenario, 'Retina Scan' has the highest reliability and lowest false-acceptance rate (FAR) among the current biometric methods.

Question, Answer & Explanation on 'Biometrics-Risks & Controls' Concept:

(1)An organization is considering implementing a biometric access control for one of its critical system. Among below mentioned biometrics, which has the highest reliability and lowest false-acceptance rate (FAR)?

A. Fingerprints
B. Retina Scan
C.Face recognition
D.Voice recognition

Answer: B. Retina Scan

Explanation:

In any given scenario, 'Retina Scan' has the highest reliability and lowest false-acceptance rate (FAR) among the current biometric methods. A retinal scan is a biometric technique that uses the unique patterns on a person's retina blood vessels. Due to its unique and unchanging nature, the retina appears to be the most precise and reliable biometric, aside from DNA. The National Center for State Courts estimate that retinal scanning has an error rate of one in ten million. This is highly reliable and has the lowest FAR among the current biometric methods.

(2) An organization is considering implementing biometric access control for one of its critical system. The auditor should be MOST concerned with which of the following?

A. False-Acceptance Rate (FAR)
B. False-Rejection Rate (FRR)
C.Equal Error Rate (EER)
D.Number of staff enrolled for biometrics.

Answer: A. False-Acceptance Rate (FAR)

Explanation:
FAR is a rate of acceptance of unauthorised person i.e. biometric will allow unauthorised person to access the system. In any given scenario, most important performance indicator for biometric system is false-acceptance rate (FAR). This is a fail-unsafe condition, i.e., an unauthorized individual may be granted access. A low FAR is most desirable when it is used to protect highly sensitive data. EER or CER is best indicator when **overall** performance is to be evaluated.

(3)The best overall quantitative performance indicator for biometric system is:

A. False-Acceptance Rate (FAR)
B. False-Rejection Rate (FRR)
C.Equal Error Rate (EER)
D.Number of staff enrolled for biometrics.

Answer: C.Equal Error Rate (EER)

Explanation:
In any given scenario, most important **overall** quantitative performance indicator for biometric system is CER or EER. A low EER is a combination of a low FRR and a low FAR. CER or EER is a rate at which FAR and FRR is equal. The most effective biometric control system is the one with lowest CER or EER. Low FRRs or low FARs alone does not measure the **overall** efficiency of the device.

(4)An organization is considering implementing a biometric access control for one of its critical system. Among below mentioned biometrics, the MOST effective biometric control system is the one:

A. with highest equal-error rate(EER).
B. with lowest equal-error rate (EER).
C. with highest cross error rate(CER).
D. which covers all the systems in the organization.

Answer: B. with lowest equal-error rate (EER).

Explanation:
CER or EER is a rate at which FAR and FRR is equal. The most effective biometric control system is the one with lowest CER or EER. Option A & C are incorrect as the biometric that has the highest EER or CER is the most ineffective. Option D is not correct as all systems may not be required to cover under biometric.

(5) Which of the following is a measure to ascertain accuracy of a biometric system?

A. response time.
B. registration time.
C. verification time.
D. false-acceptance rate.

Answer: D. false-acceptance rate.

Explanation:
Three main accuracy measures used for a biometric solution are:
(i)False-Acceptance Rate (FAR),
(ii) False-Rejection Rate (FRR),
(iii)Cross-Error Rate (CER) or Equal-Error Rate (EER)
 FAR is a measure of how often invalid individuals are accepted. Other choices are performance measures.

(6)An organization is evaluating the effectiveness of biometric systems for its extremely high security requirements. Which of the following performance indicators is MOST important?

A. False-acceptance rate (FAR)
B. Equal-error rate (EER)
C. False-rejection rate (FRR)
D. Fail to enrol rate (FER)

Answer: A. False-acceptance rate (FAR)

Explanation:
FAR is a rate of acceptance of unauthorised person i.e. biometric will allow unauthorised person to access the system. In any given scenario, most important performance indicator for biometric system is false-acceptance rate (FAR).This is a fail-unsafe condition, i.e., an unauthorized individual may be granted access. A low FAR is most desirable when it is used to protect highly sensitive data.

(7) Which of the following observations is the GREATEST concern to the auditor reviewing biometric control for a critical system?

A. Access to biometric scanner is provided through virtual private network (VPN).
B.Biometric devices are not installed in restricted area.
C.Data transferred between biometric device and access control system is not encrypted.
D.Risk analysis for biometric control is conducted before 2 years.

Answer: C.Data transferred between biometric device and access control system is not encrypted.

Explanation:
A. This is not a concern as VPN provides a secured environment.
B. This is a concern. However greatest concern should be with respect to data transmitted without encryption.
C. Data transmitted between the biometric device and the access controls system should use a securely encrypted tunnel to protect the confidentially of the biometric data.
D. This is a concern. The biometric risk analysis should be done periodically, but greatest concern should data transmitted without encryption.

(8)An IS auditor is evaluating the effectiveness of biometric systems for extremely high secured environment. Which of the following stage should be reviewed first?

A. Storage
B. Enrollment
C.Identification
D.Termination

Answer: B. Enrollment

Explanation:
Biometric life cycle comprised of enrolment, transmission and storage, verification, identification and termination processes. The users of a biometrics device must first be enrolled in the device. This occur through iterative process of acquiring sample, extracting data from sample, validating the sample and developing final template that is stored and subsequently used to authenticate the user.

(9) An organization is considering implementing access control for one of its critical system. Among below mentioned control measures, the MOST effective control is:

A. Token based PIN
B. Iris Scan
C.Photo Identification
D.Password

Answer: B. Iris Scan

Explanation:
Among all the controls, iris scan can be considered as most reliable. Fraudster finds it very difficult to bypass biometric controls. Since no two irises are alike, identification and verification can be done with confidence. Other options are not as strong as Iris Scan.

(10) An organization is considering implementing access control for one of its critical system. Among below mentioned control measures, the MOST effective control is:

A. Cipher lock
B. Fingerprint scanner
C.Photo Identification
D.Electronic door lock

Answer: B. Fingerprint scanner

Explanation:
Among all the controls, fingerprint scanner can be considered as most reliable. Fraudster finds it very difficult to bypass biometric controls. Fingerprint is harder to duplicate, easier to deactivate and individually identified. Since no two fingerprints are alike (very rare chances), identification and verification can be done with confidence. Other options are not as strong as fingerprint scanner.

(11) In which of the following attack, use of residual biometric information is done to gain unauthorized access:

A. Mimic
B. Brute-force
C. Cryptographic

D. Replay

Answer: D. Replay

Explanation:
In Replay attack, a residual biometric characteristic (example- such as fingerprints left on a biometric device) is used by an attacker to gain unauthorized access.
In a mimic attack, the attacker attempts to fake the biometric characteristics similar to those of the enrolled user, such as imitating a voice.
A brute-force attack involves sending the numerous different biometric samples to a biometric device.
A cryptographic attack targets the algorithm or the encrypted data transmitted between biometric device and access control system.

(12)In which of the following attack, the attacker reproduces characteristics similar to those of the enrolled user:

A. Mimic
B. Brute-force
C. Cryptographic
D. Replay

Answer: A. Mimic

Explanation
In a mimic attack, the attacker attempts to fake the biometric characteristics similar to those of the enrolled user, such as imitating a voice.
A brute-force attack involves sending the numerous different biometric samples to a biometric device.
A cryptographic attack targets the algorithm or the encrypted data transmitted between biometric device and access control system.
In Replay attack, a residual biometric characteristic (example- such as fingerprints left on a biometric device) is used by an attacker to gain unauthorized access.

(13)Which of the following attack targets the algorithm or the encrypted data transmitted between biometric device and access control system?

A. Mimic
B. Brute-force
C. Cryptographic
D. Replay

Answer: C. Cryptographic

Explanation:
A cryptographic attack targets the algorithm or the encrypted data transmitted between biometric device and access control system.
In a mimic attack, the attacker attempts to fake the biometric characteristics similar to those of the enrolled user, such as imitating a voice.
A brute-force attack involves sending the numerous different biometric samples to a biometric device.
In Replay attack, a residual biometric characteristic (example- such as fingerprints left on a biometric device) is used by an attacker to gain unauthorized access.

(14)Which of the following attack involves sending the numerous different biometric samples to a biometric device?

A. Mimic
B. Brute-force
C. Cryptographic
D. Replay

Answer: B. Brute-force

Explanation:
A brute-force attack involves sending the numerous different biometric samples to a biometric device.
In a mimic attack, the attacker attempts to fake the biometric characteristics similar to those of the enrolled user, such as imitating a voice.
In Replay attack, a residual biometric characteristic (example- such as fingerprints left on a biometric device) is used by an attacker to gain unauthorized access.
A cryptographic attack targets the algorithm or the encrypted data transmitted between biometric device and access control system.

(15)An organization is considering implementing access control for all PCs that access critical data. This will:

A. completely eliminate the risk of false acceptance i.e. unauthorised access will be eliminated completely.
B.require enrollment of all users that access the critical data.
C. require fingerprint reader to be controlled by a separate password.
D. provide assurance that unauthorized access will be impossible.

Answer: B. require enrollment of all users that access the critical data.

Explanation:
Setting any new biometric process requires enrollment of all users for whom access is to be provided.   The fingerprints of accredited users need to be read, identified and recorded, i.e., registered, before a user may operate the system from the screened PCs. Choice A is incorrect, as the risk of false-acceptance cannot be eliminated. Risk of a biometric device may be optimized, but will never be zero because this would imply an unacceptably high risk of false rejection. Choice C is incorrect, as the fingerprint reader does not need to be protected in itself by a password. Choice D is incorrect because the usage of biometric protection on PCs does not provide assurance that unauthorized access will be impossible.

What is Intrusion Detection System?

Intrusion Detection System is a device or software application that monitors a network (network based IDS) or monitors a system (host based IDS) for intrusive activities.

IDS is not a substitute for firewall, but it complements the function of a firewall.

Network based IDS vis-a-vis Host based IDS

Network based IDS	Host based IDS
Monitors activities on identified network.	Monitor activities on a particular single system or host.
High false positive rate. (i.e. high rate of wrong alarm)	Low false positive rate. (i.e. low rate of wrong alarm).
Better for detecting attack from outside.	Better for detecting attack from insider.
They check for attacks or irregular behaviour by inspecting the contents and header information of all the packets moving across the network.	They can detect activity on host computer such as deletion of files, modification of programs etc.

Host IDS vis-à-vis Network IDS

Monitor activities on a particular single system or host.

Monitors activities on identified network.

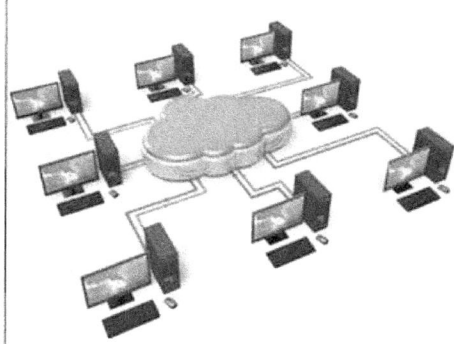

They can detect activity on host computer such as deletion of files, modification of programs etc.

They check for attacks by inspecting the contents and header information of all the packets moving across the network.

datainfosec.com

Components of Intrusion Detection System:

Components	What is does
Sensors	Collects the data. Data can be in form of network packets, log files etc.
Analyzers	Analyze the data and determine the intrusive activity.
Administration Console	To manage the IDS rules and functions.
User Interface	Enable user to view results and take necessary action.

Components of IDS

Sensors

Collects the data (in form of network packets, log files etc.)

Analyzer

Analyze the data and determine the intrusive activity.

User Interface

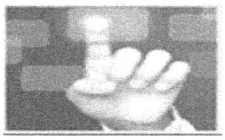

Enable user to view results and take necessary action.

Administration Console

Name	Date modified
Component Services	14/07/2009 10:16
Computer Management	14/07/2009 10:11
Data Sources (ODBC)	14/07/2009 10:11
Event Viewer	14/07/2009 10:12

To manage the IDS rules and functions

datainfosec.com

Types of Intrusion Detection System:

Types	What is does
Signature based	Intrusion is identified on the basis of known type of attacks. Such known patterns are stored in form of signature. This is also known as rule based IDS.
Statistical based	Statistical based IDS determine normal (known and expected) behaviour of the system. Any activity which falls outside the scope of normal behaviour is flagged as intrusion. Statistical based IDS generates most false positive (i.e. false alarm) as compared to other IDS. For example, if normal login timing is between 8 AM to 10 AM and on a particular day if login is done at 11 AM, it will raise alarm even if even login is done by authorized staff.
Neural network	Neural network is similar to statistical based IDS but with added self-learning functionality. IDS monitor the general pattern of activities and create a database.

Limitations of Intrusion Detection System:
(1)IDS will not able to detect application level vulnerabilities.
(2)Back doors into application.

(3)IDS will not able to detect encrypted traffic.

Placement of Intrusion Detection System:
(1)If a network based IDS is placed between Internet & the firewall, it will detect all the attack attempts (whether or not they enter the firewall).

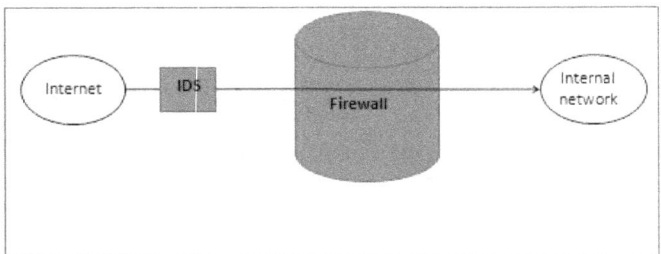

(2)If a network based IDS is placed between firewall & the corporate network, it will detect only those attack attempts which enter the firewall. (i.e. cases where firewall failed to block the attack)

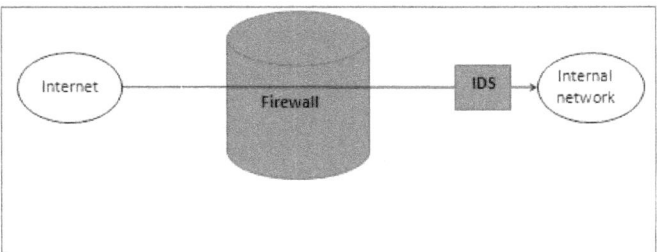

Intrusion Prevention System (IPS):
IPS not only detects the attacks but also prevent the intended victim from being affected by attempts.

Challenges in implementation of IPS:
(i)Threshold limits that are too high or too low will reduces the effectiveness of IPS
(ii)IPS may itself become a threat when attacker sends commands to large number of host protected by IPS to make them dysfunctional.

IDS   vis-à-vis   IPS

Only monitors and records the intrusion activities	Also prevents the intrusion activities

datainfosec.com

Question, Answer & Explanation:

(1)An organization has installed a IDS which monitor general patterns of activity and creates the database. Which of the following intrusion detection systems (IDSs) has this feature?

A. Packet filtering
B. Signature-based
C. Statistical-based
D. Neural networks

Answer: D. Neural networks

Explanation:

Types	What is does
Packet filtering	Packet filtering is a type of firewall and IDS.
Signature based	Signature based IDS identify the intrusion on the basis of known type of attacks. Such known patterns are stored in form of signature. This is also known as rule based IDS.
Statistical based	Statistical based IDS determine normal (known and expected) behaviour of the system. Any activity which falls outside the scope of normal behaviour is flagged as intrusion.
Neural network	Neural network is similar to statistical based IDS but with added self-learning functionality. IDS monitor the general pattern of activities and create a database.

(2) The component of an IDS that collects the data is:

A. Sensor
B. Analyzer
C. User interface
D. Administration console

Answer: A. Sensor

Explanation:

Components	What is does
Sensors	Collects the data. Data can be in form of network packets, log files etc.
Analyzers	Analyze the data and determine the intrusive activity.
Administration Console	To manage the IDS rules and functions.
User Interface	Enable user to view results and take necessary action.

(3)Even for normal activity, which of the following intrusion detection systems (IDSs) will MOST likely generate false alarms?

A. Statistical-based
B. Signature-based
C. Neural network
D. Host-based

Answer: A. Statistical-based

Explanation:
Statistical based IDS determine normal (known and expected) behaviour of the system. Any activity which falls outside the scope of normal behaviour is flagged as intrusion. Statistical based IDS is most likely to generate false positive (i.e. false alarm) as compared to other IDS. Since normal network activity may include unexpected behaviour (e.g., frequent download by multiple users), these activities will be flagged as suspicious.

(4)An IS auditor is reviewing installation of intrusion detection system (IDS). Which of the following is a GREATEST concern?

A. number of non-alarming events identified as alarming
B. system not able to identify the alarming attacks
C. automated tool is used for analysis of reports/logs
D. traffic from known source is blocked by IDS

Answer: B. system not able to identify the alarming attacks

Explanation:
Major concern will be of system not able to identify the alarming attacks. They present a higher risk because attacks will be unnoticed   and no action will be taken to address the attack. High false positive is a concern but not a major concern. Also, logs/reports are first analyzed by an automated tool to eliminate known false-positives, which generally are not a problem, and an IDS does not block any traffic.

(5)An organization wants to detect attack attempts that the firewall is unable to recognize. A network intrusion detection system (IDS) between the:

A. Internet and the firewall
B. firewall and organization's internal network
C. Internet and the IDS.
D. IDS and internal network

Answer: B. firewall and organization's internal network

Explanation:
Placement of Intrusion Detection System:

(1)If a network based IDS is placed between Internet & the firewall, it will detect all the attack attempts (whether or not they enter the firewall).

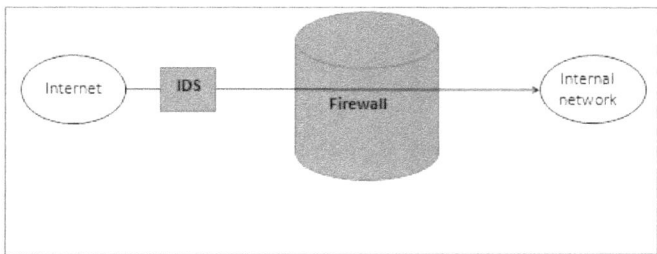

(2)If a network based IDS is placed between firewall & the corporate network, it will detect only those attack attempts which enter the firewall. (i.e. cases where firewall failed to block the attack)

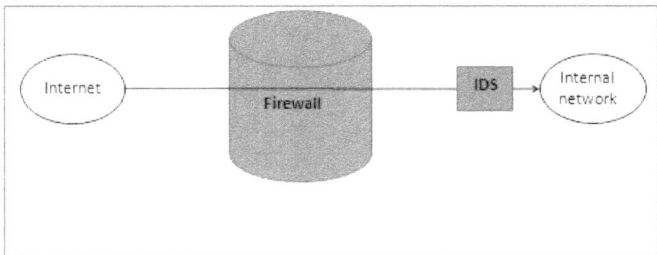

(6) Which of the following is a function of an intrusion detection system (IDS)?

A. obtain evidence on intrusive activity
B. control the access on the basis of defined rule
C. blocking access to websites for unauthorised users
D.preventing access to servers for unauthorised users

Answer: A. obtain evidence on intrusive activity

Explanation:
Obtaining evidence on intrusive activity is a function of IDS. Other options are functions of firewall.

---

(7) Which of the following is the most routine problem in implementation of   intrusion detection system (IDS)?

A. instances of false rejection rate.
B. instances of false acceptance rate.
C. instances of false positives.
D. denial-of-service attacks.

Answer: C. instances of false positives.

Explanation:
Main problem in operating IDSs is the recognition (detection) of events that are not really security incidents—false positives (i.e. false alarm). Option A & B are the concerns of biometric implementation. Denial of service is a type of attack and is not a problem in the operation of IDSs.

(8)Attempts of intrusion attacks and penetration threat to a network can be detected by which of the following by analysing the behaviour of the system?

A. Router
B. Intrusion detection system (IDs)
C. Stateful inspection
D. Packet filters

Answer: B. Intrusion detection system (IDs)

Explanation:
IDS determine normal (known and expected) behaviour of the system. Any activity which falls outside the scope of normal behaviour is flagged as intrusion. Router, Stateful inspection and packet filters are types of firewalls designed to block certain types of communications routed or passing through specific ports. It is not designed to discover someone bypassing or going under the firewall.

(9) To detect intrusion, BEST control would be:

A.Controlled procedure for granting user access
B.Inactive system to be automatically logged off after time limit.
C.Actively monitor unsuccessful login attempts.
D. Deactivate the user ID after specified unsuccessful login attempts.

Answer: C.Actively monitor unsuccessful login attempts.

Explanation: BEST method to detect the intrusion is to actively monitor the unsuccessful logins. Deactivating the user ID is preventive method and not detective.

(10)An IS auditor reviewing the implementation of IDS should be most concerned if:

A. High instances of false alarm by statistical based IDS.
B.IDS is placed between firewall and internal network.
C.IDS is used to detect encrypted traffic.
D.Signature based IDS is not able to identify new threats.

Answer: C.IDS is used to detect encrypted traffic.

Explanation:

IDS cannot detect attacks which are in form of encrypted traffic. So if organization has misunderstood that IDS can detect encrypted traffic also and accordingly designed its control strategy, then it is major concern.

(11)Of all three IDS (i.e. (i) signature (ii) statistics and (iii) neural network), neural network is more effective in detecting fraud because:

A. Intrusion is identified on the basis of known type of attacks.
B. Any activity which falls outside the scope of normal behaviour is flagged as intrusion.
C. IDS monitor the general pattern of activities and create a database and attacks problems that require consideration of a large number of input variables.
D.IDS solves the problem where large and where large database is not required.

Answer: C. IDS monitor the general pattern of activities and create a database and attacks problems that require consideration of a large number of input variables.

Explanation:
Neural networks monitor the general pattern of activities and create a database and attacks problems that require consideration of a large number of input variables. They are capable of capturing relationships and patterns often missed by other statistical methods. Option A is feature of signature based IDS. Option B is feature of statistics based IDS.

Last Minute Revision:

- In any given scenario, out of all three IDS (i.e. (i)signature (ii)statistics and (iii) neural network), neural network creates its own database.
- Of all three IDS (i.e. (i)signature (ii)statistics and (iii)neural network), neural network is more effective in detecting fraud.
- In any given scenario, out of all three IDS (i.e. (i)signature (ii)statistics and (iii) neural network), statistical based IDS generates most false positives (false alarms).
- In any given scenario, out of four components of IDS (i.e. (i)sensor (ii)analyzer (iii)admin console and (iv)user interface) sensor collects the data and send to analyzer for data analysis.
- In any given scenario, most important concern of IDS implementation is that attacks not identified/detected by IDS.

What is single sign on?

Single sign-on (SSO) is a user authentication service that permits a user to use one set of login credentials (e.g., name and password) to access multiple applications.

Advantages of Single Sign On:

- Multiple passwords not required. This encourages user to select a stronger password.
- Improves administrator's ability to manage user's accounts.
- Reduces administrative overhead cost in resetting passwords due to lower number of IT help desk calls about passwords.
- Reduces time taken by users to log into multiple applications.

Disadvantages of Single Sign On:

- SSO acts as a single authentication point for multiple applications which constitute risk of single point of failure.
- Support of all major operating system environments is difficult.

Single Sign on vis-à-vis Reduced Sign on:

In SSO user needs to log in just one time for all the applications. In RSO, users need to sign in individually for each application (with same user ID & password).

In layman's term, unlike SSO where a user logs on just one time, RSO challenges the user again for higher risk applications while keeping the frequency of authentication low.

Kerberos:

- One Example of SSO is Kerberos.

- Kerberos is an authentication service used to validate services and users in distributed computing environment (DCE).
- In client server environment, only users are authenticated however in distributed computing environment (DCE) both users and servers authenticate themselves.
- At initial logon time, Kerberos third party application is used to verify the identity of the client.

Question, Answer & Explanation:

(1) An organization is introducing a single sign-on (SSO) system. Under the SSO system, users will be required to enter only one user ID and password for access to all application systems .A major risk of using single sign-on (SSO) is that it:

A. acts as a single authentication point for multiple applications.
B. acts as a single point of failure.
C. acts as a bottleneck for smooth administration.
D. leads to a lockout of valid users in case of authentication failure.

Answer A. acts as a single authentication point for multiple applications.

Explanation:
SSO acts as a single authentication point for multiple applications which constitute risk of single point of failure. The primary risk associated with single sign-on is the single authentication point. A Single point of failure provides a similar redundancy to the single authentication point. However, failure can be due to any other reasons also. So more specific answer to this question is option A.

(2)An organization is introducing a single sign-on (SSO) system. In SSO, unauthorized access:

A. will have minor impact.
B. will have major impact.
C. is not possible.
D. is highly possible.

Answer: B. will have major impact.

Explanation:
Single sign-on (SSO) is a user authentication service that permits a user to use one set of login credentials (e.g., name and password) to access multiple applications. This constitutes risk of single point of failure. The impact will be greater since the hacker needs to know only one password to gain access to all the related applications and therefore, cause greater concerns than if only the password to one of the systems is known. Introduction of SSO will not have any relevance on possibility (higher or lower) of unauthorized access.

(3)An organization is introducing a single sign-on (SSO) system. Under the SSO system, users will be required to enter only one user ID and password for access to all application systems .A major risk of using single sign-on (SSO) is that:

A. It increases security administrator work load.
B. It reduces administrator's ability to manage user's accounts.
C. It increases time taken by users to log into multiple applications.
D. Unauthorized password disclosure can have greater impact.

Answer: D. Unauthorized password disclosure can have greater impact.

Explanation:
Single sign-on (SSO) is a user authentication service that permits a user to use one set of login credentials (e.g., name and password) to access multiple applications. This constitutes risk of single point of failure. The impact will be greater since the hacker needs to know only one password to gain access to all the related applications and therefore, cause greater concerns than if only the password to one of the systems is known.SSO improves the administrator's ability to manage user's accounts. SSO reduces time taken by users to log into multiple applications and work load of security administration.

(4)An organization is introducing a single sign-on (SSO) system. Under the SSO system, users will be required to enter only one user ID and password for access to all application systems. To prevent unauthorized access, the MOST important action is to:

A. to monitor all failed attempts.
B. regular review of log files.
C. implement a strong password policy.
D. to deactivate all unused accounts.

Answer: C. implement a strong password policy.

Explanation:
A strong password policy is better preventive control. Other options are good practice but may not able address the risk of unauthorized access if password is compromised.

(5)Which following is most important benefit of Single Sign On?

A. Easier administration of password management.
B. It can avoid a potential single point of failure issue
C. Maintaining SSO is easy as it is not prone to human errors
D. It protects network traffic

Answer: A. Easier administration of password management.

Explanation:
Easier administration of changing or deleting passwords is the major advantage of implementing SSO. The advantages of SSO include having the ability to use stronger passwords, easier administration of changing or deleting the passwords, and requiring less time to access resources.

(6)Risk of unauthorised access can be best control by:

A. Before-image/after-image logging
B. Vitality detection
C. Multimodal biometrics
D. Kerberos

Answer: D. Kerberos

Explanation:
Kerberos is a network authentication protocol for client-server applications that can be used to restrict access to the database to authorized users. Vitality detection and multimodal biometrics are controls against spoofing and mimicry attacks. Before-image/after-image logging of database transactions is a detective control, as opposed to Kerberos, which is a preventative control.

Last Minute Revision:

- When CISA question is about major risk of SSO, our answer should be:

    - SSO acts as single authentication point for multiple applications.
    - SSO acts a single point of failure.

    If both the options are there, please select 'SSO acts as single authentication point for multiple applications. This is more specific answer as compared to 'SSO acts a single point of failure'.

- When CISA question is about most important control for SSO, our answer should be implementation of strong password policy.

CRM covers following types of Fire Suppression System:

- Water-Based Systems
- Dry-Pipe Sprinkling Systems
- Halon Systems
- FM-200
- Argonite
- Carbon Dioxide -CO_2

www.cisaexamstudy.com

Difference between Wet (water based) and Dry Sprinkling System:

CISA Aspirant should be aware about difference between Wet & Dry Sprinkling System:

Water-Based Systems (WBS)	Dry-Pipe Sprinkling Systems (DPSS)
In WBS, water always remains in the system piping.	DPSS do not have water in the pipes until an electronic fire alarm activates the water pump to send water into the system.
WBS is more effective and reliable.	Comparatively less effective and reliable.
Disadvantage of exposing the facility to water damage if pipe leaks or breaks.	Advantage of not exposing the facility to water damage even if pipe leaks or breaks.

www.cisaexamstudy.com

What is Halon Gas System?

- Halon gas removes oxygen from air thus starving the fire.
- They are not safe for human life.
- There should be audible alarm and brief delay before discharge to permit time for evacuation.
- Halon gas is banned as its adversely effects the ozone layer.
- Popular replacements are FM-200 & Argonite.

What is FM-200 Gas?

- FM-200 is colorless & odorless gas.
- FM-200 is safe to be used when people are present.
- FM-200 is environment friendly.
- It is commonly used as a gaseous fire suppression agent.

What is Argonite Gas?

- Argonite is a mixture of 50% Argon & 50% Nitrogen.
- It is used as a gaseous fire suppression agent.
- Though environment friendly & non-toxic, people have suffocated by breathing argon by mistake.

What is CO_2 ?

- CO_2 Systems release pressurized CO_2 gas in the area protected to replace the oxygen required for combustion.
- Unlike Halon, FM-200 & Argonite, CO_2 is unable to sustain Human life.
- In most countries, it is illegal for such systems to be set to automatic release if any human may be i the area.
- CO_2 installations are permitted where no humans are regularly present such as unmanned data centers.

Which gas is Safe for Human Life?

- As per CRM, FM-200 & Argonite gases are safe for human life. However, it must be noted that Argonite, though environment friendly & non-toxic, people have suffocated by breathing argon by mistake.
- CO_2 & Halon gases are not safe for human life.

Safe for Human Lives

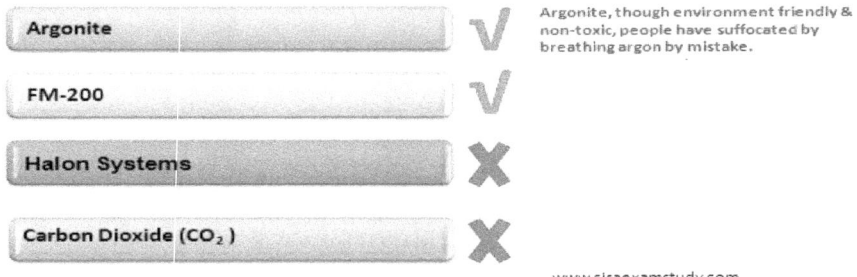

Argonite, though environment friendly & non-toxic, people have suffocated by breathing argon by mistake.

Argonite ✓

FM-200 ✓

Halon Systems ✗

Carbon Dioxide (CO_2) ✗

www.cisaexamstudy.com

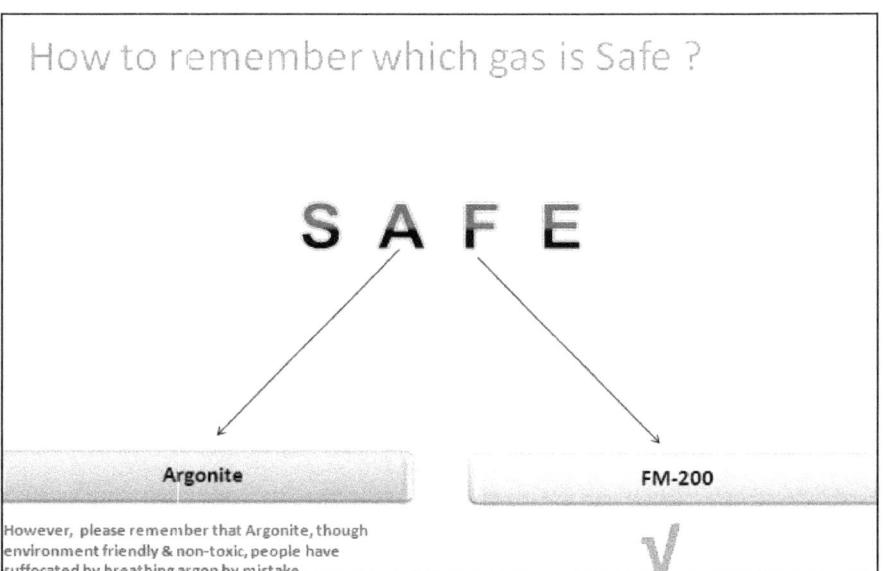

How to remember which gas is Safe ?

S A F E

Argonite

FM-200 ✓

However, please remember that Argonite, though environment friendly & non-toxic, people have suffocated by breathing argon by mistake.

Point to remember for CISA Exam:

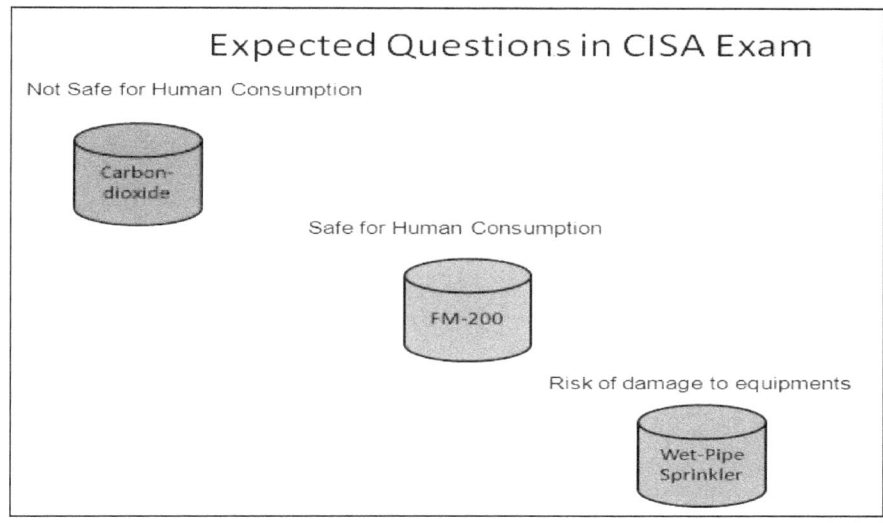

Question, Answer & Explanation:

(1) An IS Auditor is reviewing fire safety arrangement in data centre. Which of the following is the MOST effective and environmentally friendly?

A. Carbon dioxide gas
B. Dry-pipe sprinklers
C. Wet-pipe sprinklers
D. Halon gas

Answer: B. Dry-pipe sprinklers

Explanation:
Carbon dioxide is accepted as an environmentally acceptable gas, but it is not safe for human life. Also, Halon has certain side effects and not safe for human life. Both Dry-pipe and Wet-pipe are effective and environment friendly. However, Sprinklers must be dry pipe to prevent the risk of leakage in data centre.

(2) An IS Auditor is reviewing fire safety arrangement in data centre where dry-pipe sprinklers are installed. A dry-pipe fire extinguisher uses:

A. Halon gas.
B. CO_2
C. Water resides in the pipe with special water-tight sealants.
D. Water, but it enters the pipe only when fire has been detected.

Answer: D. Water, but it enters the pipe only when fire has been detected.

Explanation:
Sprinklers can be of two types i.e. dry pipe and wet pipe. Both uses water. In Wet System, water always remains in the system piping. Dry pipe does not have water in the pipes until an electronic fire alarm activates the water pump to send water into the system.

(3) An IS Auditor is reviewing fire safety arrangement in data center where wet-pipe sprinklers are installed. A wet-pipe fire extinguisher uses:

A. Water, but it enters the pipe only when fire has been detected.
B. CO_2
C. Water resides in the pipe with special water-tight sealants.
D. Halon gas

Answer: C. Water resides in the pipe with special water-tight sealants.

Explanation:
Sprinklers can be of two types i.e. dry pipe and wet pipe. Both uses water. In Wet System, water always remains in the system piping. Dry pipe does not have water in the pipes until an electronic fire alarm activates the water pump to send water into the system.

(4) Which of the following is the Highest risk (to be given priority) with respect to use of CO_2 and Halon gas as fire extinguishers:

A. Halon gas has negative impact on the ozone layer.
B. CO_2 is not effective for solid combustible.
C. Halon is not effective for solid combustible.
D.Both present a risk to human life if used in closed room.

Answer: D. Both present a risk to human life if used in closed room.

Explanation:
Both CO_2 and Halon gas reduces the oxygen ratio in atmosphere and hence they are risk to human life if used in closed room.   Protecting people's life should always be of highest priority in fire suppression activities. In many countries installing or refilling halon fire suppression systems is not allowed. Although, both gases are effective for synthetic combustibles they are ineffective on solid combustibles.

(5) An IS Auditor is reviewing fire safety arrangement in data center. Which of the following is the area of MOST concern?

A. Use of FM-200 gas in a manned data centre.
B. Use of Dry-pipe sprinklers in an expensive data centre facility.
C. Use of Wet-pipe sprinklers in an expensive data centre facility.
D. Use of Carbon dioxide gas in a manned data centre.

Answer: D. Use of Carbon dioxide gas in a manned data centre.

Explanation:
Carbon dioxide is not safe for human life. FM-200 is a safe to use where people are present. Both Dry-pipe and Wet-pipe are effective and environment friendly. Generally, Sprinklers must be dry pipe to prevent the risk of leakage in data centre. However, major risk is use of CO_2 where human life in present.

(6) Which of the following gases is safest to be used in presence of human life?

A. CO_2.
B. FM-200
C. Halon gas
D. Argonite gas.

Answer: B. FM-200

Explanation:
CO_2 & Halon are not safe for human life. Argonite, though environment friendly & non-toxic, people have suffocated by breathing argon by mistake. FM-200 is environment friendly and safe to be used when people are present.

Last Minute Revision:

- Carbon dioxide is not safe for human life.
- FM-200 is a safe to use where people are present.
- Sprinklers can be of two types i.e. dry pipe and wet pipe. Both uses water. In Wet System, water always remains in the system piping. Dry pipe does not have water in the pipes until an electronic fire alarm activates the water pump to send water into the system.
- Protecting people's life should always be of highest priority in fire suppression activities.

Introduction:

- Cloud computing is the practice of using remote servers hosted on the Internet to store, manage, and process data, rather than a local server or a personal computer.
- Cloud computing, simply means the use of computing resources as a service through networks, typically the Internet.
- The Internet is commonly visualized as clouds; hence the term "cloud computing" for computation done through the Internet.
- With Cloud Computing, users can access database resources via the Internet from anywhere, for as long as they need, without worrying about any maintenance or management of actual resources.
- Cloud computing relies on sharing of resources to achieve coherence and economies of scale, similar to a public utility.

Characteristics of Cloud Computing:

- Ability to automate computing capabilities (network, storage, server etc.) without any human interaction.
- Ability to be accessed anywhere, anytime and by almost any device.
- Ability to provide rapid and scalable capabilities.
- Ability to monitor, control and report the usage of the resource.
- Resources such as storage, processing, memory, network bandwidth and virtual machines can be used through cloud computing.

Cloud Computing – Service Models:

(1) Infrastructure as a Service (IaaS):

- IaaS provides computing resources such as processing power, memory, storage, and networks for users.
- IaaS facilitates optimum utilization of computing resources without having to own and manage their own resources.
- The end-users or IT architects will use Virtual machines (VMs) as per their requirements.
- User need not maintain the physical servers as it is maintained by the service providers.
- Examples of IaaS providers include Amazon Web Services (AWS), Google Compute Engine, OpenStack etc.

(2) Software as a Service (SaaS):

- SaaS provides ability to the end users to access an application over the Internet.
- Application is hosted and managed by the service provider.
- Users are not required to maintain or control application development platform and related infrastructure.
- For example, one can make own word document in Google docs online without having installed office software or one can edit a photo online on pixlr.com without installing any editing software.

(3) Platform as a Service (PaaS):

- PaaS provides platform to the users to develop and deploy an application on the development platform provided by the service provider.
- In traditional application development, the application will be developed locally and will be hosted in the central location.
- PaaS changes the application development from local machine to online.
- For example- Google AppEngine, Windows Azure Compute etc.

Cloud Computing – Deployment Models

Private Cloud	Public Cloud	Hybrid Cloud	Community Cloud
This cloud is used exclusively for the benefit of particular organization. It resides within boundaries of organization.	This cloud is for open use of general public. This service is offered on the basis of pay per use basis.	In this environment, there is combination of private and public cloud computing. In this method initially, private cloud is used and then for additional resources public cloud is used.	In this environment, cloud is used by specific community of consumers that have shared concerns.
Characteristics of Private Cloud is as follow: i. More secure environment and very less chances of data leakage. ii. Centralized Control of cloud by organization itself. iii. In private cloud, Service Level Agreement either does exit or are very weak.	Characteristics of Public Cloud is as follow: i. Highly Available ii. Highly Scalable iii. Affordable cost iv. Less Secure as compared to other models v. Strict SLAs are followed in public cloud arrangement.	Characteristics of Hybrid Cloud is as follow: i. Complex cloud management as more than 1 model is involved. ii. Less secured than private cloud. However more secured than public cloud. iii. Highly Scalable iv. Better SLA as compared to private cloud.	Characteristics of Community Cloud is as follow: i. Collaborative Maintenance is required. No single company has control over cloud. ii. Less secured than private cloud. However more secured than public cloud. iii. Cost effective: As cloud is shared by few organizations, it becomes cost effective.

Cloud Computing – Risk & Control

Risk	Control
Compliance with Legal Requirements	• To verify whether regulations of the locations (where infrastructure is located) is aligned with the enterprise's requirements. • Contract to include term to restrict movement of assets within approved locations. • To prevent disclosure, encrypt the asset prior to migration to the CSP.
Physical Security	• Verify the CSP's physical security policy and ensure that it is aligned with the enterprise's security policy. • Obtain copy of independent security reviews or audit reports of CSP. • Bind the CSP through contract to align with the enterprise's security policy and to implement necessary controls to ensure it. • Verify CSP's disaster recovery plans and ensure that they contain the necessary arrangement to protect assets.
Data Disposal	• Verify CSP's technical specifications and controls that ensure that data are properly wiped off as per requirement. • Contract should specify that upon contract expiration a mandatory data wipe carried out in presence of representative of enterprise.
Application Disposal	• Contract should specify requirement for proper disposal of applications including objects, source and backups. • Contract should also include non-compete clause.
Identity and Access Management	• Contract should include 'right to audit' clause. • Contract should specify implementation of necessary controls to ensure access to only authorized users. • Obtain copy of independent security reviews or audit reports of CSP.
Collateral Damage	• Control should specify requirement of notification to enterprise in case of any event. • Contract should specify availability of contracted capacity and same should not be directed to other tenants without approval. • To use a private cloud deployment (no multi tenancy)
Hypervisor Attacks	• Contract should include 'right to audit' clause. • Contract should require CSP to align with enterprise's security policy and implementation of necessary controls to ensure.

Following security objective is required to be met for smooth functioning of cloud computing:

- To ensure availability of information systems and data on continuous basis.
- To ensure the integrity and confidentiality information and sensitive data while stored and in transit.
- To ensure compliance to relevant laws, regulations and standards.

IS Auditor should consider following parameters regarding cloud computing:

- Clarity with respect to data ownership, data custody and security administration related to cloud deployment models.
- To consider legal requirements, laws, regulations and unique risk in the cloud environment. Regulations.
- Limitations to 'right to audit' clause as it may not be possible to audit physical perimeters of cloud environment.

Questions, Answer & Explanation:

(1) Which of the following is the best way to verify cloud service provider's physical security arrangements?

(A)Verify the CSP's physical security policy and ensure that it is aligned with the enterprise's security policy.
(B)Verify copy of independent security reviews or audit reports of CSP.
(C)Bind the CSP through contract to align with the enterprise's security policy and to implement necessary controls to ensure it.
(D)Verify CSP's disaster recovery plans and ensure that they contain the necessary arrangement to protect assets.

Answer: (B)Verify copy of independent security reviews or audit reports of CSP.

Explanation: Best way to ensure is to obtain and verify independent security review or audit report of CSP. Other options are not sufficient in themselves to verify the physical security arrangements.

(2) Which of the following is the most important clause in a contract with cloud service provider?

(A)Contract should specify that upon contract expiration a mandatory data wipe carried out in presence of representative of enterprise.
(B)Contract should also include non-compete clause.
(C)Contract should include 'right to audit' clause.
(D)Contract should restrict movement of data within territory allowed as per relevant law or regulation.

Answer: (D)Contract should restrict movement of data within territory allowed as per relevant law or regulation.

Explanation: It is very important to validate and verify whether regulations of the locations (where infrastructure is located) is aligned with the enterprise's requirements. Contract to include term to restrict movement of assets within approved locations. Other options are also important but option (D) should be considered as most important clause in a contract with cloud service provider.

(3) IS auditor is reviewing terms of contract with Cloud Service Provider. Which of the following is most important consideration?

(A)Clarity with respect to data ownership, data custody and IPR related requirements.
(B)Clarity with respect to non-disclosure requirements.
(C)Clarity with respect to data backup requirements.
(D)Clarity with respect to data access requirements.

Answer: (A)Clarity with respect to data ownership, data custody and IPR related requirements.

Explanation: It is very important that contract should have proper clarification with respect to data ownership, data custodian and other IPR related requirements.

(4) Which of the following would be of most concern to the IS auditor with respect to storage of personal customer information in cloud environment?

(A)Inadequate disaster recovery procedure.
(B)The data in the multi-tenancy environment being accessed by competitors.
(C)Inadequate incident management procedure.
(D)Inadequate business continuity arrangements.

Answer: (B)The data in the multi-tenancy environment being accessed by competitors.

Explanation: Considering various laws and regulations that require privacy/confidentiality of customer information, unauthorized access to information and data leakage are the major concerns.

(5) IS auditor is reviewing terms of contract with Cloud Service Provider. Which of the following is most important consideration?

(A)Physical Security
(B)Compliance with Legal Requirements
(C)Data disposal policy
(D)Application disposal policy

Answer: (B)Compliance with Legal Requirements

Explanation: Most important consideration is to consider legal requirements, laws and regulations. Other options are also important but option (B) should be considered as most important clause in a contract with cloud service provider.

(6) Which cloud deployment method is considered as most secured and have very less chances of data leakages?

(A)Public cloud
(B)Private cloud
(C)Community cloud
(D)Hybrid cloud

Answer: (B)Private cloud

Explanation: Private cloud is considered as most secure deployment method.

Introduction:

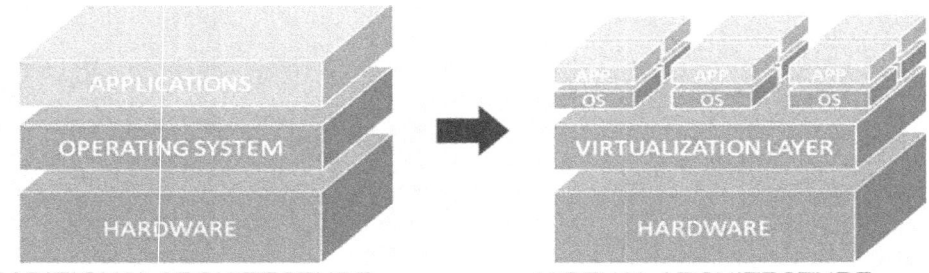

TRADITIONAL ARCHITECTURE   VIRTUAL ARCHITECTURE

- Virtualization allows users to run multiple operating systems simultaneously on a single machine.
- In other words, virtualization refers to the creation of a virtual resource such as a server, desktop, operating system, file, storage or network.
- The main goal of virtualization is to manage workloads by transforming traditional computing to make it more scalable.
- It allows using a physical machine's full capacity by distributing its capabilities among many users or environment.
- Virtualization provides an enterprise with a significant opportunity to increase efficiency and decrease costs in its IT operations.
- Virtualization creates a layer between the hardware and the guest OSs to manage shared processing and memory resources on the host.

Elements of Virtualization:

- Server or other hardware product
- Virtualization hypervisor: Also known as 'host' – a software, firmware or hardware that creates and runs virtual machine environment.
- Guest machine: Virtual environment elements (e.g., OS, switches, routers, firewalls, etc.) residing on the computer on which a hypervisor host machine has been installed.

Deployment Methods:

- **Bare metal/native virtualization:** Hypervisor runs directly on the underlying hardware without a host OS.
- **Hosted virtualization:** Hypervisor runs on top of the host OS.
- **Containerization:** Containers run as an isolated process in user space on the host operating system.

Disadvantages of Virtualization:

- Poor configuration of the host may create vulnerabilities for host as well as guest.
- Any attack against host could affect all the guests.

- Inadequate security of management console can have risk of unapproved administrative access to the host's guests.
- Performance issues of the host's own OS could impact each of the host's guests.
- Risk of data leakage between guests if there is poor control for memory release and allocation.

Key risk areas of Virtualization:

- Installation of rootkits as a hypervisor below the Operating System and thus risk of interception of guest OS. As malware runs below OS, antivirus software may not able to detect this.
- Risk of improper configuration of the hypervisor partitioning resources (CPU, memory, disk space and storage). This allows for unauthorized access to resources by guest OS.
- On hosted virtualization, mechanisms called guest tools can allow an attacker to gain access to particular resources.
- On hosted virtualization, products rarely have hypervisor access controls. Anyone who can launch an application on the host OS can run the hypervisor.

Controls in Virtual Environment:

- Secure configuration and hardening of hypervisors and guest images.
- Encrypt hypervisor management communications.
- Ensure regular patch updates for the hypervisor.
- Synchronized the virtualized infrastructure to a trusted timeserver.
- Disconnect all unused physical hardware system.
- Disable hypervisor services such as clipboard- or file-sharing between the guest OS and the host OS, if not required.
- Log and monitor security events of each guest OS.
- File integrity monitoring of the hypervisor should be used to monitor for signs of compromise.

9 781983 328343